Gahan Wilson's Out There

FANTAGRAPHICS BOOKS

THE MAGAZINE OF
Fantasy AND
Science Fiction

A MERCURY PUBLICATION

JANUARY   50¢

A Meeting of Minds
by ANNE McCAFFREY

Santa Claus Vs. S.P.I.D.E.R.
by HARLAN ELLISON

GahanWilson

GAHAN
*WILSON'S
*IN HERE *

INTRODUCTION BY GARY GROTH

he *Magazine of Fantasy & Science Fiction* (*F&SF*) was one of a number of fantasy and science fiction digests—successors to the pulps—published in the '50s and '60s, which included, among others, *Galaxy*, *Amazing*, and *Fantastic*. Gahan Wilson was a cartoonist, but he was also a hardcore science fiction, fantasy, and horror aficionado, reading voluminously, attending SF conventions, and writing short stories: *F&SF* was his favorite of the monthly digests. "I was just delighted when it came out because they were working at a higher level than an awful lot of the other stuff [being published]," he said. "A real grown-up fantasy and science fiction magazine. I loved the magazine from the start because it was [editor Anthony] Boucher and all these guys who really were opening their gates to more variety; it was a lot better than the other science fiction magazines."

Wilson's first published work in *F&SF* was not a cartoon, but a one-page short story, "Beware of the Dog," in the April 1964 issue. Two more one-page short stories appeared in rapid succession in the June and July issues; his next contribution was his first gag cartoon, which appeared in the April 1965 edition. (He hadn't initially submitted cartoons because they didn't publish cartoons at the time.) He published a full-page cartoon in every issue of *F&SF* from then until October 1981 (when he stopped contributing to the magazine for reasons he no longer remembers).

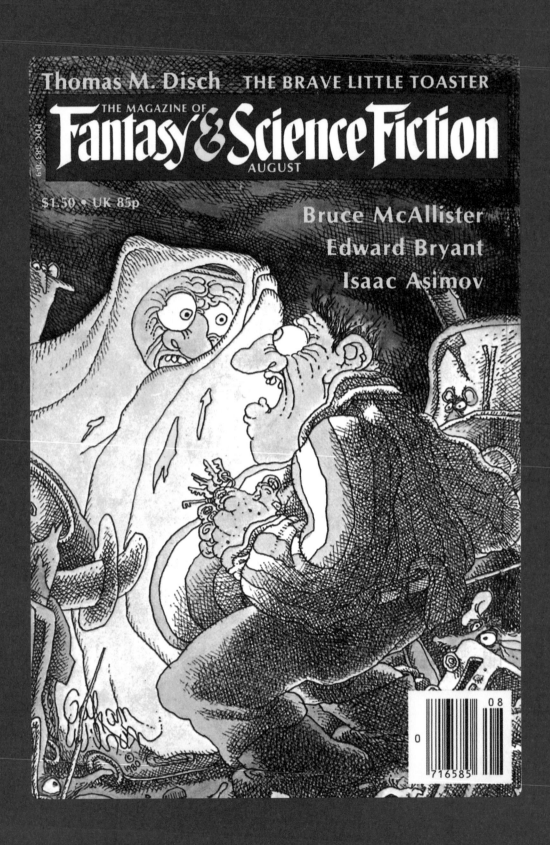

Thomas M. Disch   THE BRAVE LITTLE TOASTER

THE MAGAZINE OF
Fantasy & Science Fiction
AUGUST

$1.50 • UK 85p

Bruce McAllister

Edward Bryant

Isaac Asimov

Wilson established a close and collegial working relationship with those at the magazine. "I had been a regular reader of the magazine for years and knew Ed Ferman's father Joseph." He worked primarily with Ed, who took over the editorial reins from his father, and served as its editor from 1966 to 1991. Wilson described the staff as "very friendly. I would visit Ed at the magazine's office [in Manhattan] and it was a nice, cozy, comfy bunch there." "They were quite receptive from the get-go," he says about their editorial interaction. "We'd have an occasional back and forth, they would make occasional suggestions this way and that, and they were all good ones. I can't remember any kind of conflict of opinion, I never had anything even the tiniest bit unpleasant—I was never thinking, '"Oh, gee, why are they saying that?' 'Cause they were intelligent, helpful suggestions."

Between 1964 and October 1981, Wilson published nine short stories and 197 full-page gag cartoons as well as numerous decorative illustrations. In the October 1968 issue, he began writing a book review column titled "The Dark Corner."

It may surprise those who know Gahan Wilson only as a brilliant cartoonist to learn that he is an accomplished prose writer as well. His short stories are characterized by a piquant prose style, a pukish sense of humor, a leisurely pace, a playful imagination, and a distinct avoidance of cliché. A prairie dog is not simply disintegrated, for example, it is "reduced . . . to a cloud of idly drifting ash." Nothing is rushed, yet the stories zip right along. He clearly had a good time invigorating the tropes of the fantasy genre with lightness of touch and an off-kilter sense of humor. The genre conventions he employs aren't mocked, either; they are bent to his will and put in the service of a fresh and unjaded vision. Despite the amount of death and dismemberment, his stories are downright charming, or, at least, told with a degree of restrained, albeit sinister, suavity. Violence is calmly, dispassionately considered, and occasionally executed. "I wiped the palms of my hands carefully with my napkin and cleared my throat," says one of his characters. "I could think of nothing else to do, short of leaping over the table and crushing in the top of Aladar Rakas's skull." His "M-1," about which I dare not say any more for fear of spoiling your initial reading of it, is a miniature masterpiece that can in fact sustain multiple pleasurable readings.

Wilson's column "The Dark Corner" is a model of appreciative book reviewing. He demonstrates a true connoisseurial passion for and a deep knowledge

THE MAGAZINE OF
Fantasy AND
Science Fiction

MARCH   50¢

HARVEY JACOBS
THE EGG OF THE GLAK

MIRIAM ALLEN deFORD
ROBERT SHECKLEY
L. SPRAGUE DE CAMP
ISAAC ASIMOV

A MERCURY PUBLICATION

of the overlapping genres he discusses—fantasy, horror, the supernatural, ghost stories, et al. Wilson considered the fantasy genre (and the subgenres) as literarily legitimate as mainstream fiction. "I very much enjoy fantasy and horror literature and enjoy doing cartoons along the same lines," he said. "It's always—not annoyed me—but puzzled me that the fantasy or science fiction wasn't taken seriously as a category, and looked upon disdainfully because it was a genre. I don't feel there's a big heavy line between fantasy and science fiction and everything else. Short stories are short stories and cartoons are cartoons." He tackled a vast array of authors, including Arthur Machen, Richard Matheson, Colin Wilson, Ramsey Campbell, Manly Wade Wellman, and one with the unlikely name of Oliver Onions (apparently a master of the ghost story). His breezy, cheerful, and lighthearted tone belies sharp observations and marvelously subtle, clear-eyed distinctions. Consider, for example, his comparison of Clark Ashton Smith and Ambrose Bierce: "The vast difference between them was that Bierce's understanding of man's sublime futility infuriated him and made him bitter, whereas Smith's clear vision of it braced and cheered him and spurred him on to endless, lively speculations on the awesome possibilities of impartial disaster."

His descriptions of authors are juicily novelistic as well as admirably succinct; here he is on H. P. Lovecraft: "His cool cockiness against a background of dismayed nihilism has a recognizably John Barrymorian swagger to it."

He could be unpretentiously scholarly, too. I bet you didn't know that:

> One of the most legendary vampire books in English literature, and certainly one of the most baroquely titled, is *Varney the Vampire; or, the Feast of Blood* by Thomas Preskett Prest. Varney first made his appearance in 1847, and thus stands chronologically midway between Polidori's *The Vampyre* (1819)—whose Byronic and Byron-based antihero, Lord Ruthven, pretty much established the breed as we know it—and Stoker's winner and still champion, *Dracula* (1897), who, some scholars maintain, might never have risen from his grave without Varney's example to lead the way.

I didn't.

THE MAGAZINE OF
Fantasy AND
Science Fiction

AUGUST   50¢

PIERS ANTHONY
BRIAN CLEEVE
ISAAC ASIMOV
K. M. O'DONNELL

Samuel R. Delany and
Ed Emshwiller on
2001: A Space Odyssey

A MERCURY PUBLICATION

And, being Gahan Wilson, he can't resist injecting a little larksome badinage into an otherwise serious undertaking. Referring to a book under review, he admonishes the reader parenthetically: "Your friendly book dealer knows how to get hold of it, don't let him tell you he doesn't. He's lying if he tells you he doesn't. Show him who's boss, show a little guts."

And then there are the cartoons—197 of them, published here for the first time since their original appearance thirty to fifty years ago. (Not to mention a half-dozen book covers, also reproduced here, making over 200 pages of previously inaccessible, prime Wilson images.) Wilson was building a successful career as a gag cartoonist, contributing regularly to such magazines as *Playboy* and *Collier's*, by the time he published his first work in *F&SF*, but he was not yet a seasoned vet. The ink line of his earliest work is somewhere between Feiffer's nervous, febrile line and Gluyas Williams's highly controlled line, but quickly evolves into the self-assured groove that is recognizably Wilson's own. All the cartoons published in *F&SF* were done specifically for the magazine. "I made up all the cartoons myself," he says, "but sometimes a conversation over lunch with Ed Ferman about some topic led to another idea."

What is perhaps most remarkable about the cartoons in this volume is how contemporary they feel, how universal their themes and subject matter are. Their settings may lean toward the more phantasmagoric, but they are filled with the same obsessions that have fueled Wilson's cartoons throughout his life: atomic holocaust, the Taylorized business mentality, marital difficulties and domestic contention, judicial absurdities, the obscenities of the medical profession, environmental despoliation, a punitive and retributive social order, and the flimsy nature of reality. There is also a walking bathtub, a *Lifeboat* homage, Superman and a phone booth, possible evidence of a Mickey Mouse obsession, and—proving that Basil Wolverton had nothing on him—a virtual gallery of grotesque visages throughout.

In one of his book reviews, he describes the author Mary E. Wilkins Freeman as "not only a sharp examiner of what went on about her, she saw it all with a lovely sense of humor, gentle, but most ironic, solidly based on human foolishness seen through clear but wonderfully understanding eyes." Which happens to be a perfect description of the creative lens through which Gahan Wilson's sees the world.

‡

CARTOONS

— BY —

Gahan Wilson

"This is Willy, and this is Willy's imaginary playmate."

"Boy—you talk about your lucky timing!"

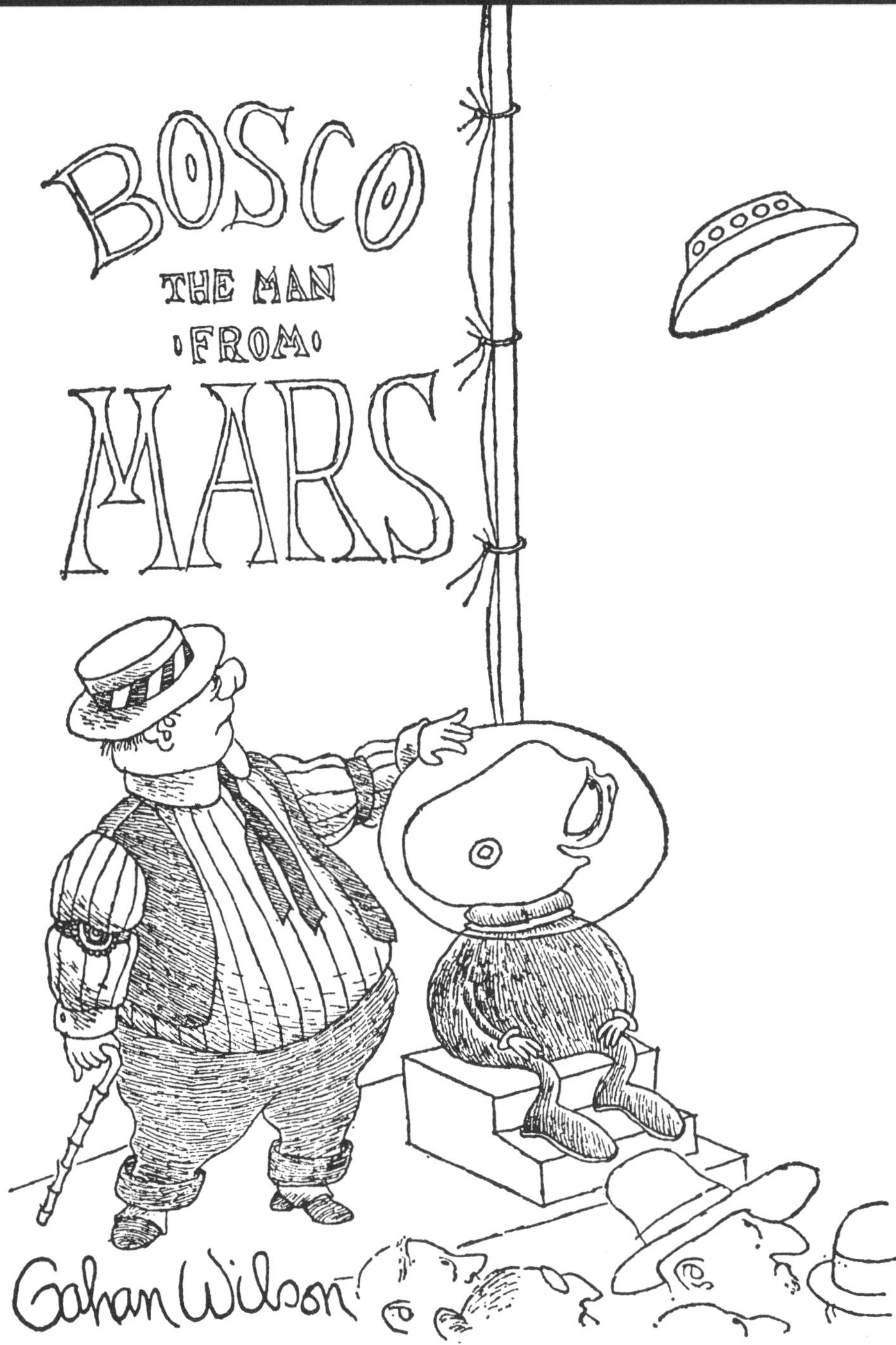
BOSCO
THE MAN
FROM
MARS
Gahan Wilson

"Thank God!"

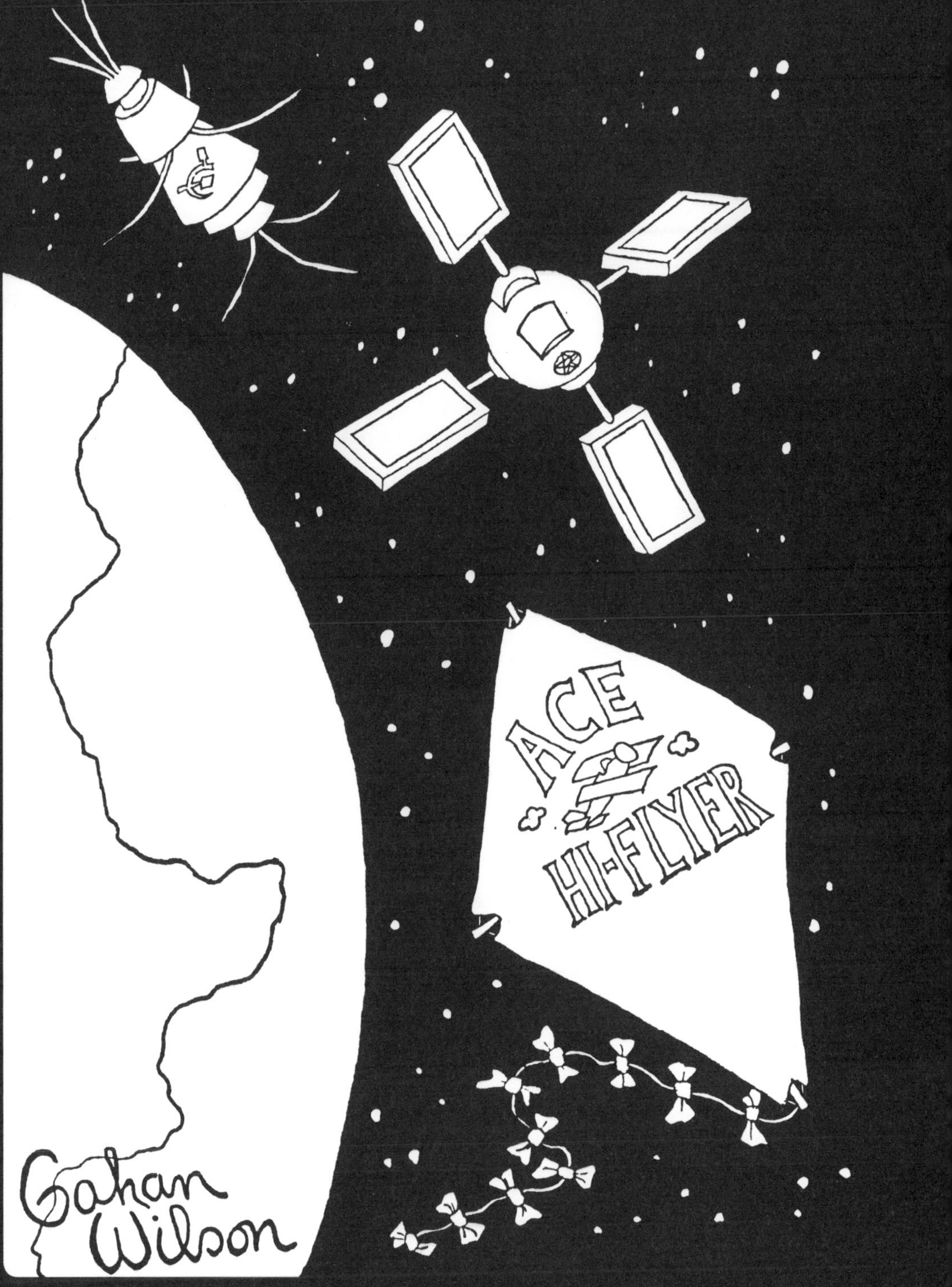
ACE
HI-FLYER
Gahan Wilson

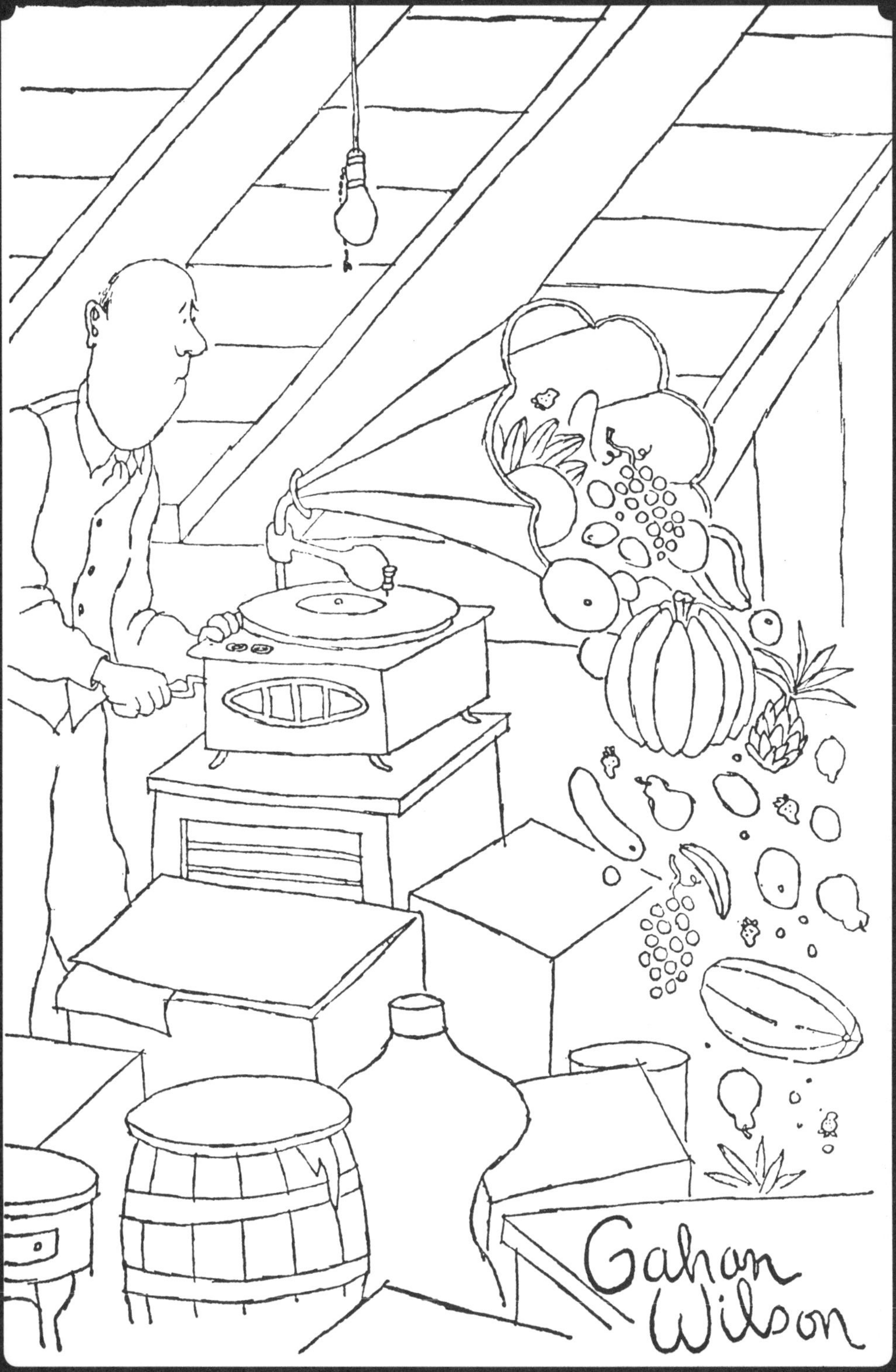
Gahan Wilson

"Marsha, you're tending to lead again!"

FUNNY FOTOS 25¢
FUNNY FOTOS 25¢
Gahan Wilson

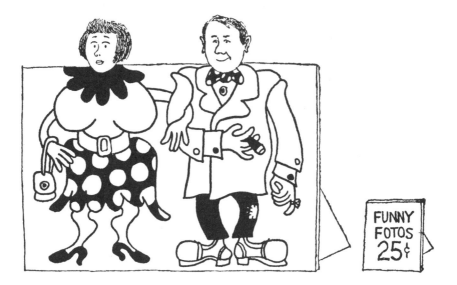

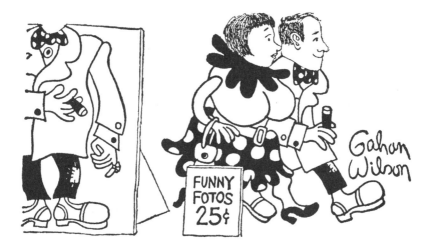

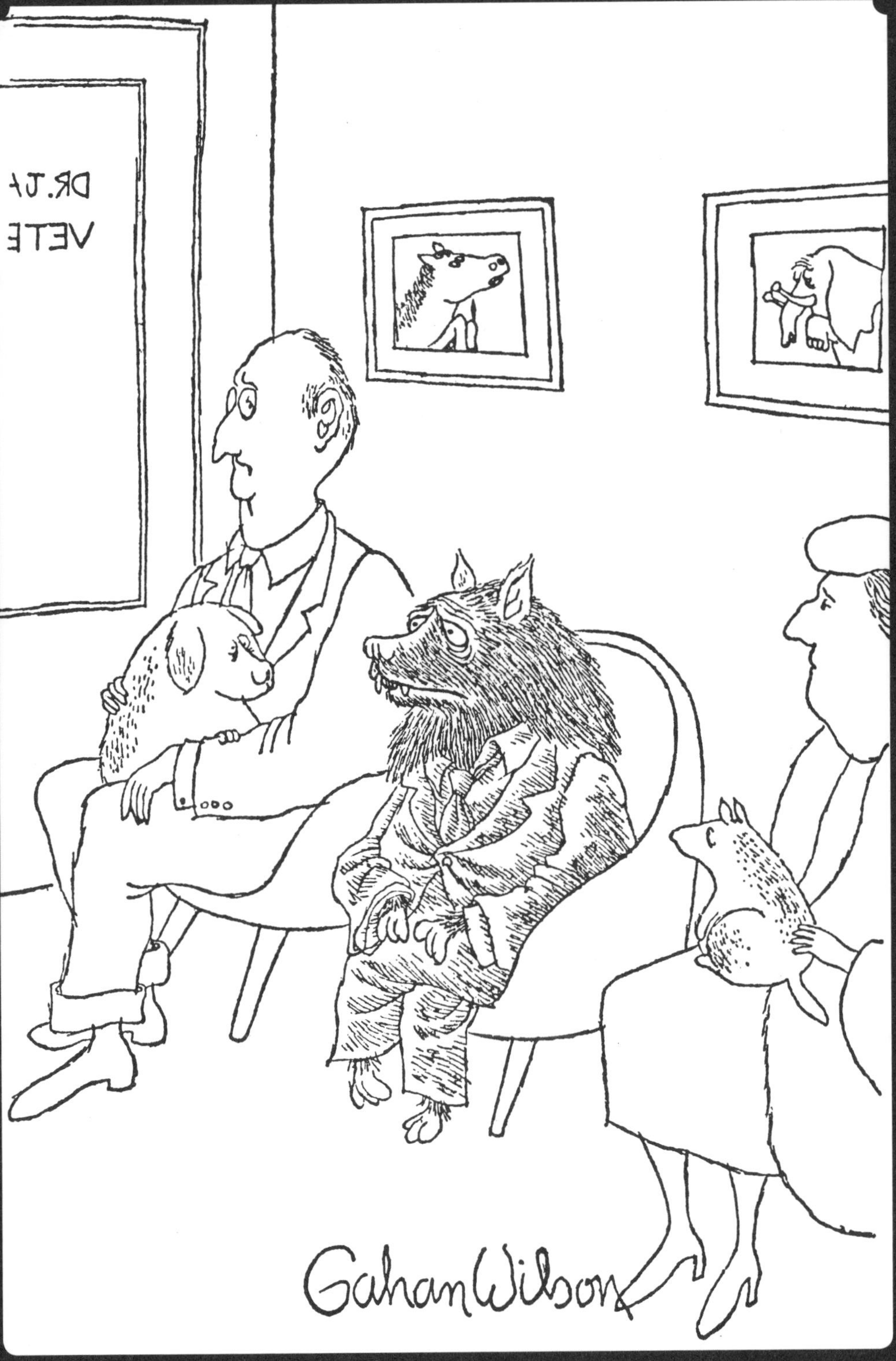
Gahan Wilson

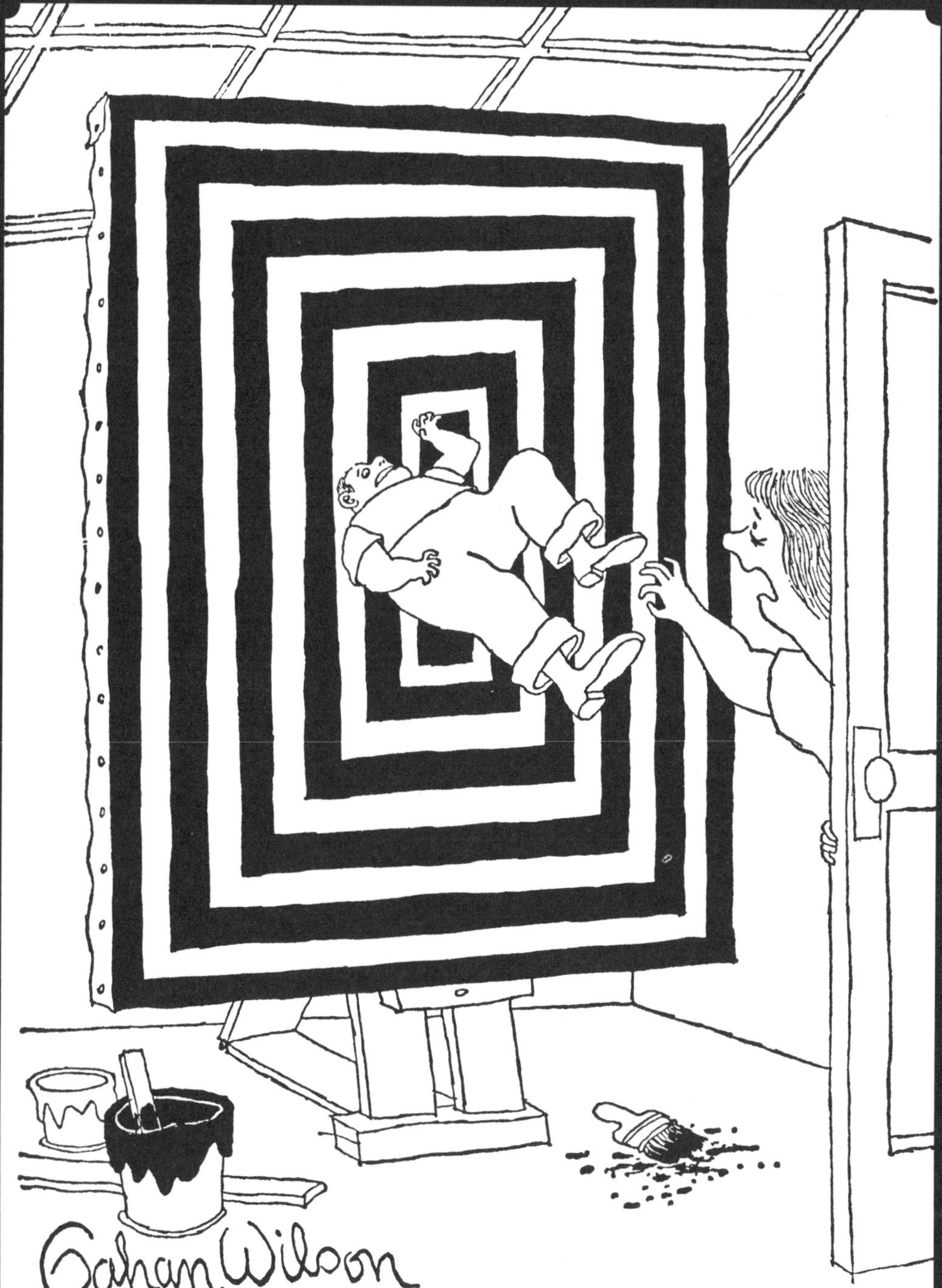
Gahan Wilson

"Harry!"

"It's a grand little ice breaker I picked up in London."

"*Your only worry is the bill, Jack.*"

"I knew you'd missed Long Island Sound!"

"There's that funny noise again!"

"I expect one seldom encounters the older,
traditional hazards on your American courses."

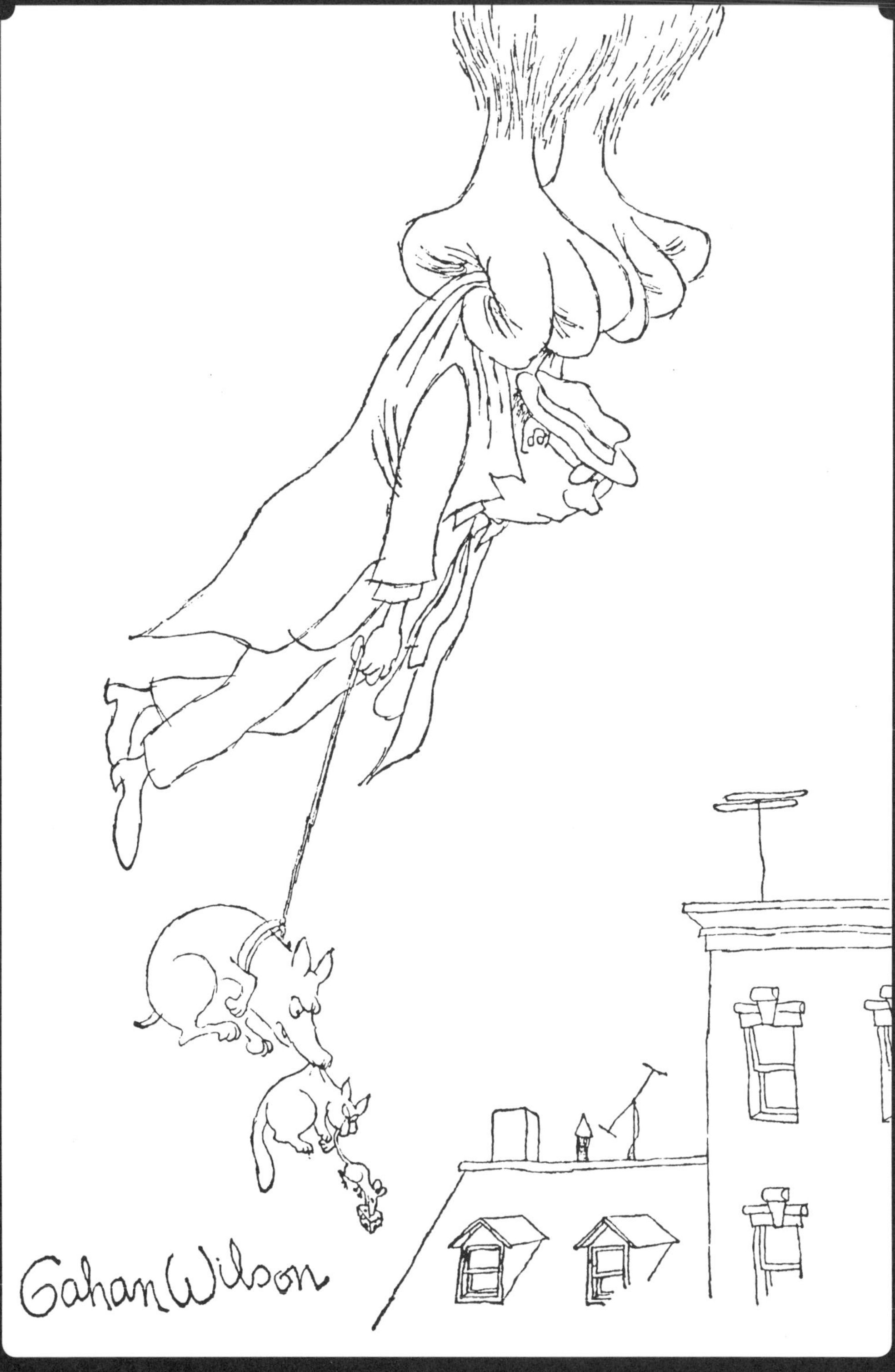
Gahan Wilson

"Of course, once the plaque's done, we're both out of a job."

"Look—in this world you don't get something for nothing!"

"It's just as I'd always hoped it would be."

"I must confess that the terms of Dr. Asimov's
will are unique in my experience."

*"I think you'll agree with me, Chief, that this time
we've really put our finger on the bottleneck."*

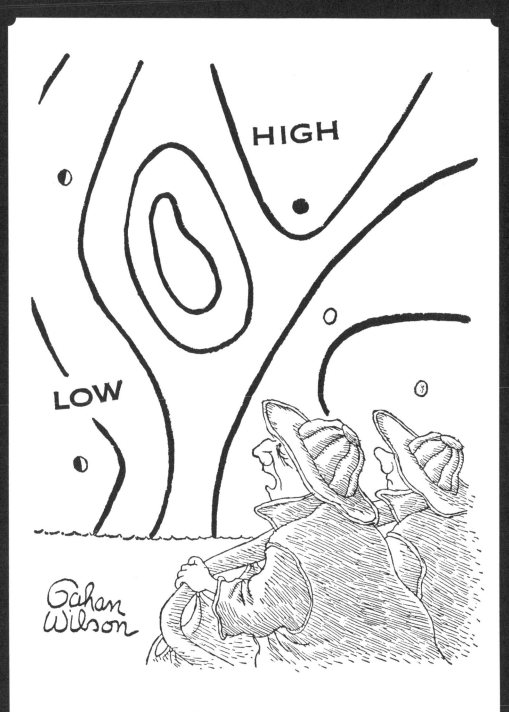

"Looks like a storm tomorrow, sure."

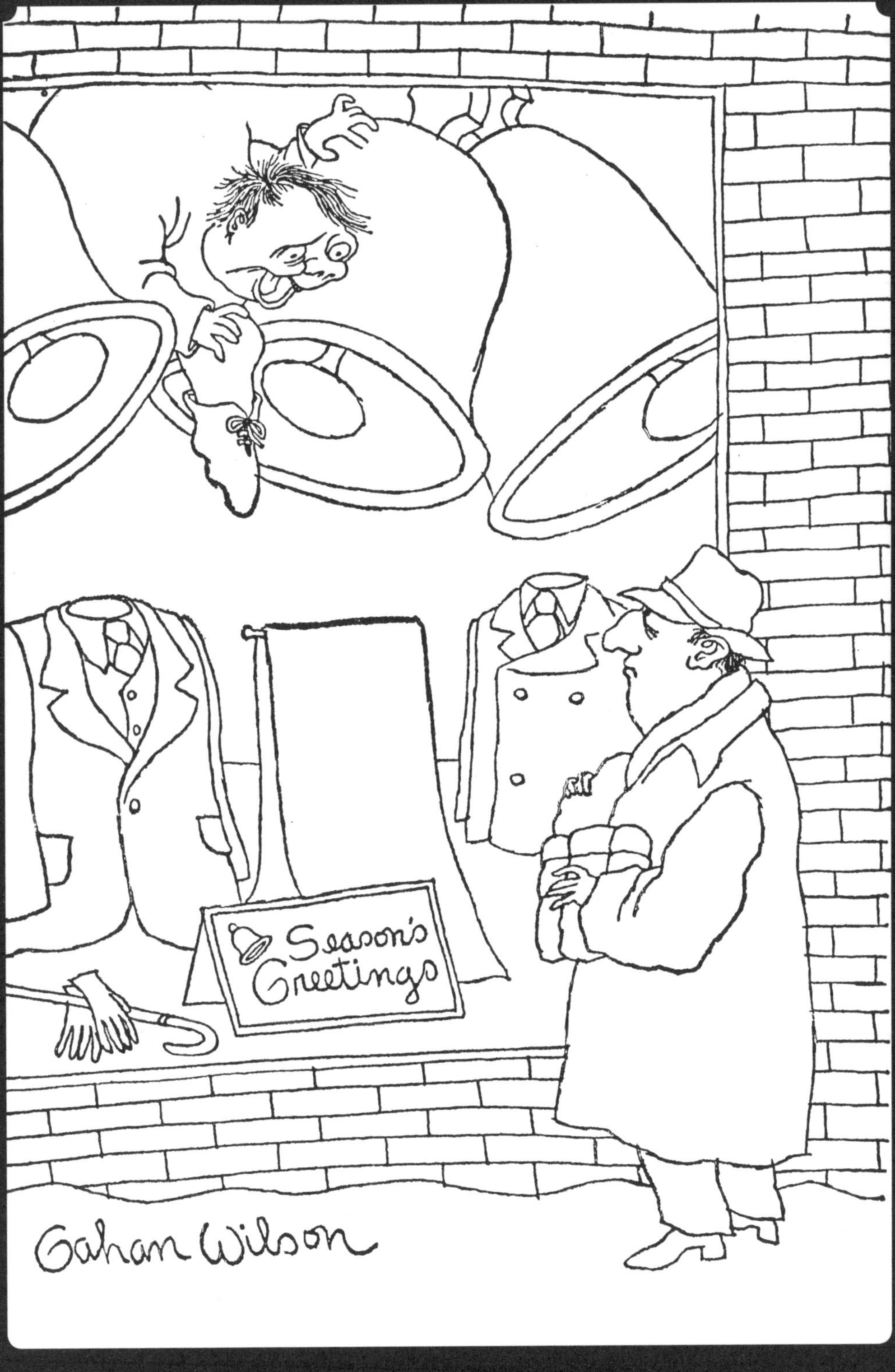
Season's
Greetings
Gahan Wilson

"*You can tell she's thinking it over.*"

"It's the one attack the country wasn't prepared for, Mr. President!"

"Now I think you'll find this one is something rather special, sir."

"Ding dong the witch is dead!"

"Oh, will I be glad when those blasted summer people are gone!"

"No fair turning yourself off, Mr. Hasbrow!"

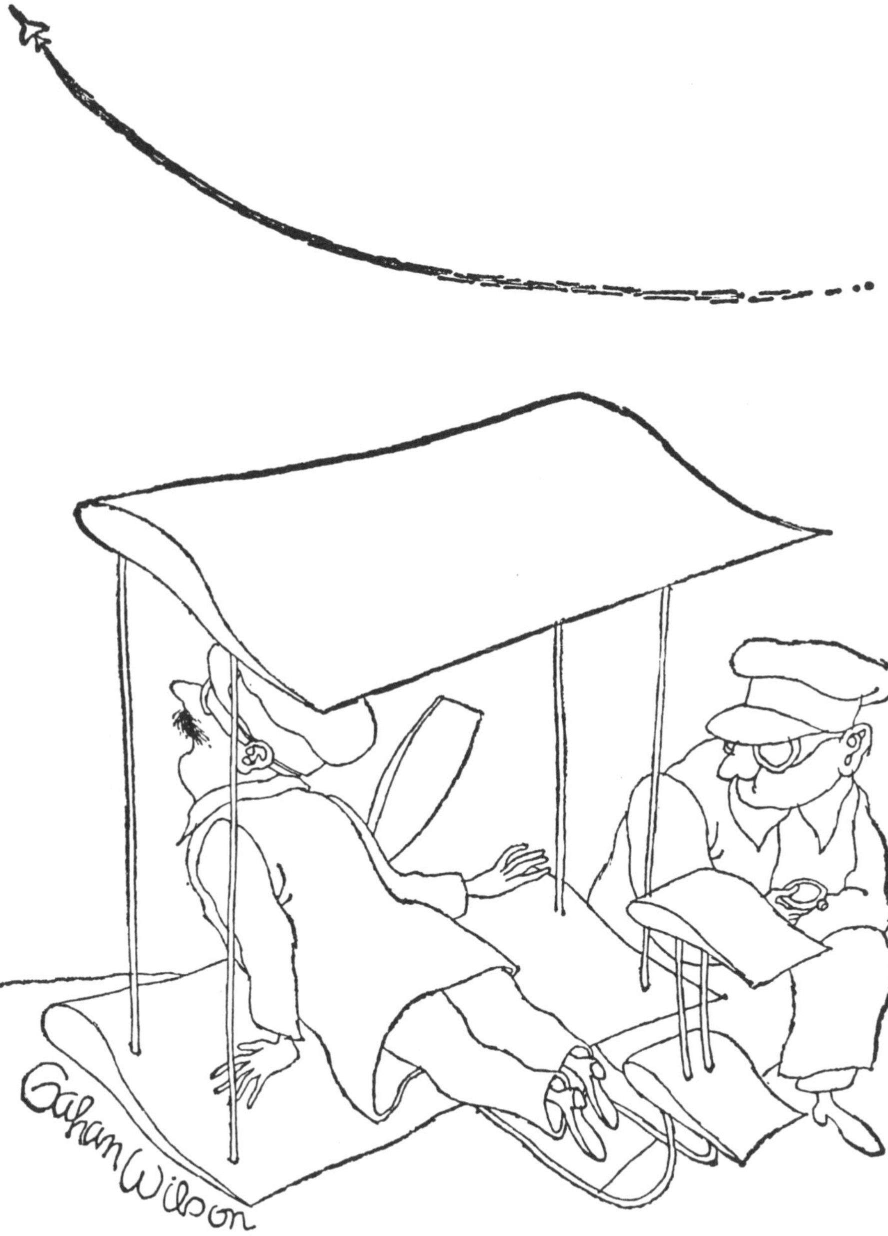
Gahan Wilson

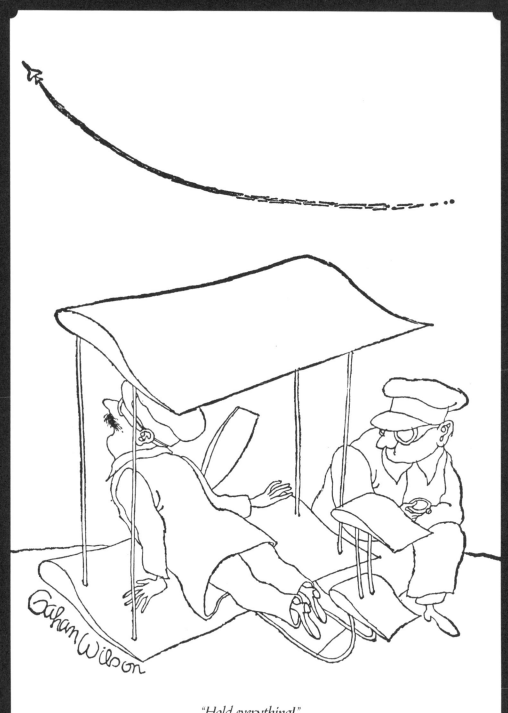

"Hold everything!"

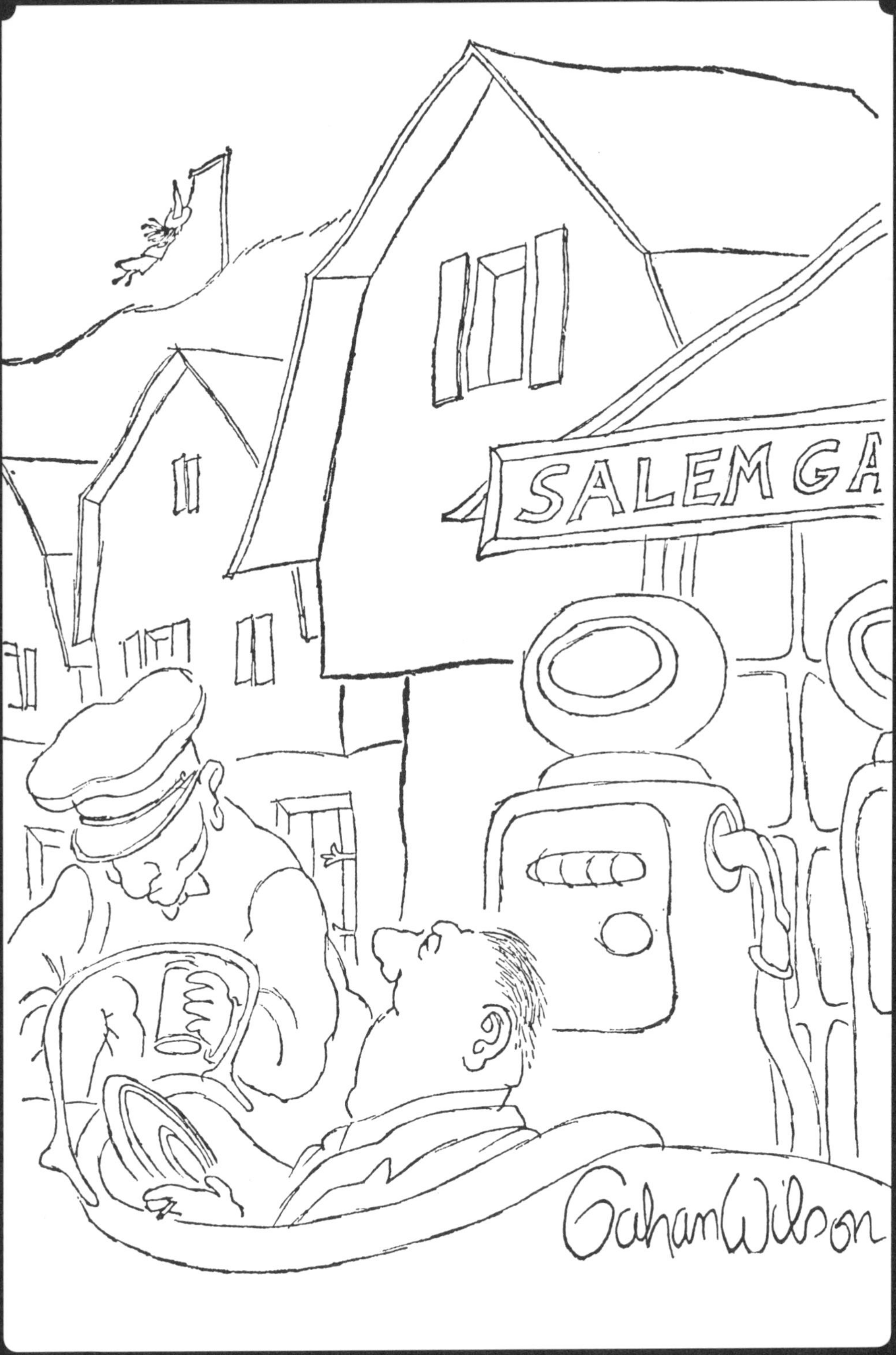
SALEM GA
Gahan Wilson

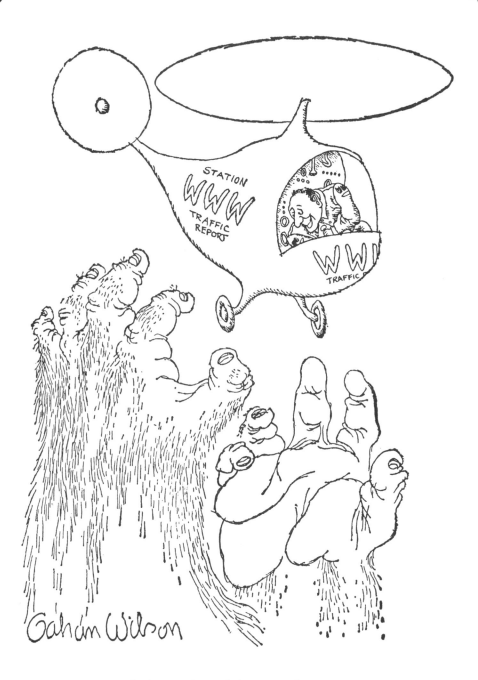

"I think we've located the cause of that tie-up
at Thirty-fourth Street and Seventh Avenue!"

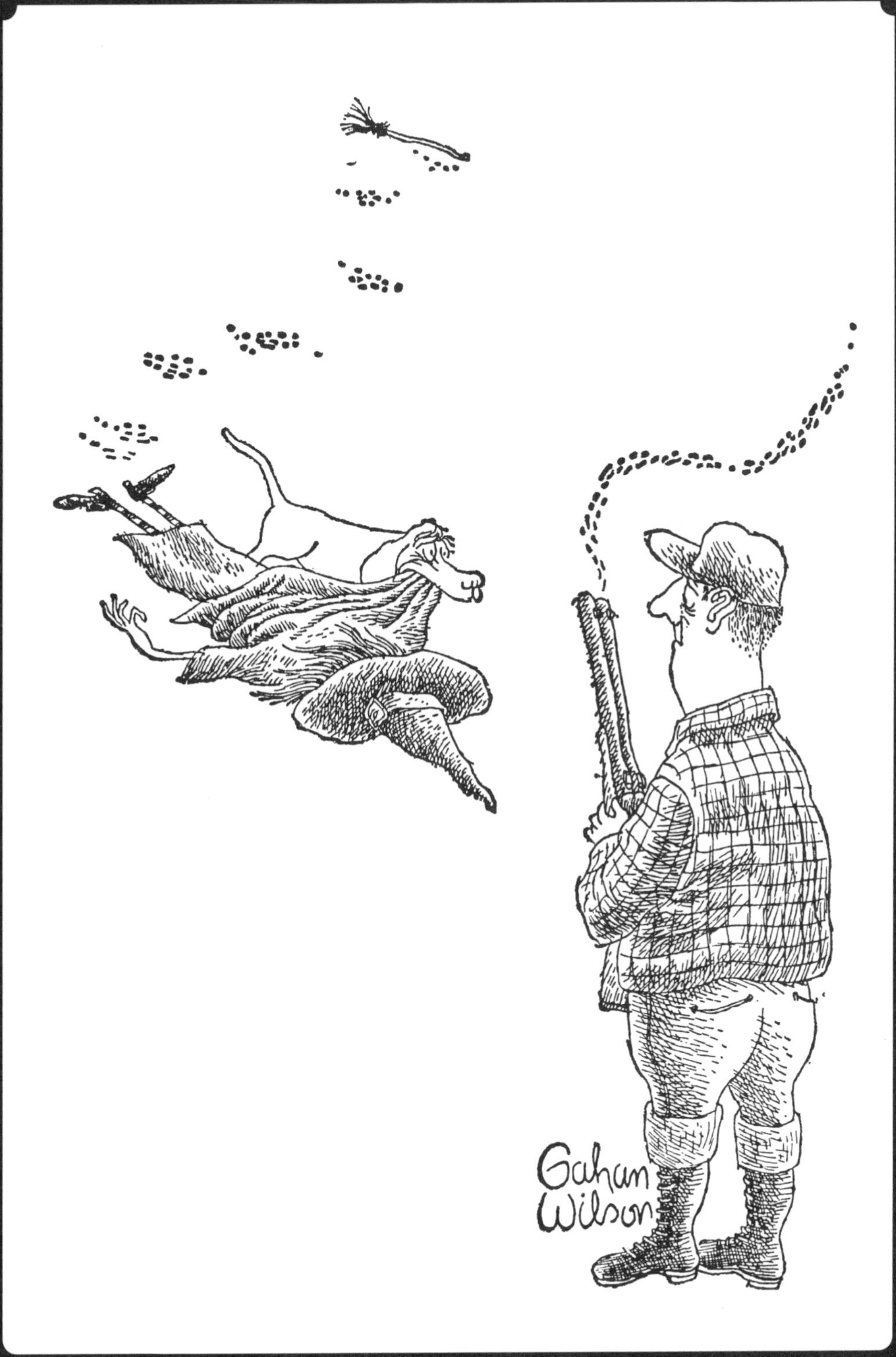
Gahan Wilson

"But surely it must have occurred to you that the wide differences in your backgrounds would make your marriage more than ordinarily difficult!"

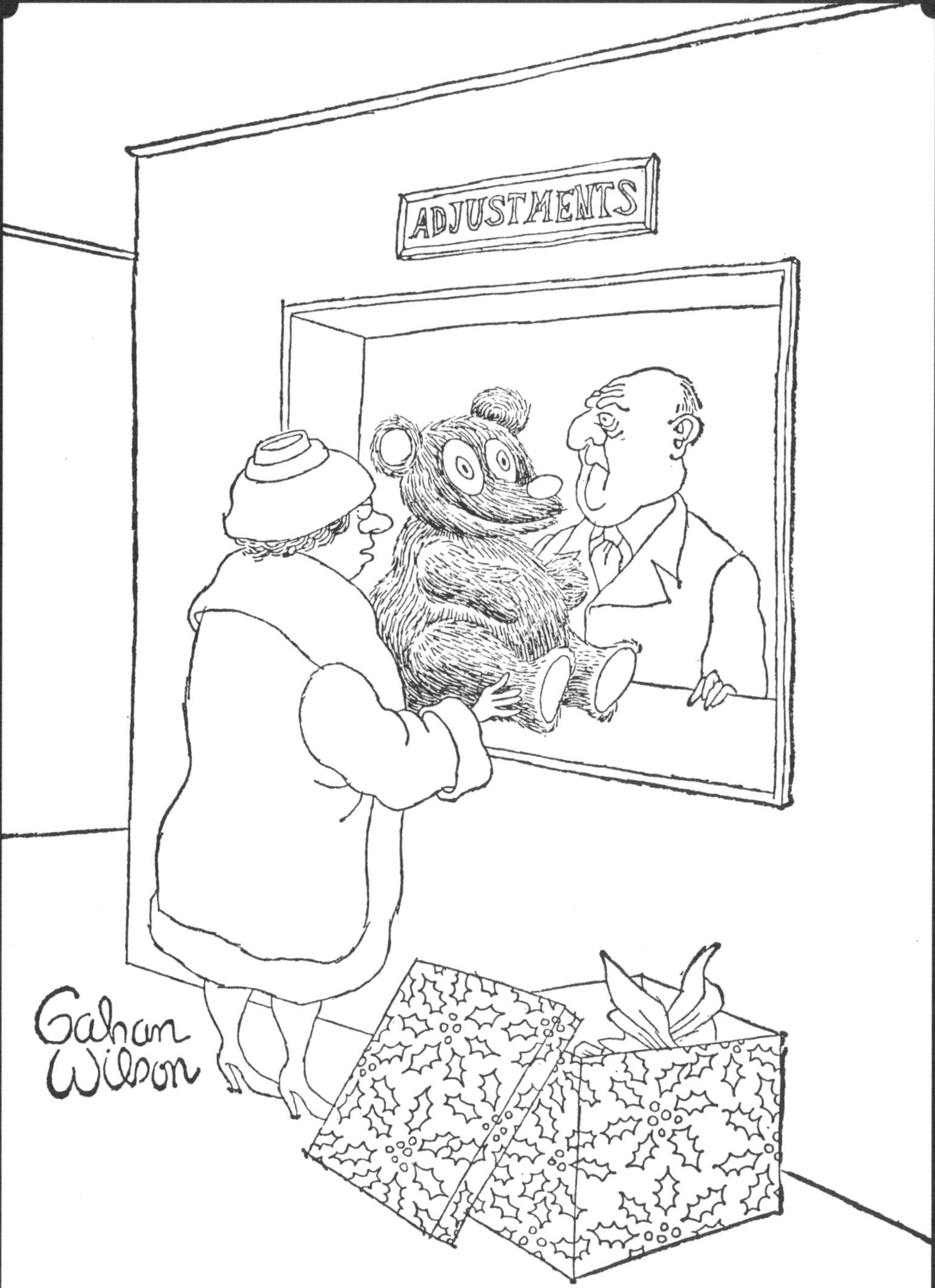
ADJUSTMENTS
Gahan Wilson

"It bites!"

"Better give the missus a touch, too."

"You've got to come over at once, sir! Something
terrible's happening in the hall of eggs!"

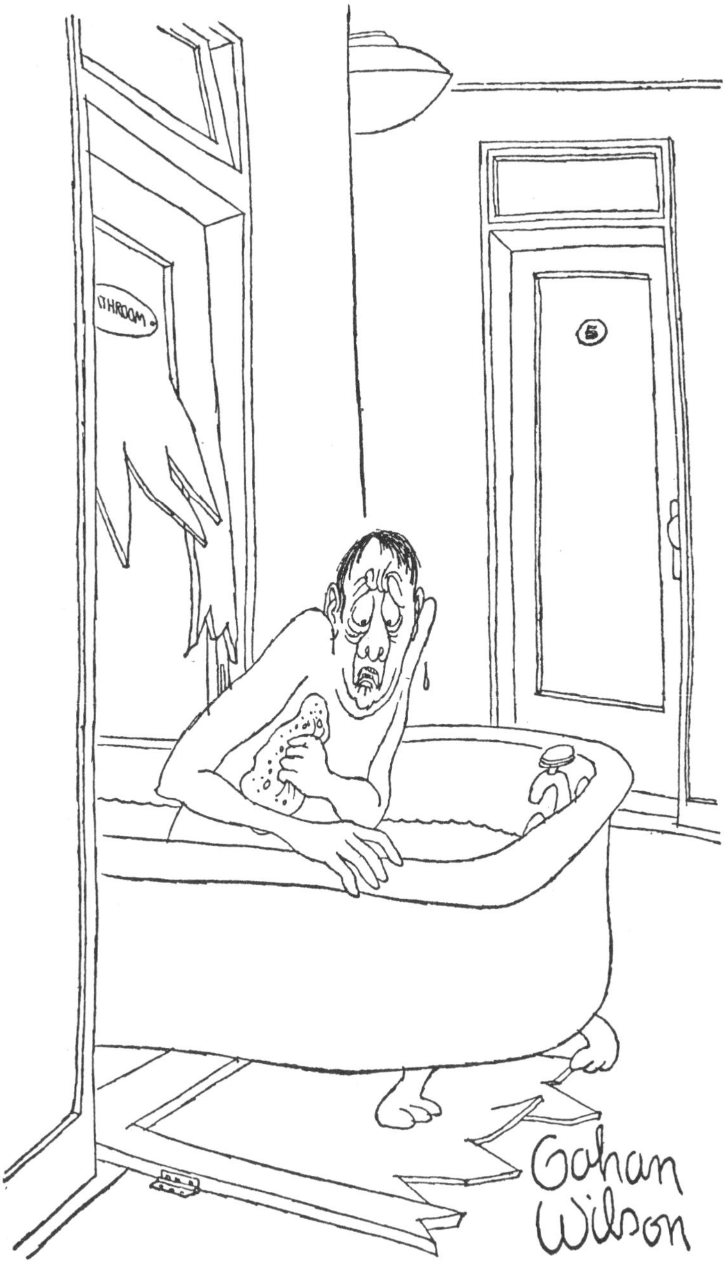
THROOM
5
Gahan Wilson

"Where are you taking me?"

"How come we all draw all the shaggy dog cases?"

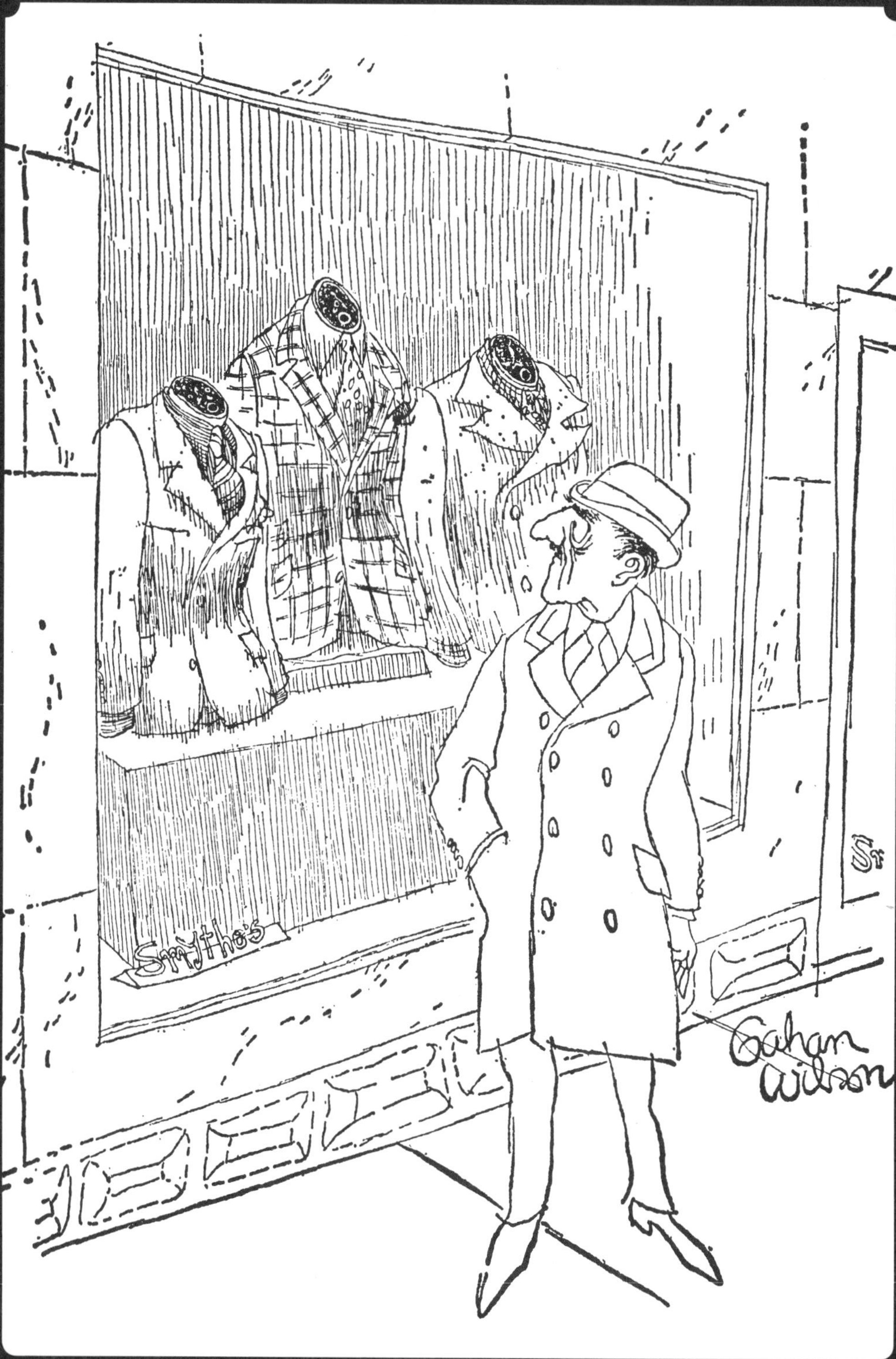
Smythe's
Gahan Wilson

"Well, I guess that pretty well takes care of my anemia diagnosis."

"Funny thing. Eddie was always sure a meteor would get him."

*"I think we have just the thing for that upset tummy
of yours, Mrs. Starbright…"*

"First time I've seen that."

"Here she comes again, and she's got another poodle!"

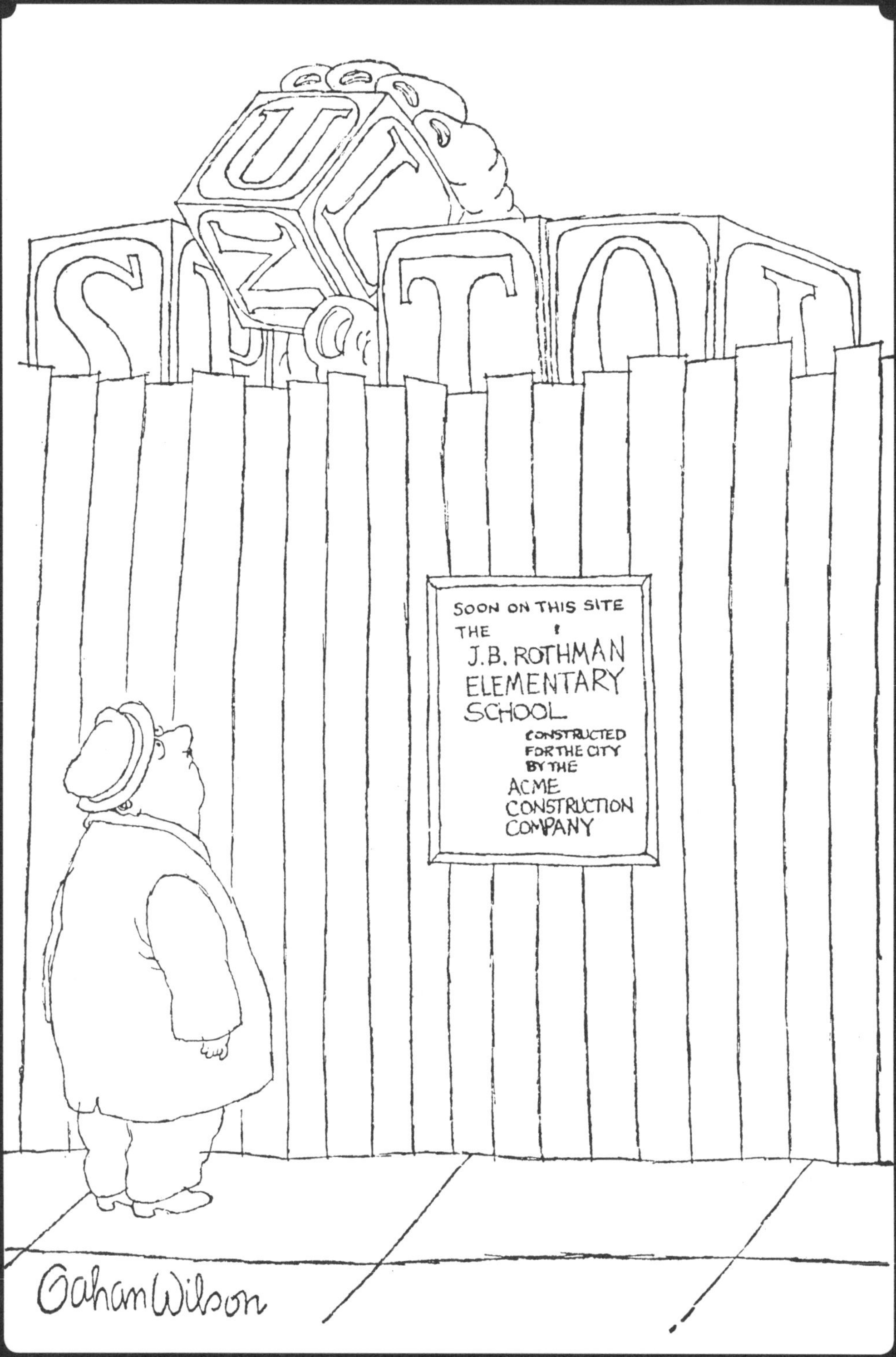
SOON ON THIS SITE
THE
J.B. ROTHMAN
ELEMENTARY
SCHOOL
CONSTRUCTED
FOR THE CITY
BY THE
ACME
CONSTRUCTION
COMPANY
Gahan Wilson

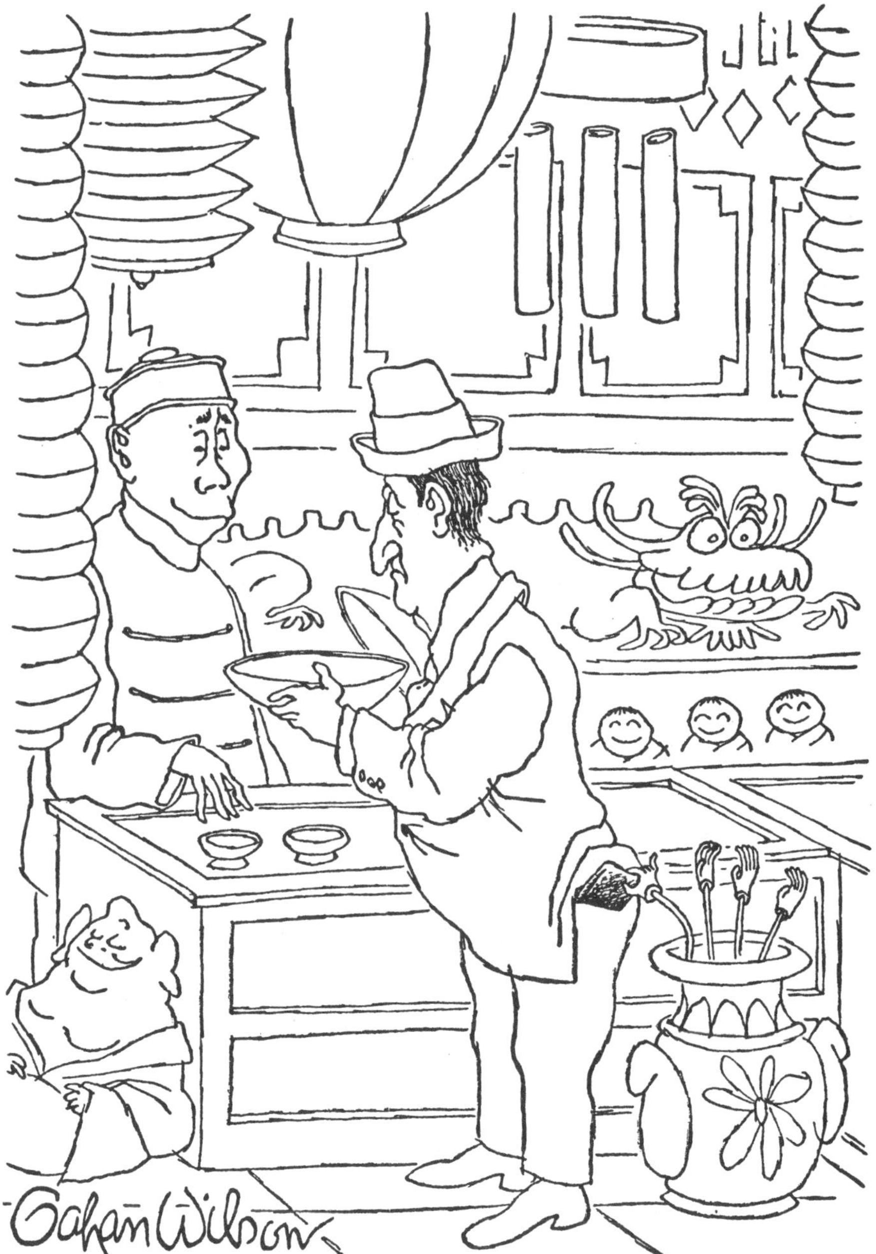
Gahan Wilson

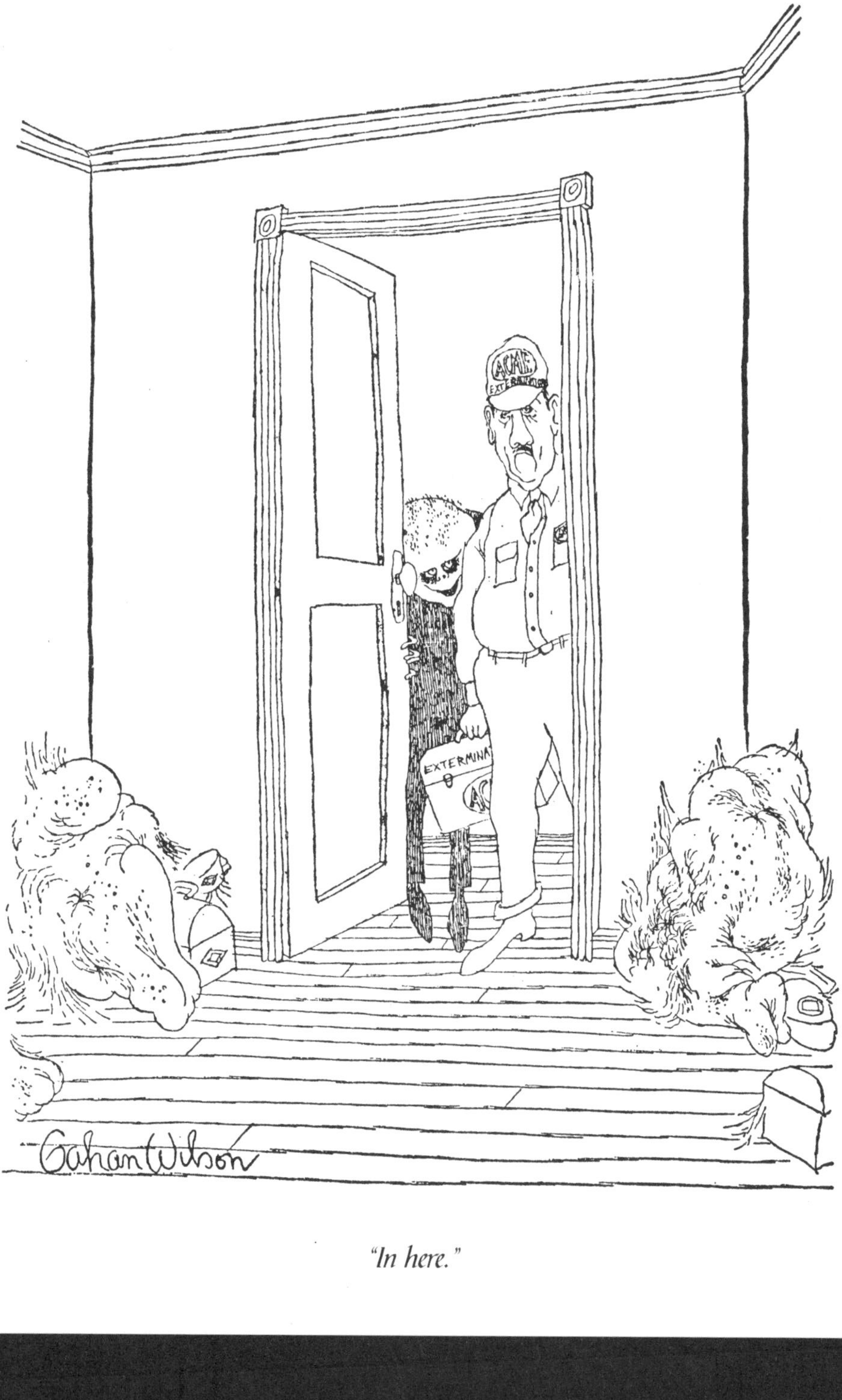
ACME
EXTERMINAT
Gahan Wilson

"In here."

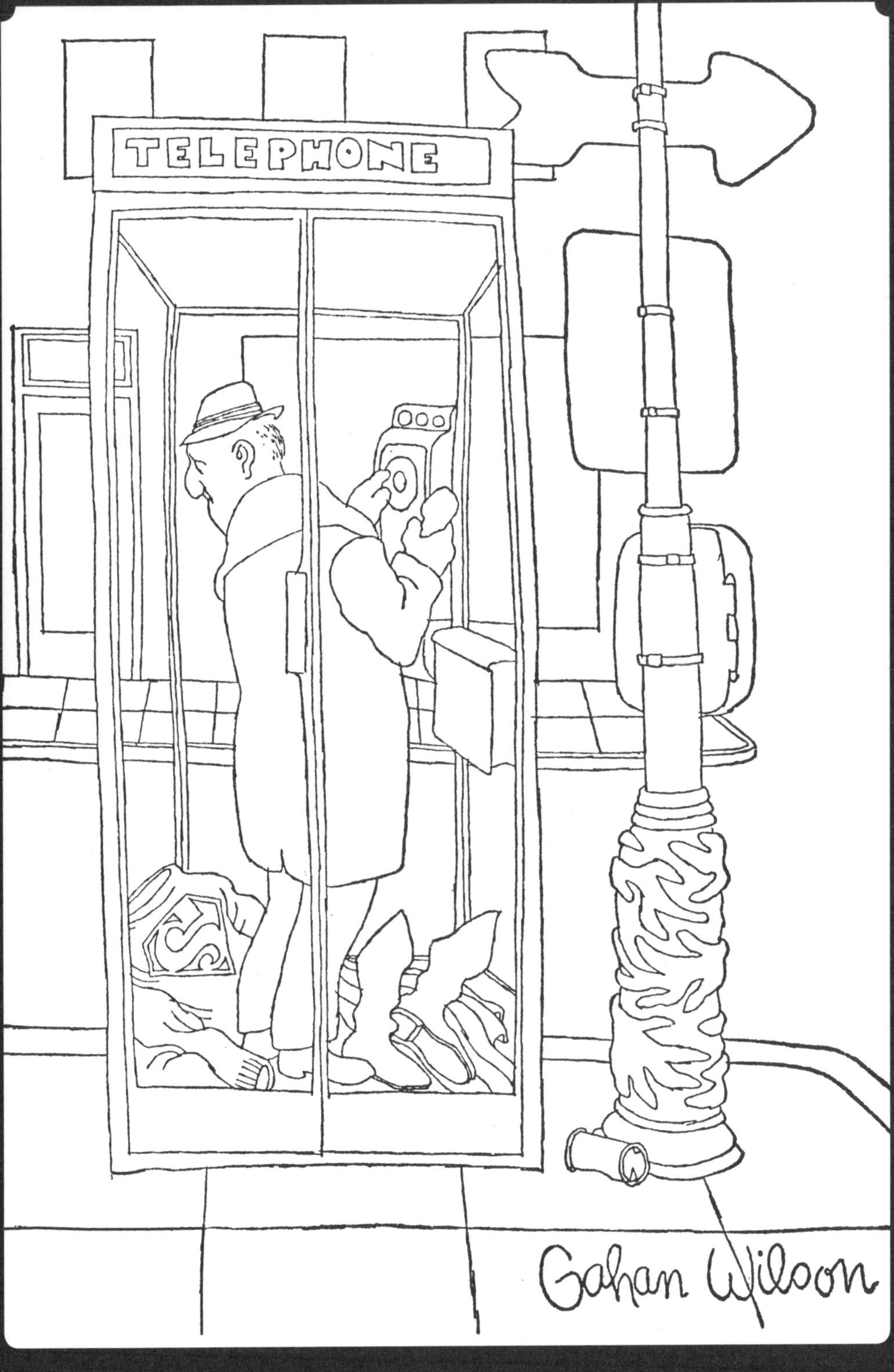
TELEPHONE
Gahan Wilson

"I tell you, Shirley, there's something funny about this place!"

"*I just don't understand it, Captain. Equal shares of food and water to all, yet those two thrive while we wither away.*"

Gahan Wilson

"It's working!"

"Hold it, Newton. We've been barking up the wrong tree."

"Whoever they are, they've sold out."

"The sandwich man killer has struck again!"

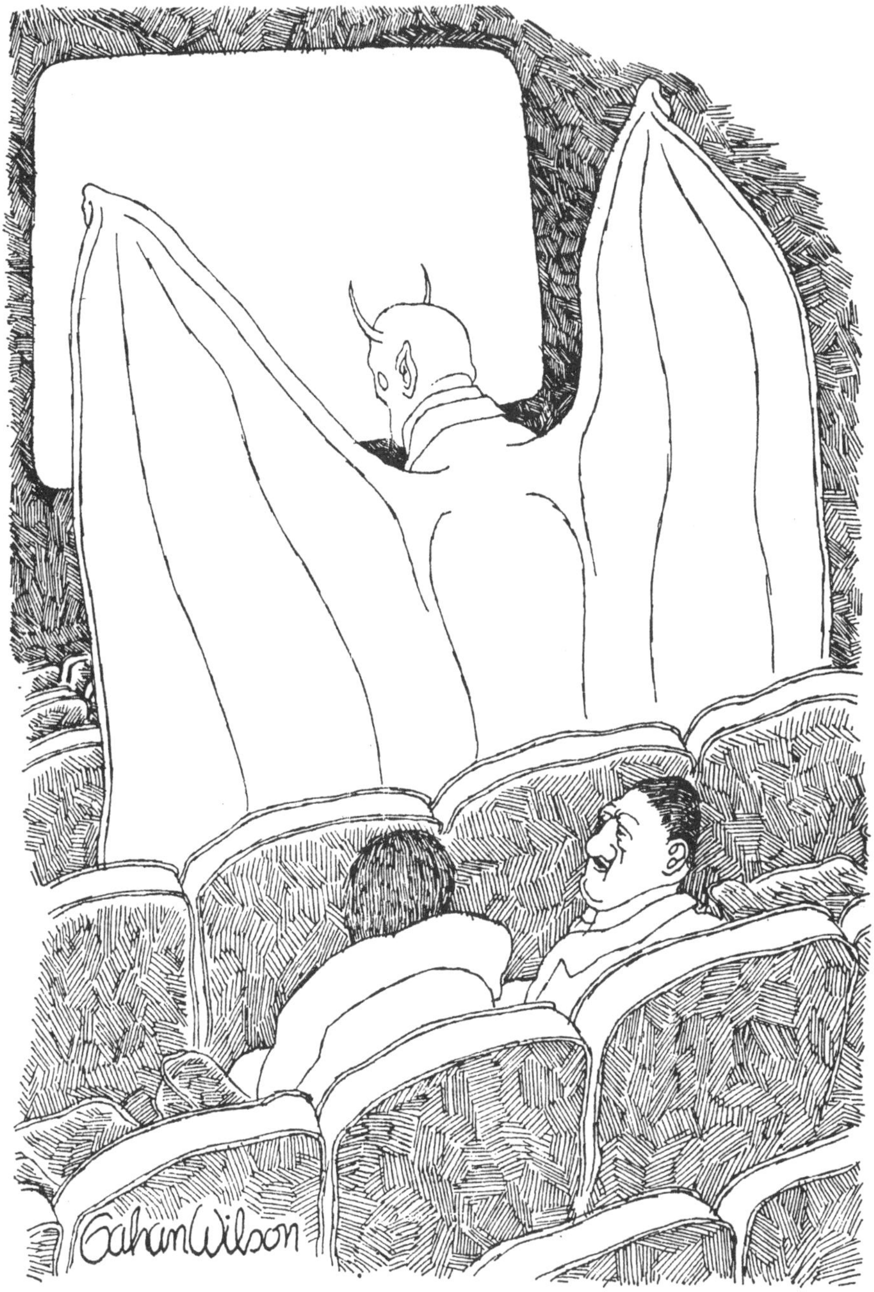
Gahan Wilson

"My usual luck."

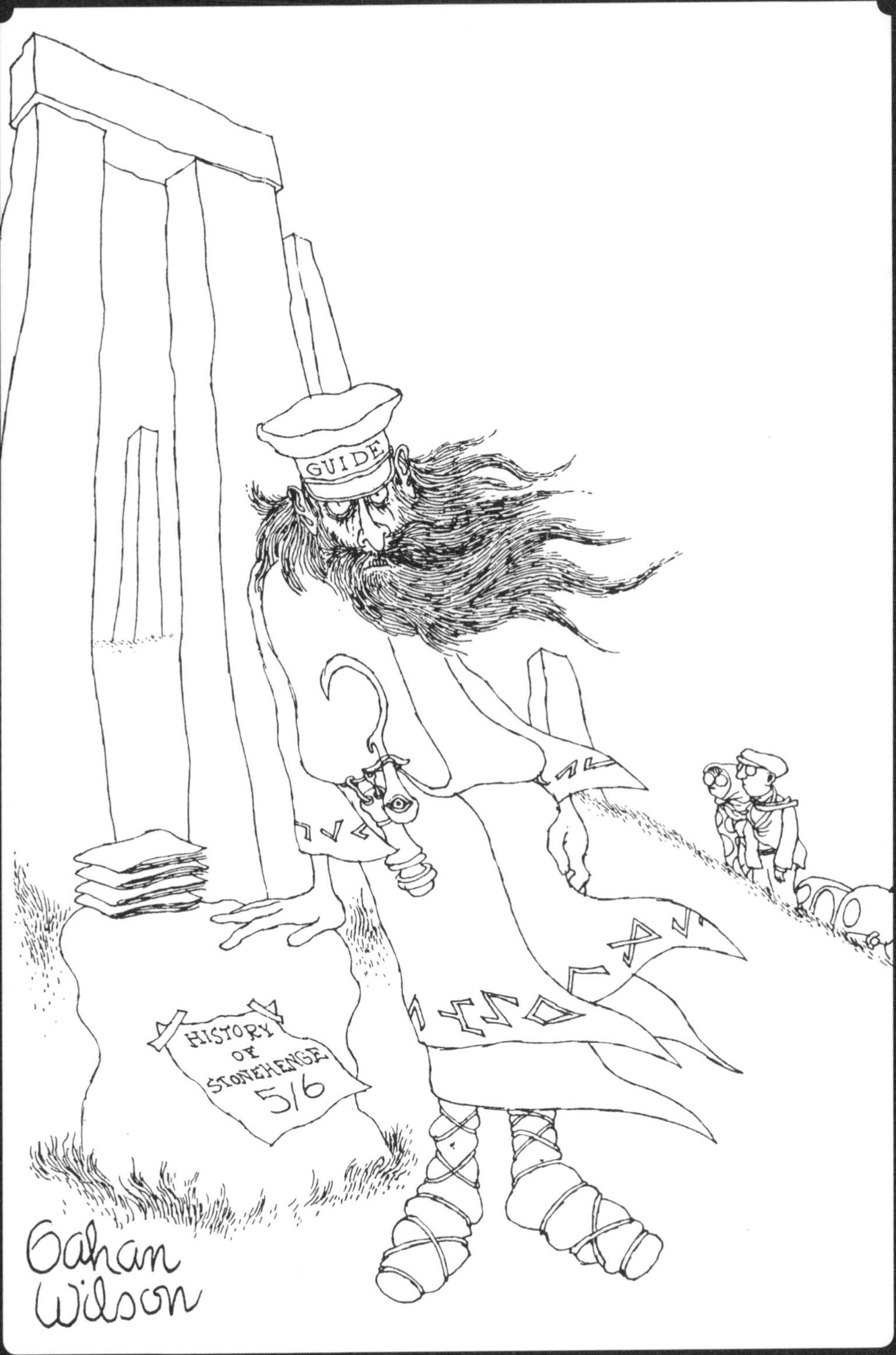
GUIDE
HISTORY OF STONEHENGE 5/6
Gahan Wilson

"The thing that gets me is I sent boxtops in to everyone of these bums!"

"Best damn special effects man in the business!"

"Very well, Miss Apple—call my broker."

*"I'm afraid this simulator test indicates Commodore Brent
would be a poor choice for the Lunar Expedition."*

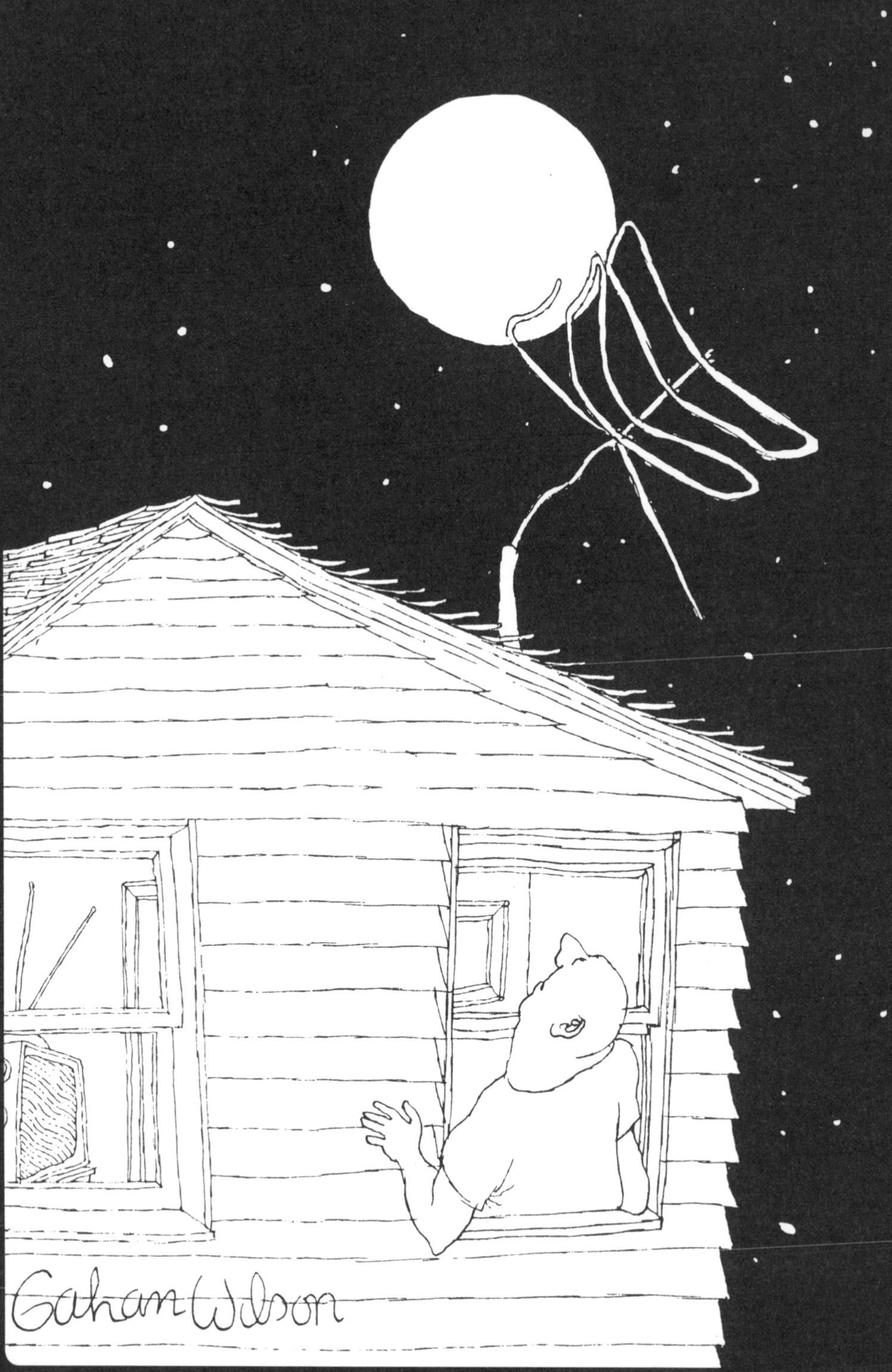
Gahan Wilson

"I don't like the looks of that, at all!"

"That's alright, boy! Here, boy! Forget it, boy! C'mon, boy…"

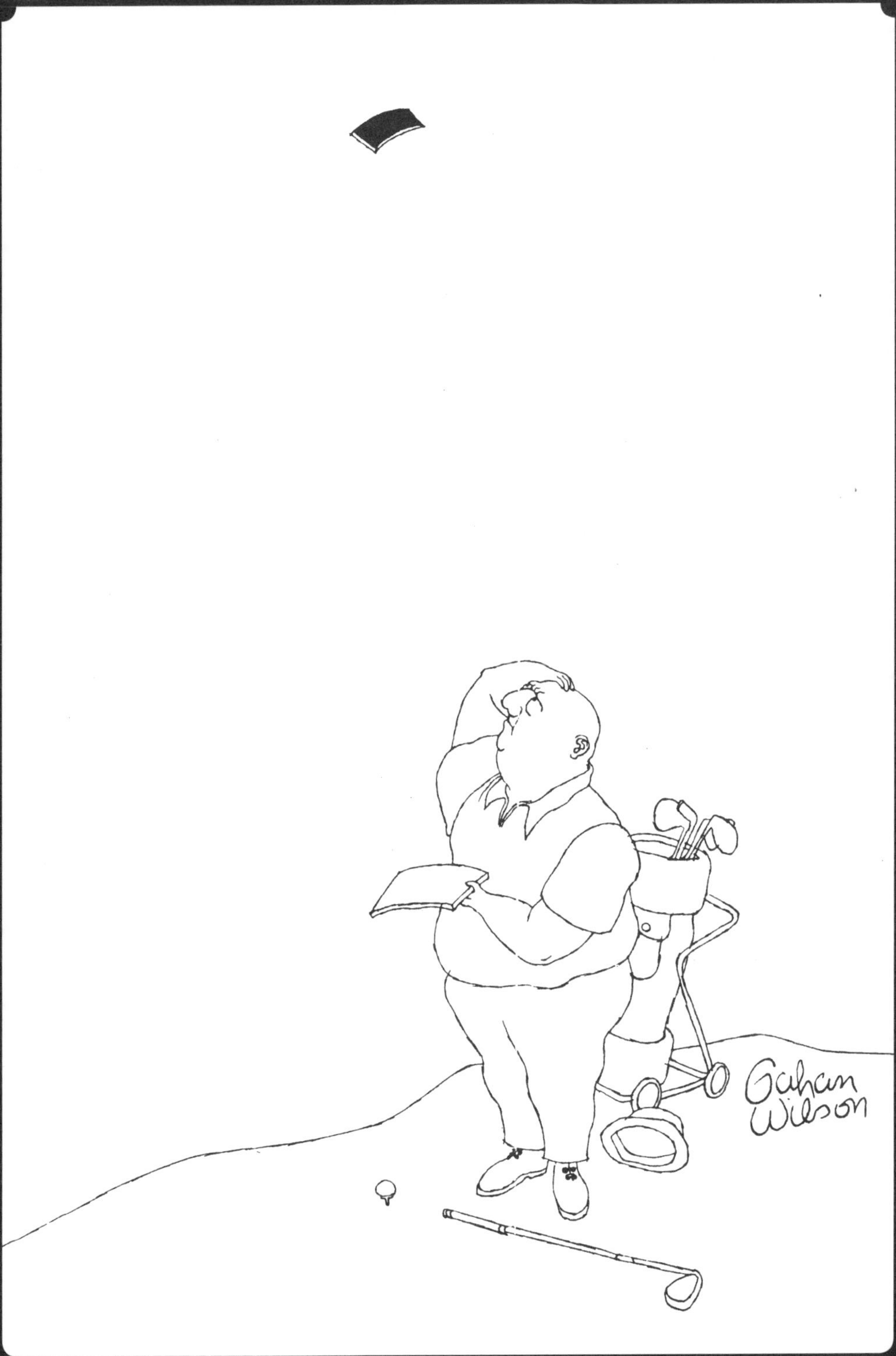
Gahan Wilson

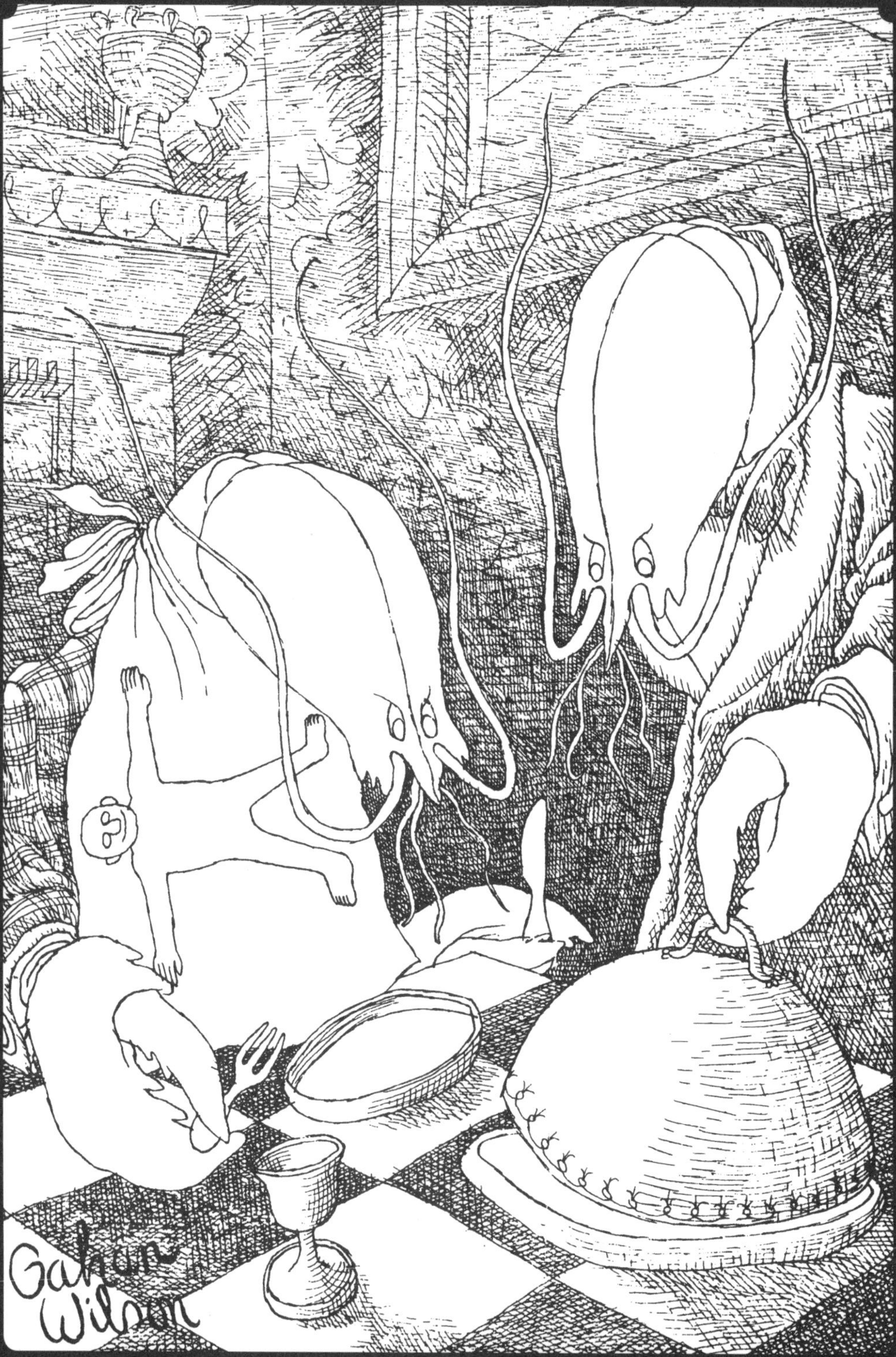
Gahan Wilson

"Why, that's the Edison's Boy!"

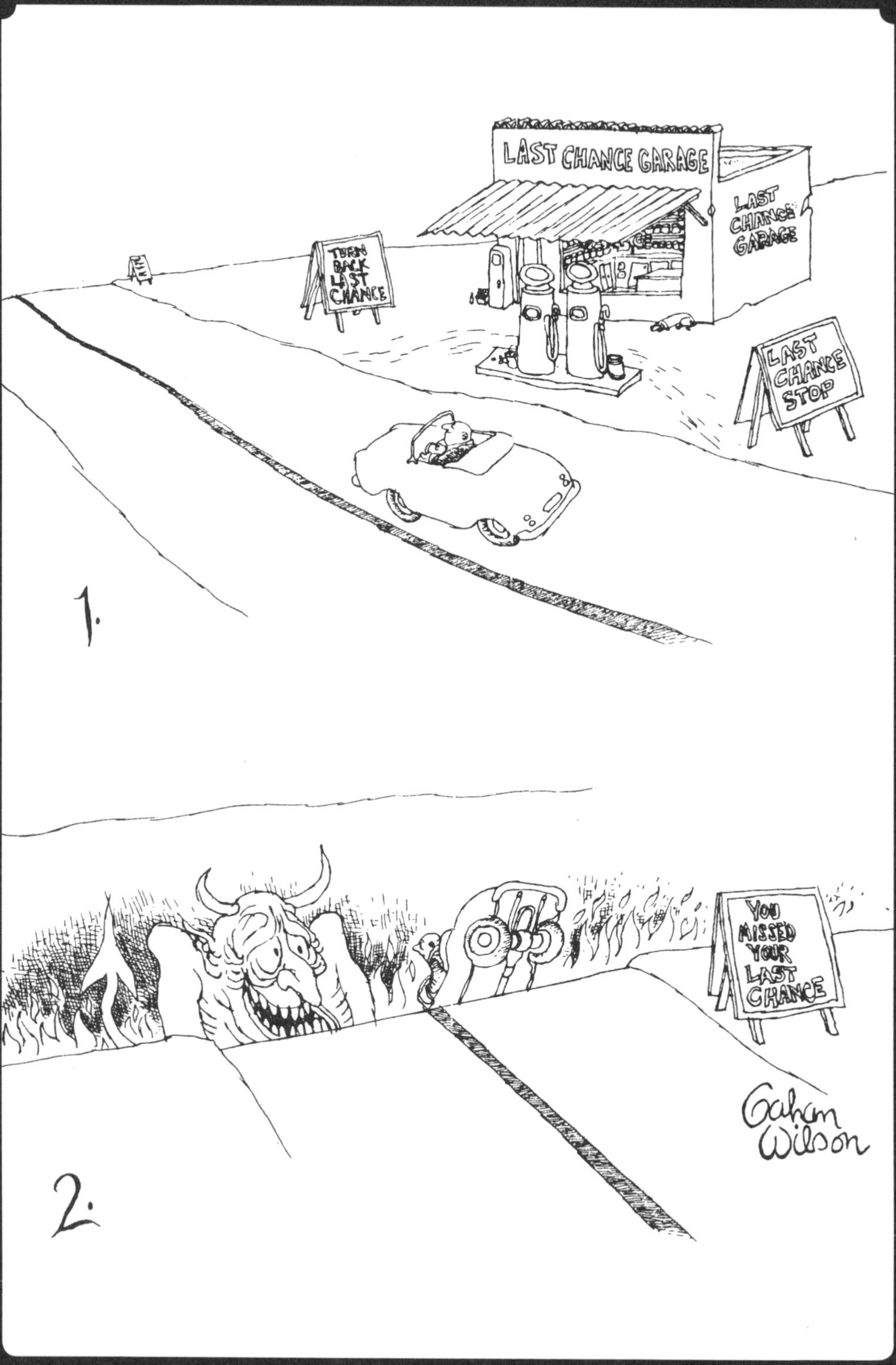
LAST CHANCE GARAGE
LAST CHANCE GARAGE
TURN BACK LAST CHANCE
LAST CHANCE STOP
1.
YOU MISSED YOUR LAST CHANCE
Gahan Wilson
2.

"Oh, my God—we completely forgot about Uncle Fred!"

"We three kings of Orient are…"

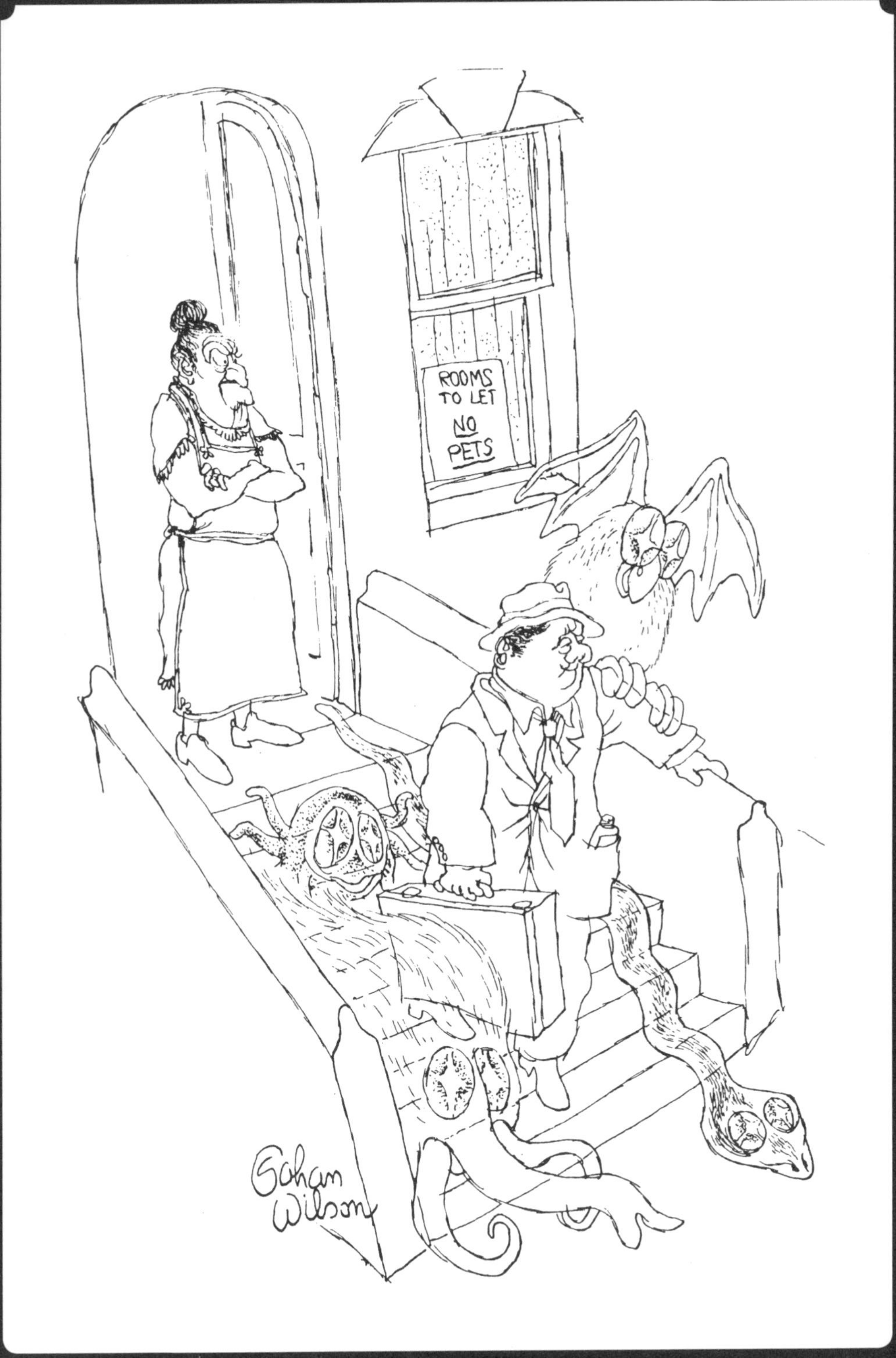
ROOMS
TO LET
NO
PETS
Gahan
Wilson

"I suppose the least we can do is name the damned thing after poor Dembar."

"Doesn't look like such a bad sort."

"*Your husband is with a lady named Claire Belle Webster at the*
Whispering Pines Motel near Akron, Ohio."

"Yes, the public _did_ put up with color TV's radiation, but I think this is really asking an awful lot of them. Even for 3-D."

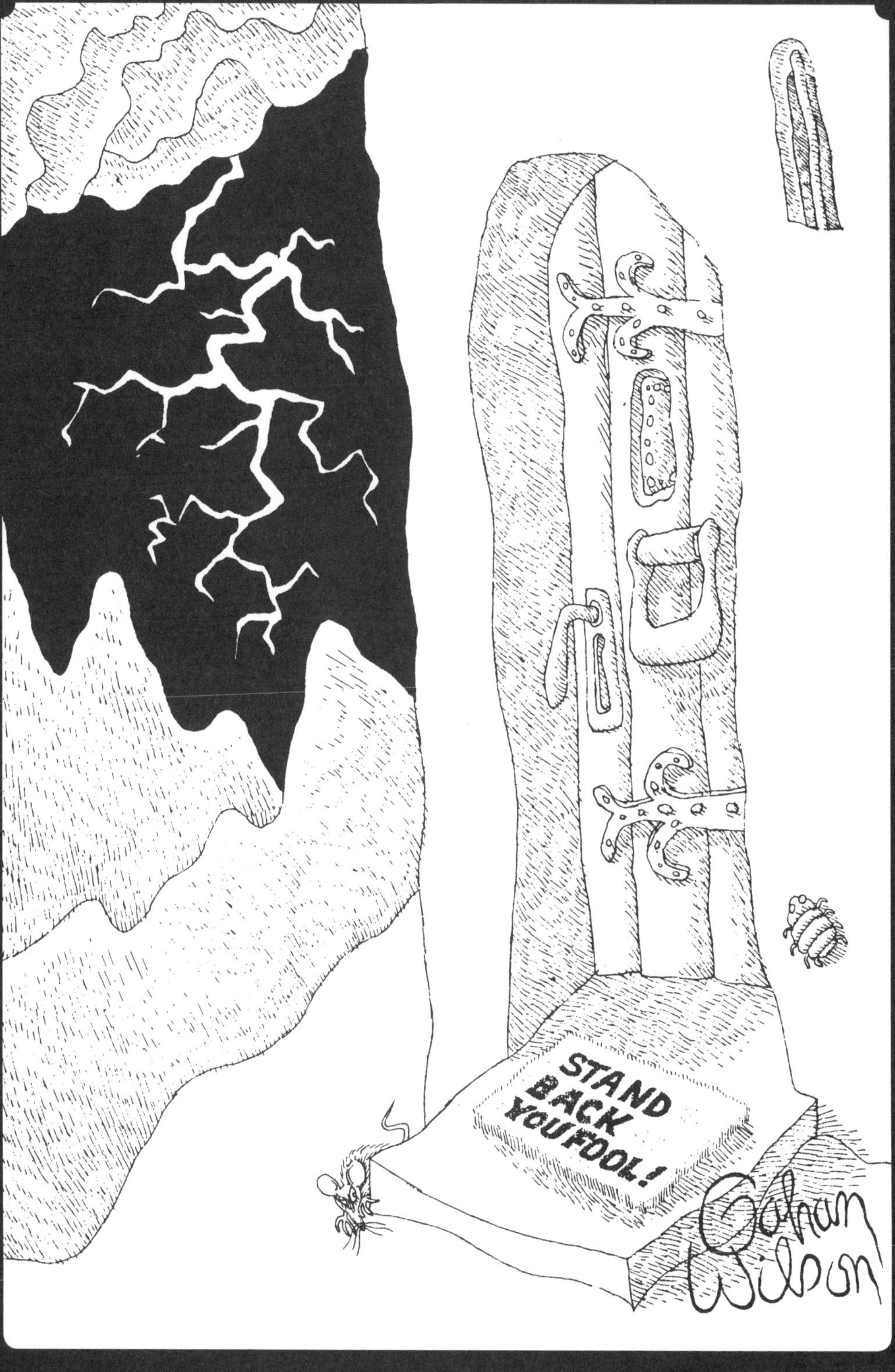
STAND
BACK
YOU FOOL!
Gahan
Wilson

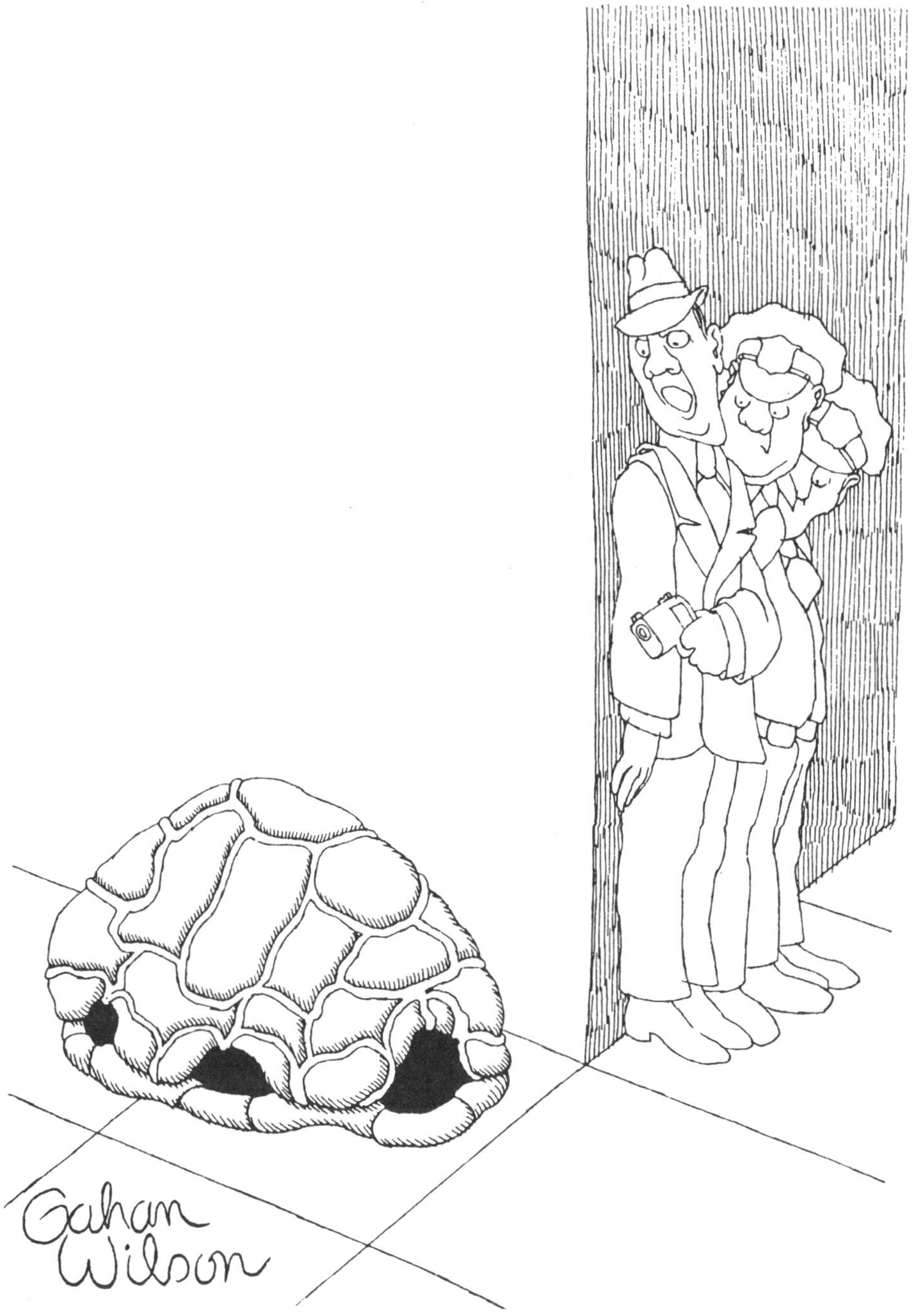
Gahan Wilson

"We know you're in there!"

"I don't know how we ever got along without the stuff."

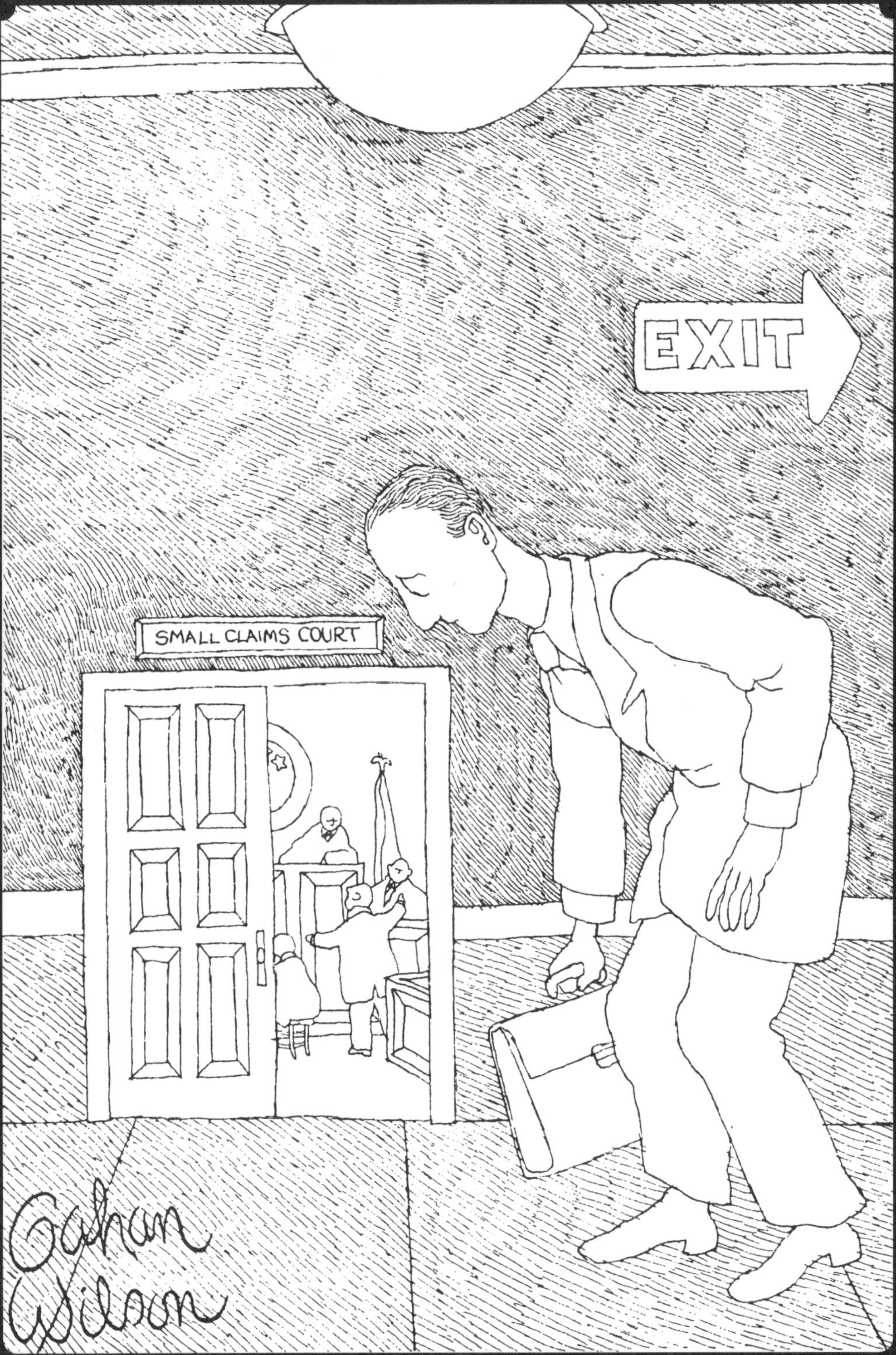
EXIT
SMALL CLAIMS COURT
Gahan Wilson

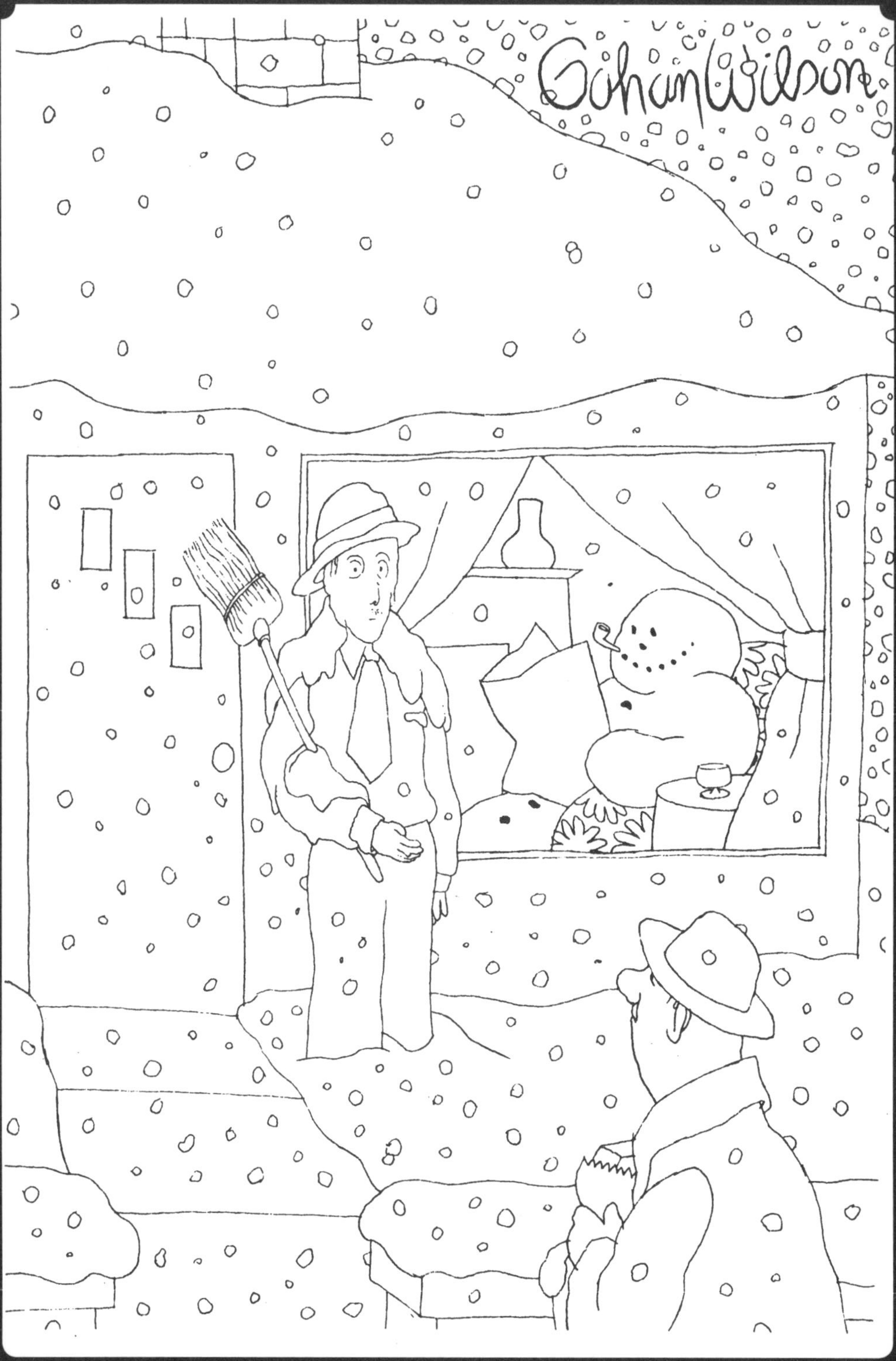
Gahan Wilson

"*Where were you for all those years?*"

"I can never sell ticket one in this Goddam town."

"Listen. There it goes again!"

"How do you suppose young Ainsworth's so damned
sharp at spotting tombs?"

"Oh? And what sort of sacrifices are you going to make
to your snow idol, Timmy?"

"Trying to bolster one of your shabby little theories, Carson?"

"O.K., they've signed the release."

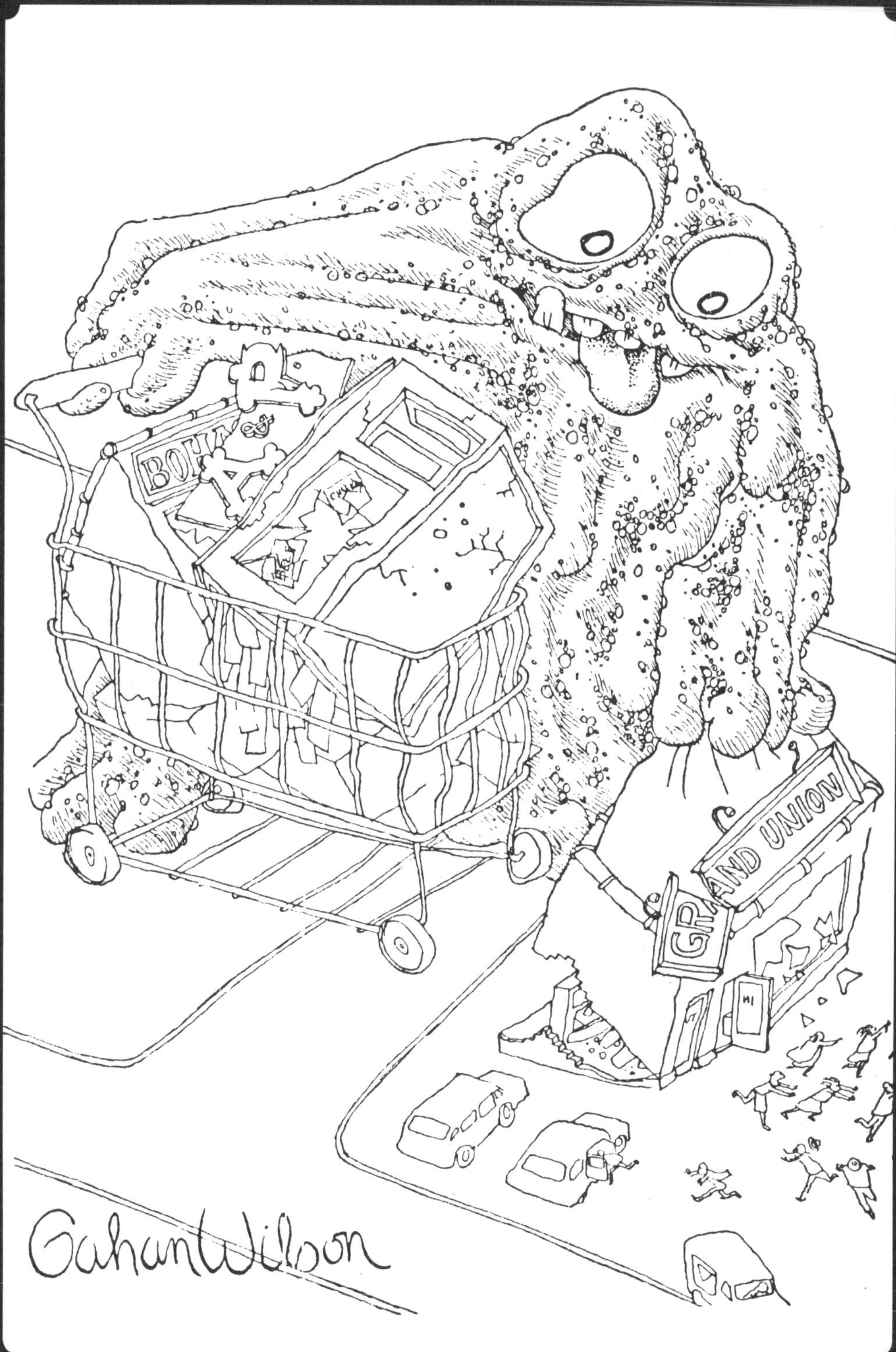
A&P
GRAND UNION
Gahan Wilson

"Being the first astronaut to play golf on the Moon is one thing, men;
being the first to shoot crap is quite another!"

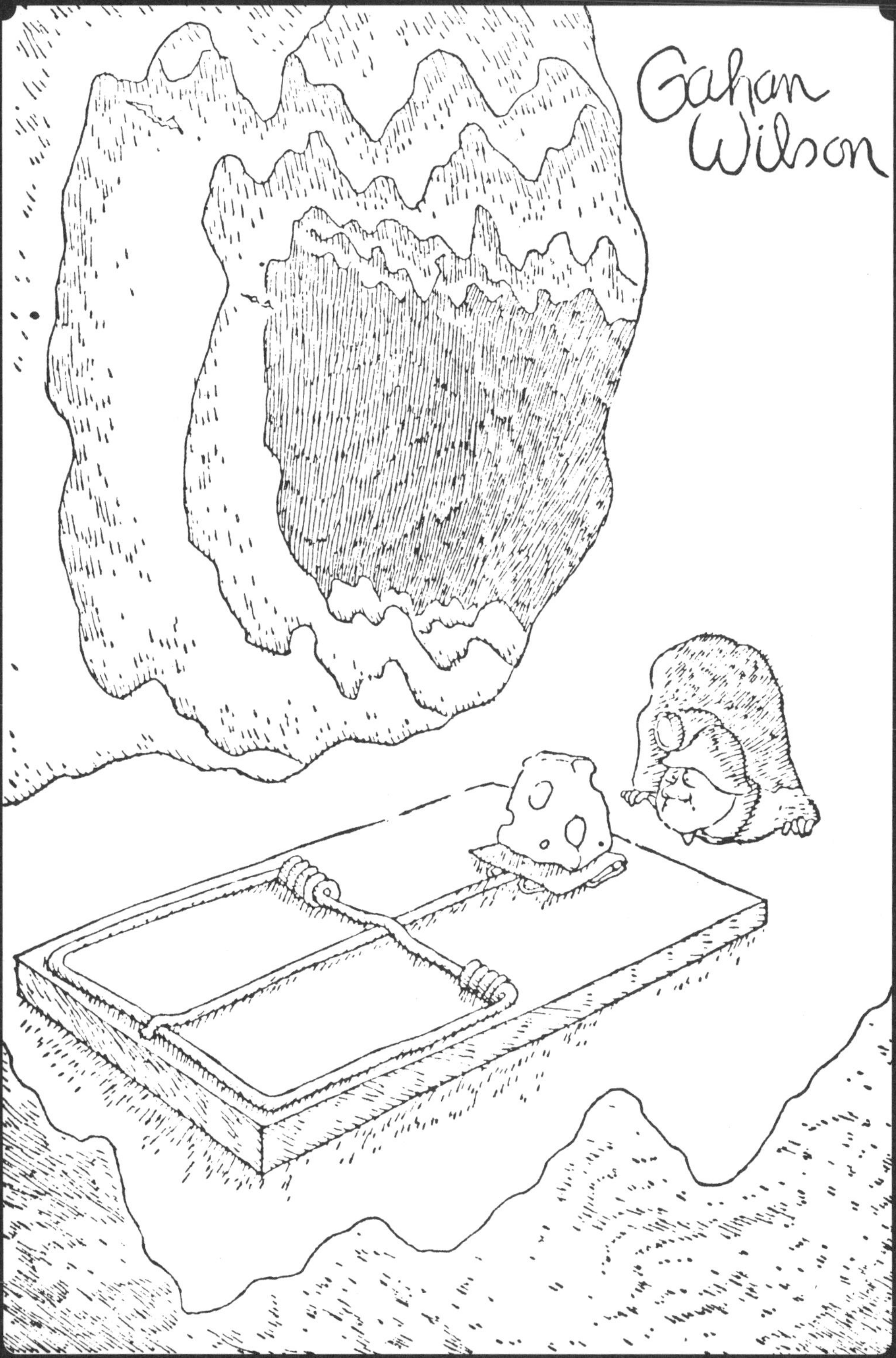
Gahan
Wilson

"It's just wonderful how the doctors have
managed to keep him going!"

"Just exactly what are you teaching these children, Miss Rawley?"

"Never mind, Nurse, I've spotted the boy!"

"*You know, Phil, you've really done very well for a walrus—*""

"You know, Larry, with a smart lawyer
you could make a lot of money!"

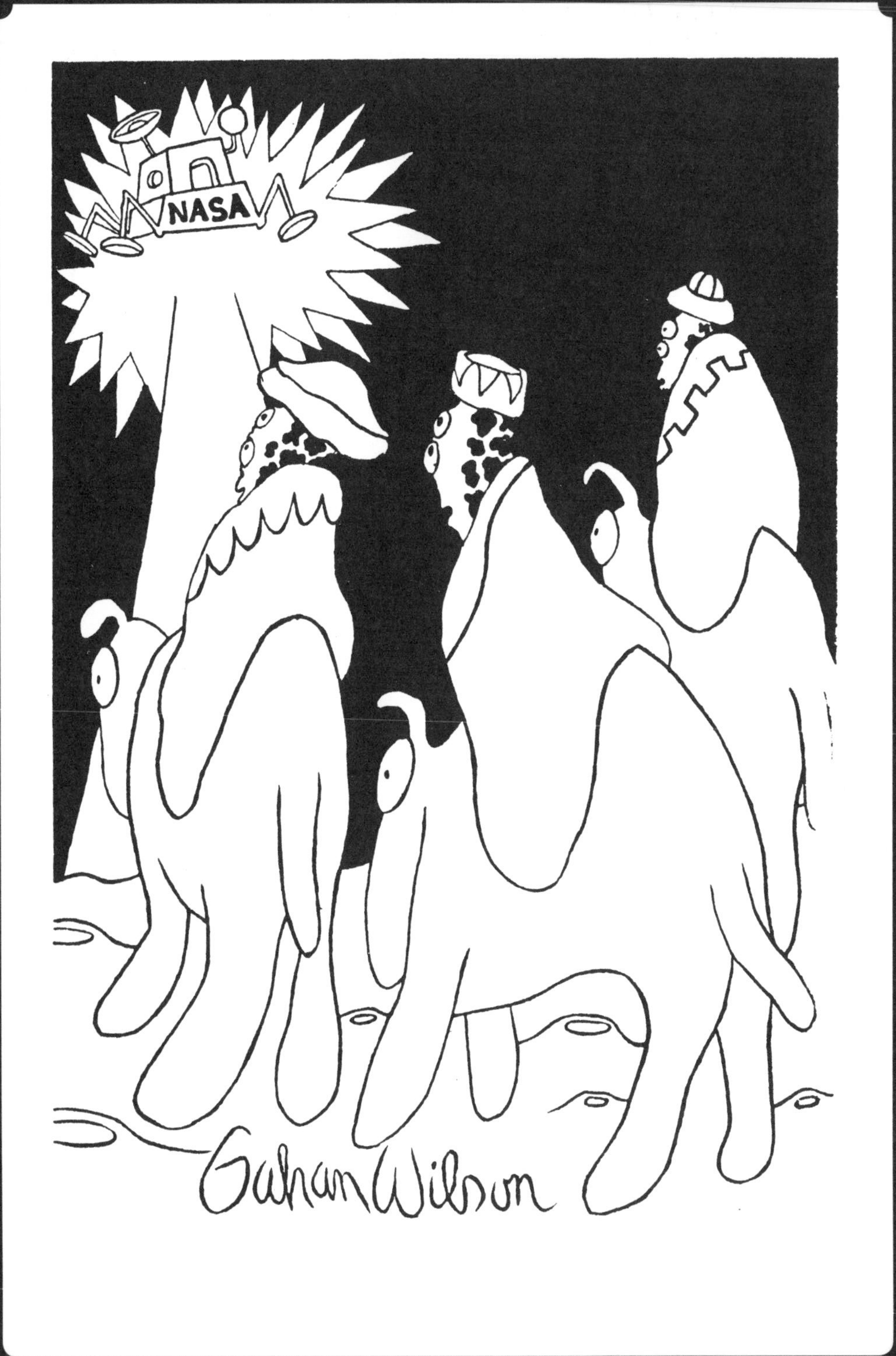
NASA
Gahan Wilson

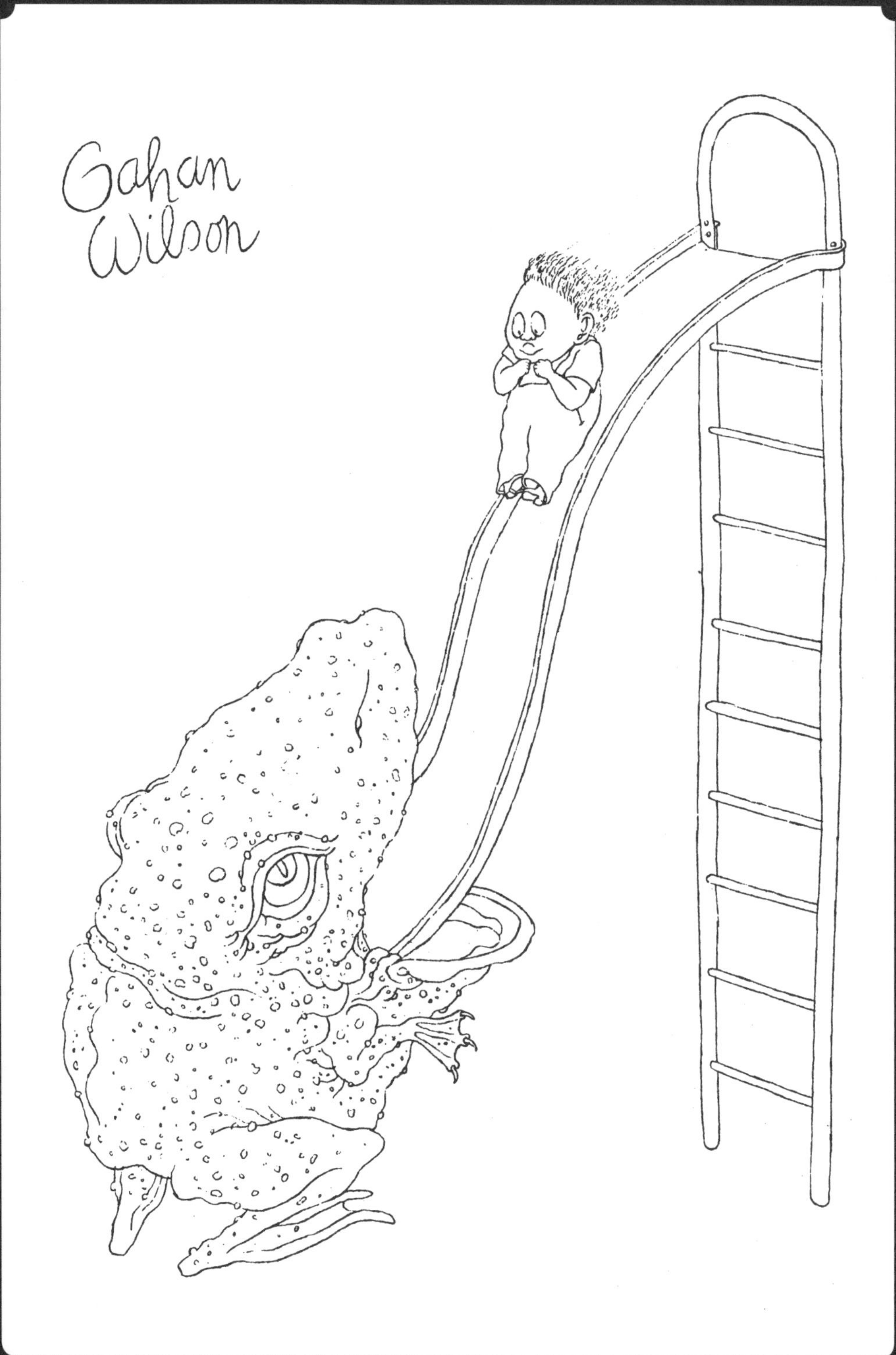
Gahan
Wilson

"I don't like the looks of your face, Mac!"

"*Grand dad, Marylin and I were curious about this old scrapbook of yours…*"

"We…the members…of…the jury…find…
the defendent…not guilty."

"This is the place, driver."

"First, I'd like to take this opportunity to clear up these silly rumors about my having made a deal with the devil…"

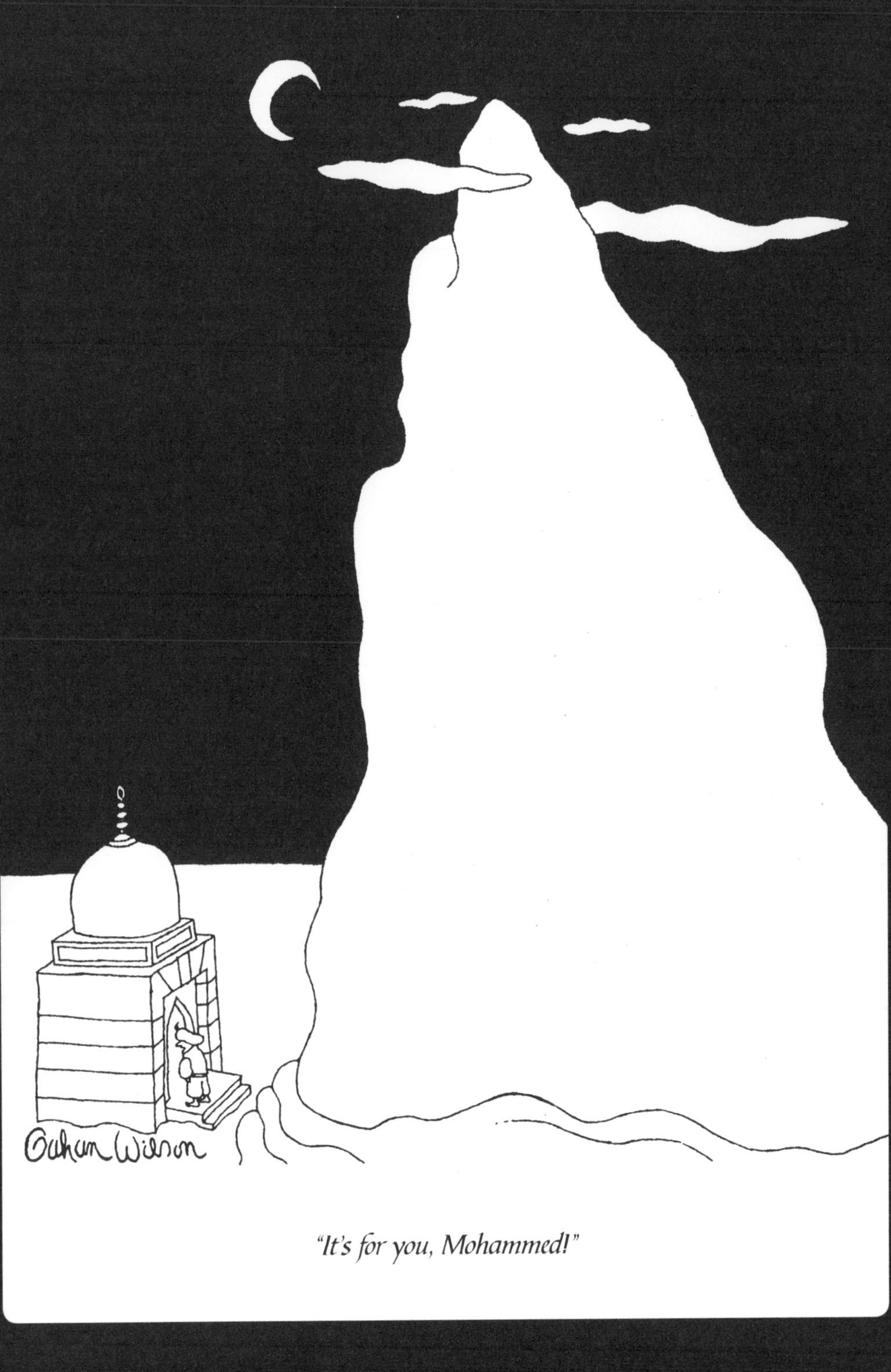
Gahan Wilson

"It's for you, Mohammed!"

"How's every little thing, Carter?"

"Oh, no, Ma'm—I can assure you the spray is perfectly harmless!"

"Hello! You have reached the number of Harold Mayberry. I am sorry,
but Mr. Mayberry is not in. I am a simulation of Mr. Mayberry.
Please leave your name and number and Mr. Mayberry will
call you back when he gets in. Thank you very much!"

"Sorry I'm not making myself clearer, but it's hard to express yourself in a language as crude and primitive as ours."

"You never know when he'll fall off the wagon."

"Take it from me, Mr. Kirby—you're an eye, ear and throat man's dream."

"*Good grief—he's writing out Lucille!*"

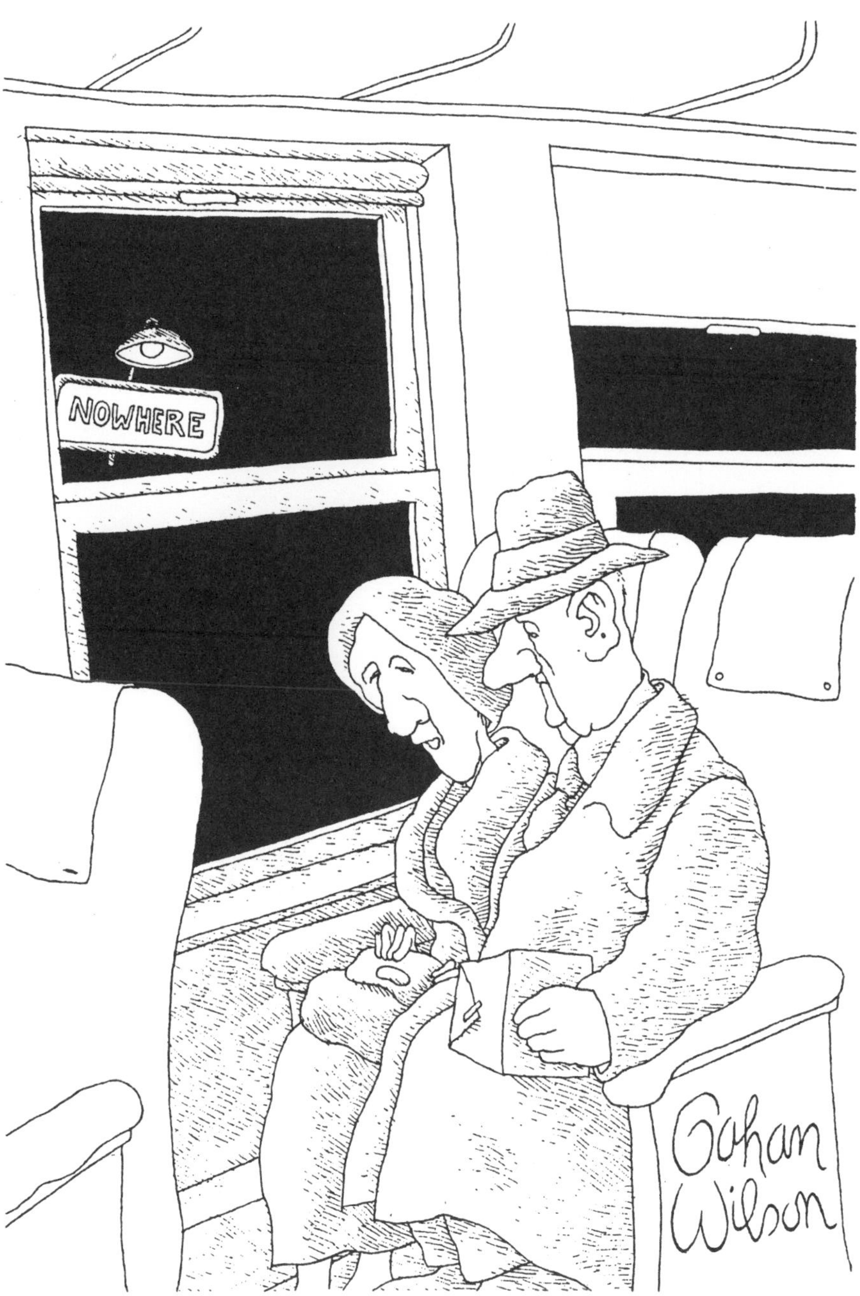
NOWHERE
Gahan Wilson

"We're there."

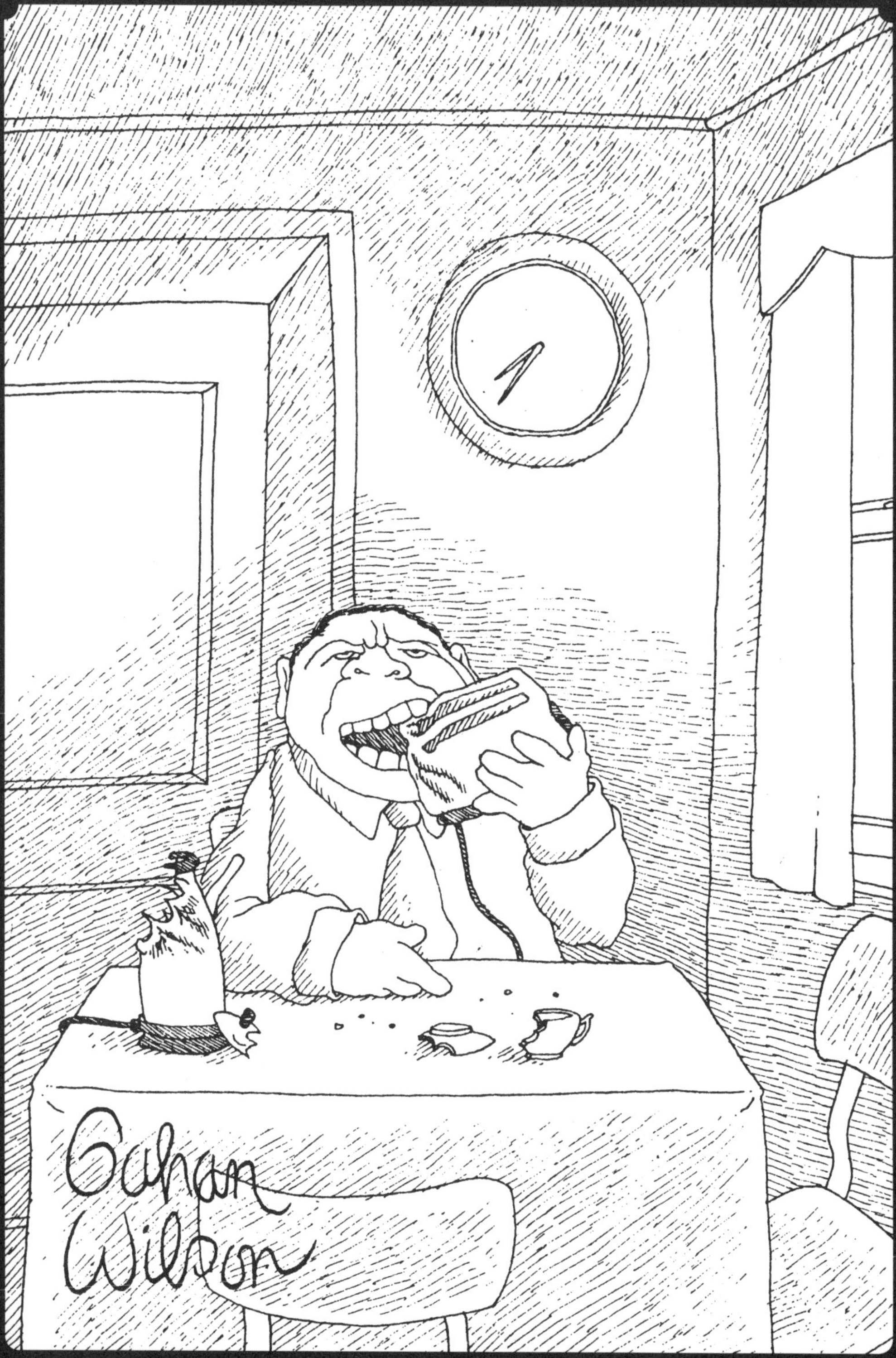
Gahan Wilson

"We're getting nowhere with this one. How you doing with his buddy?"

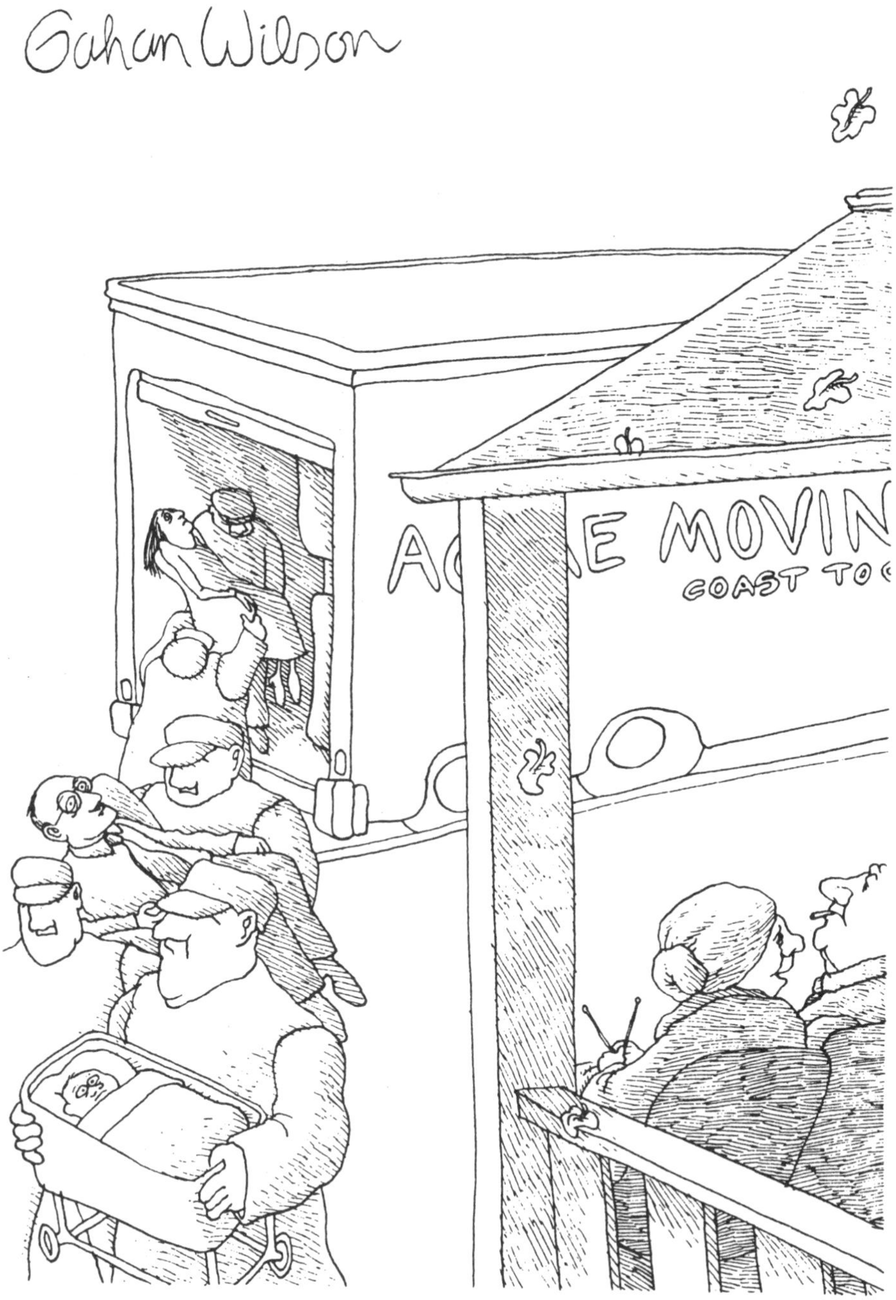
Gahan Wilson
AC
E MOVIN
COAST TO

"Look like nice folks—"

"At least they're a quiet bunch!"

"Of course the animators' union is giving us a lot of flack."

"I've the strangest feeling I _know_ this place!"

"Your mother and I think he's very nice, dear—but is he human?"

"Would you mind hanging around somewhere else, buddy?"

"Now just a goddamn minute!"

"Our people have many sayings on the vanity of haste, effendi…"

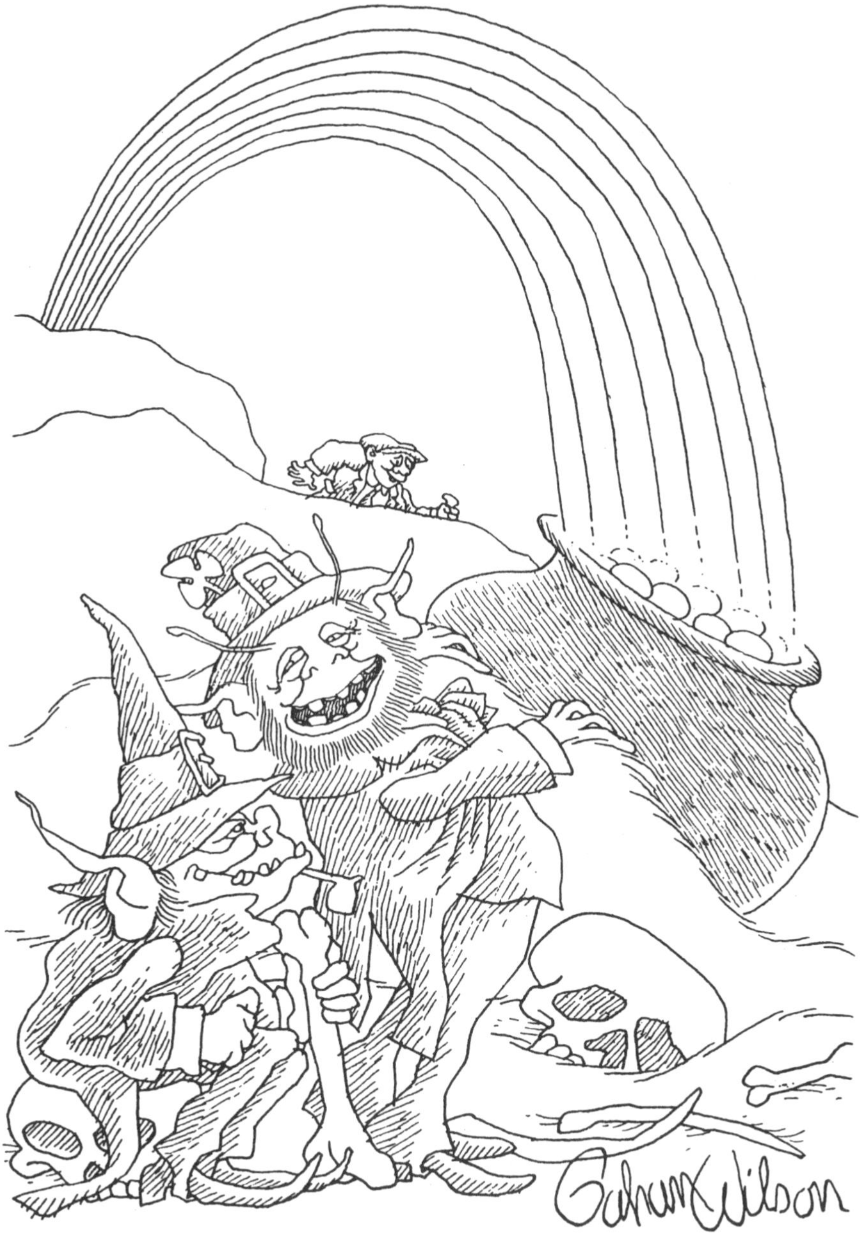
Gahan Wilson

"Here comes another!"

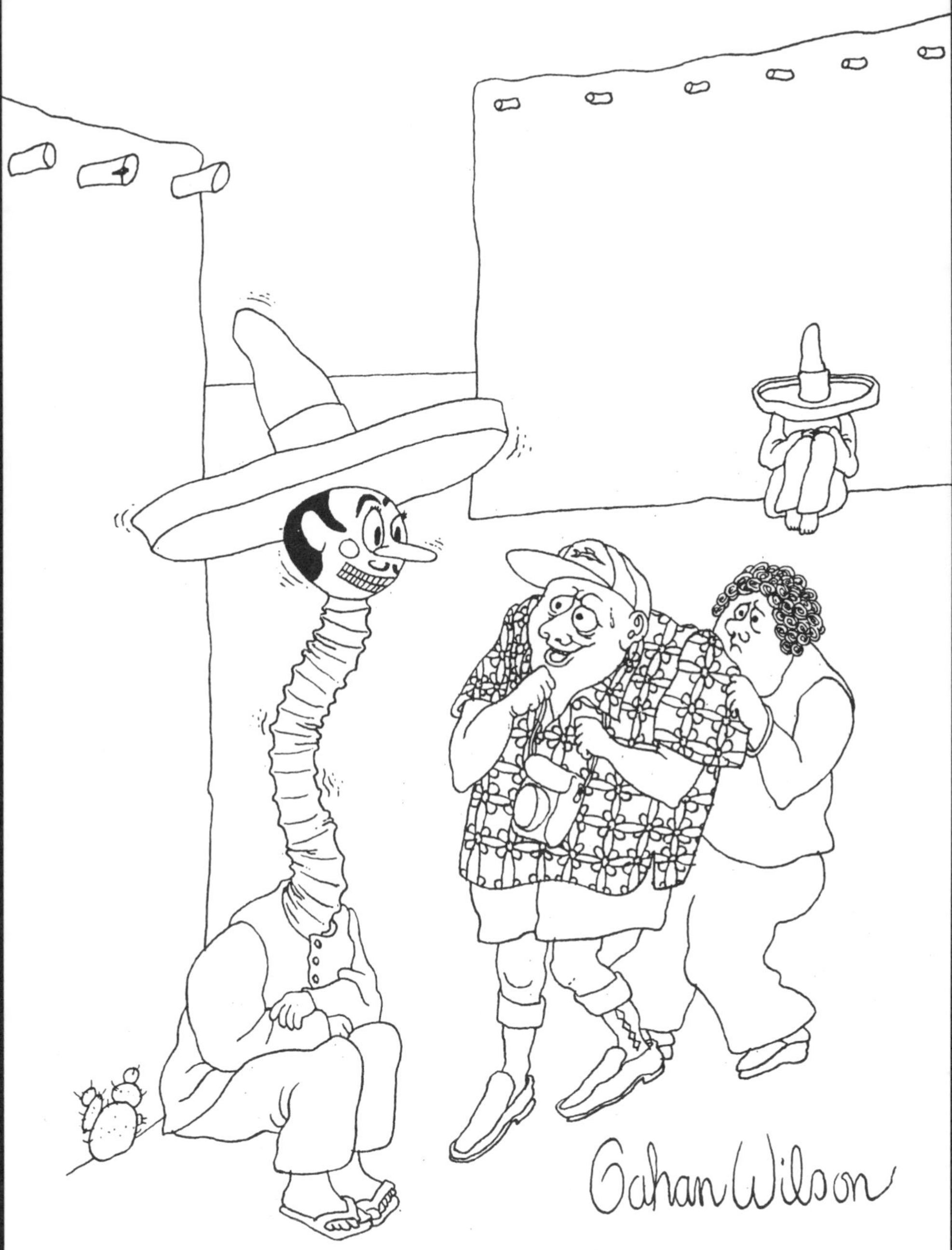
Gahan Wilson

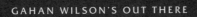

"Really gave me a turn!"

"First, retirement—and now, this!"

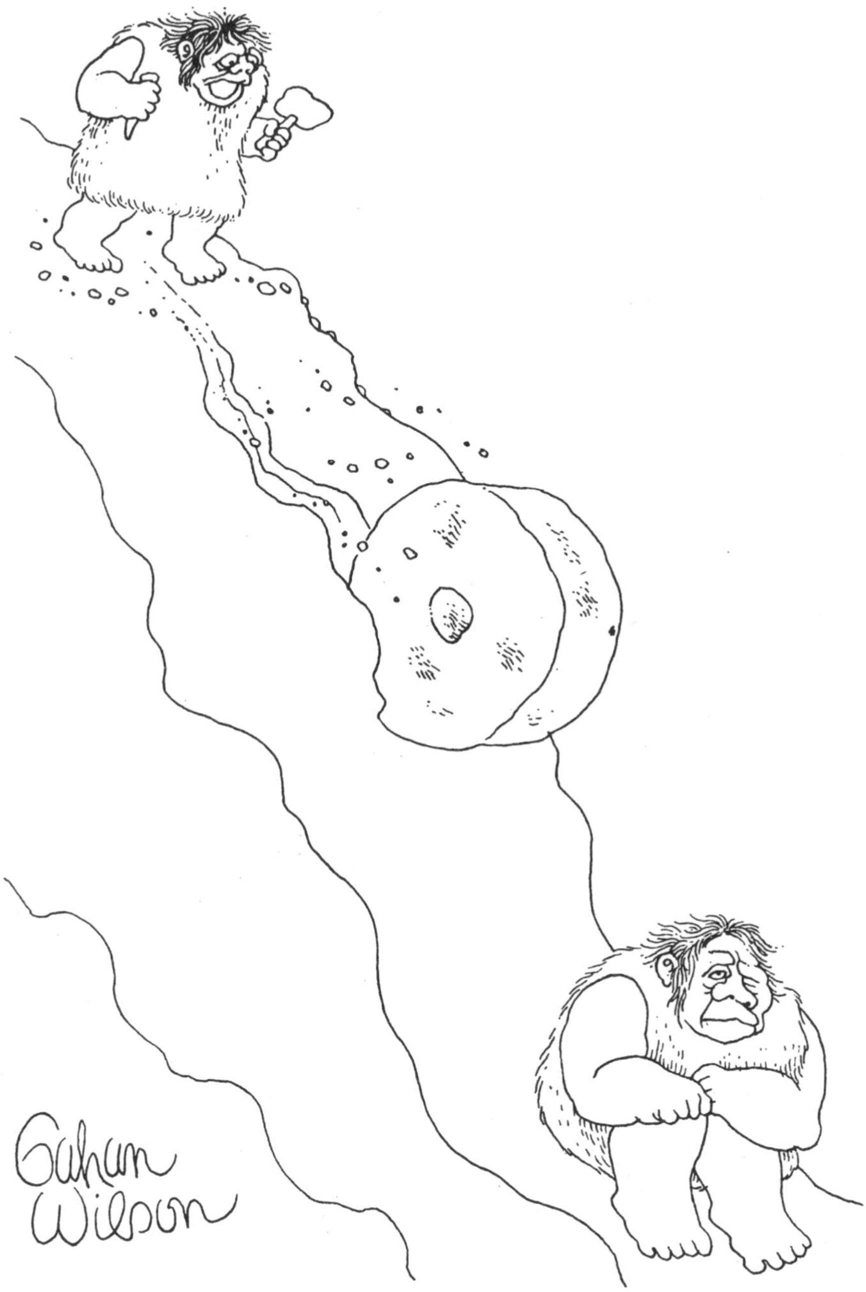
Gahan Wilson

"Watch out!"

"...and this looks like a tiny pair of aqualungs!"

"Remember when we used to let the oil slick get us down?"

"He hasn't touched a thing for weeks!"

"Must be some kind of queer!"

"The hell with this stuff!"

"First they guess wrong on Kohoutek, and now this!"

"You any idea what these stains are, sir?"

"Lamont Cranston? No, there's no Lamont Cranston here."

"This particular gem has an interesting curse attached to it…!"

"What is it? What do you see?"

"Better get a replacement for Parker."

"Better get a replacement for Parker."

"I'm sorry, Mr. Cheever, but there's absolutely nothing in your warranty about the howler turning into a pumpkin."

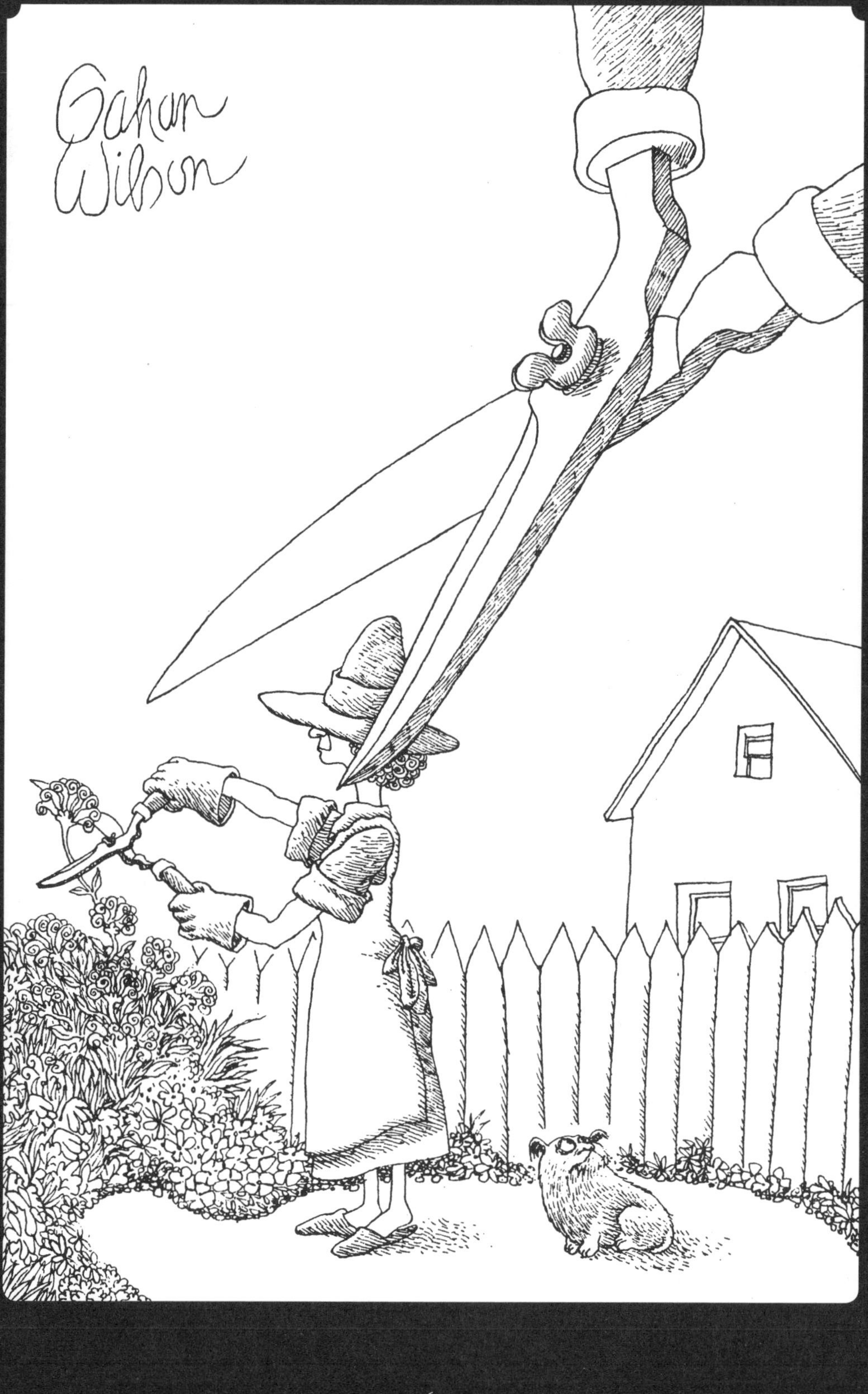
Gahan Wilson

"What is it? What do you see?"

"I don't think those are birds at all—I think
they're just little curved lines!"

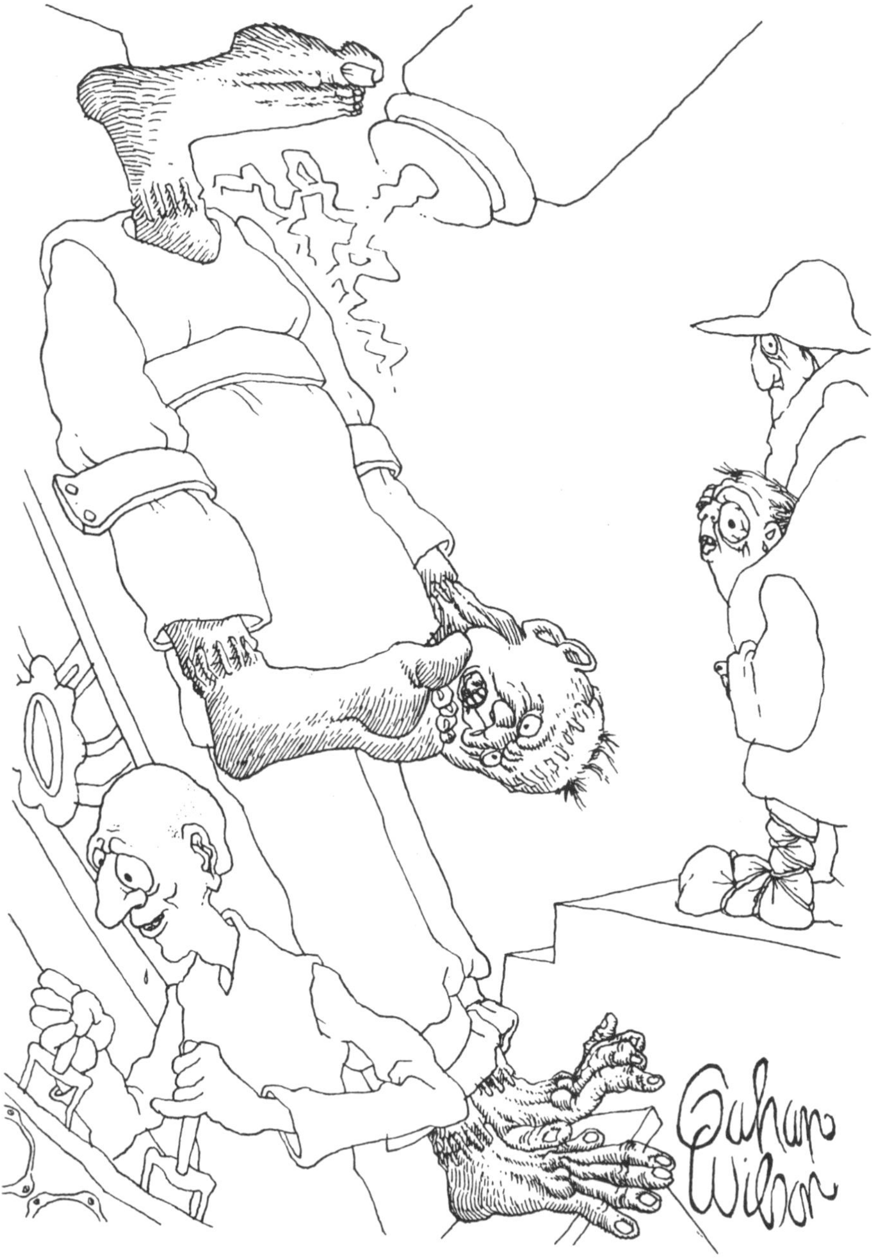

"I think he's gone soft!"

"…but then I realized in order to make it work I'd have to invent a socket and God knows what else."

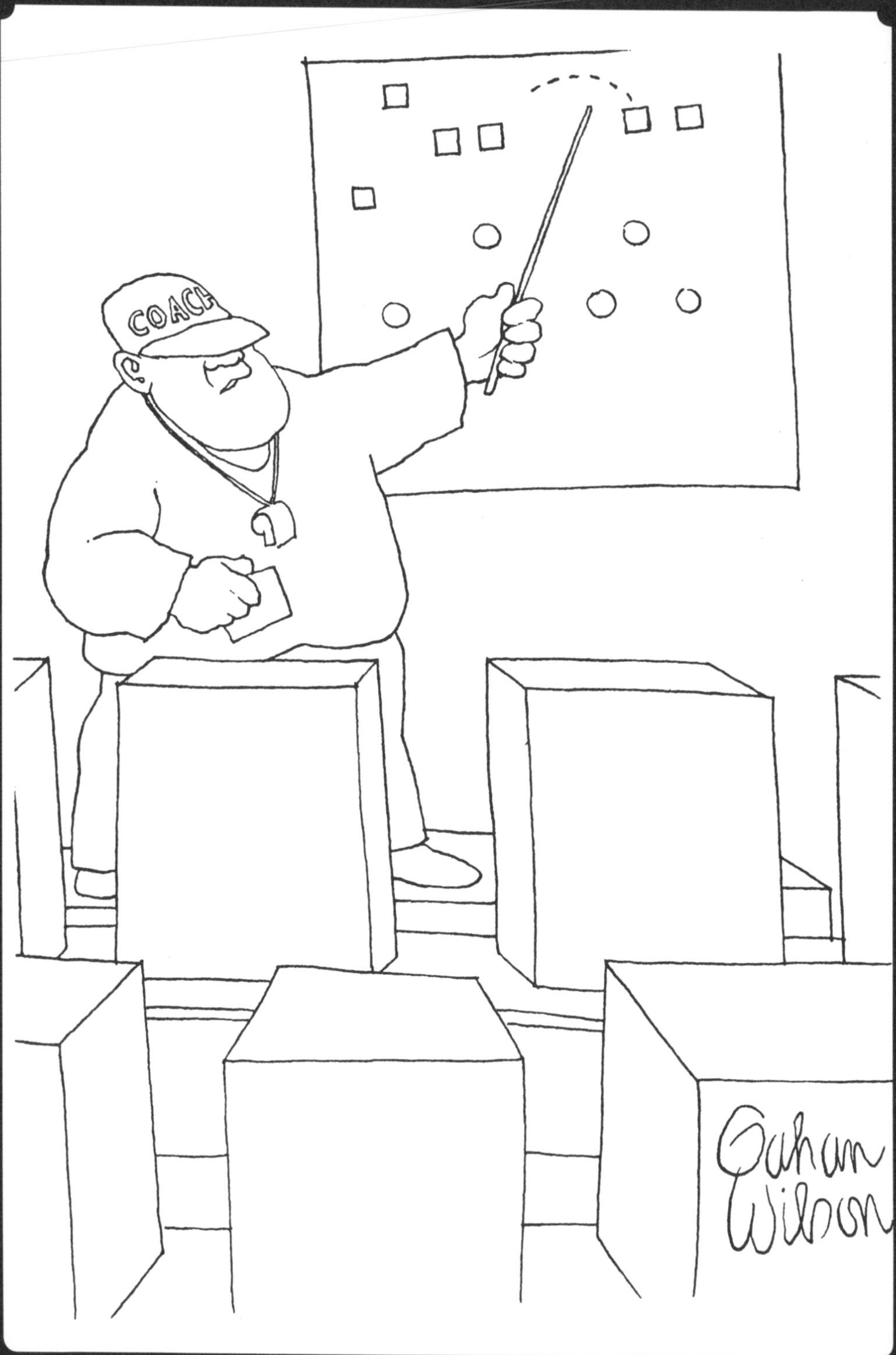
COACH
Gahan Wilson

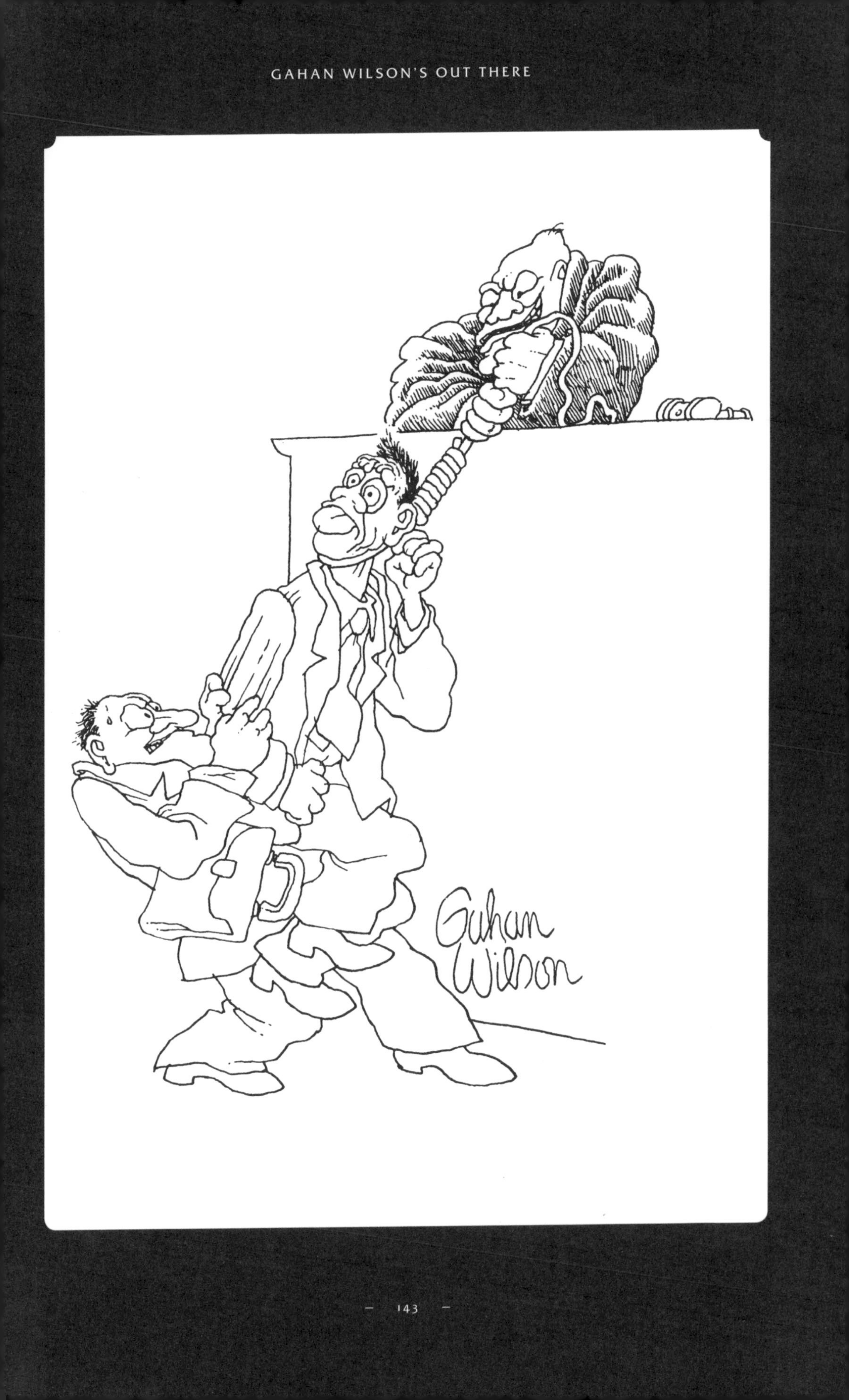
Gahan Wilson

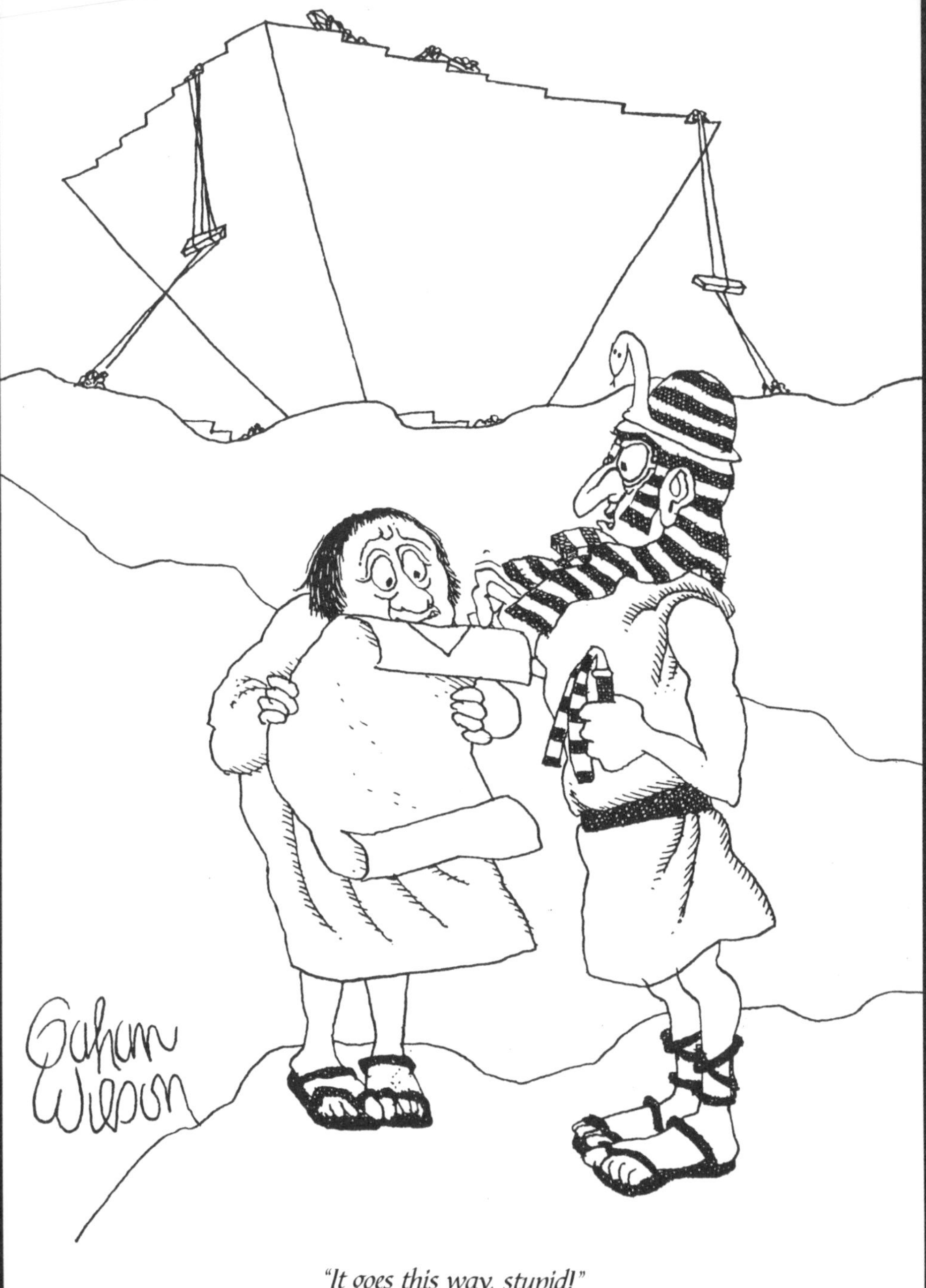
Gahan Wilson

"It goes this way, stupid!"

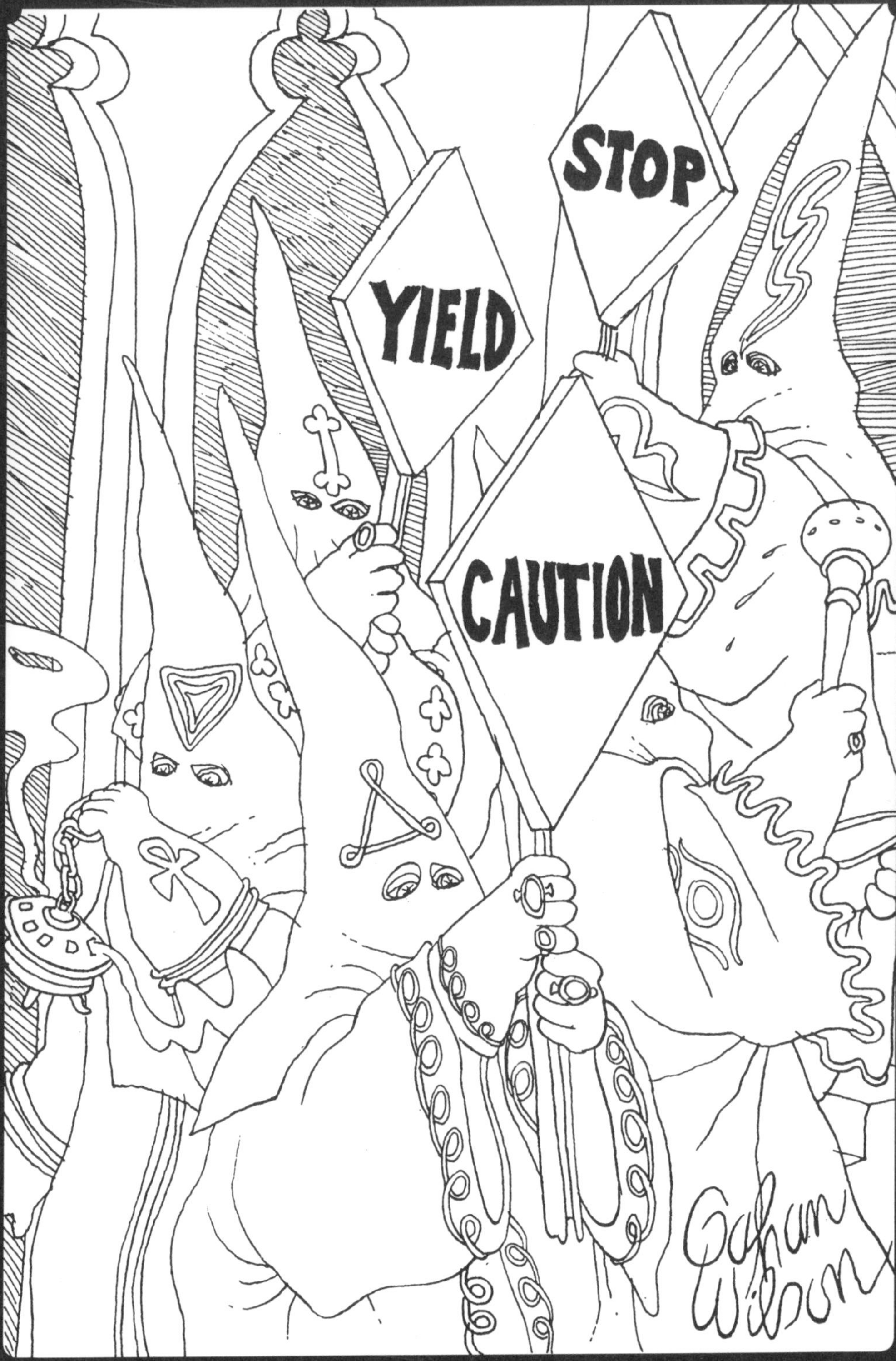
STOP
YIELD
CAUTION
Gahan Wilson

"Yes, I'd say you have the basis for a really sweet malpractice suit!"

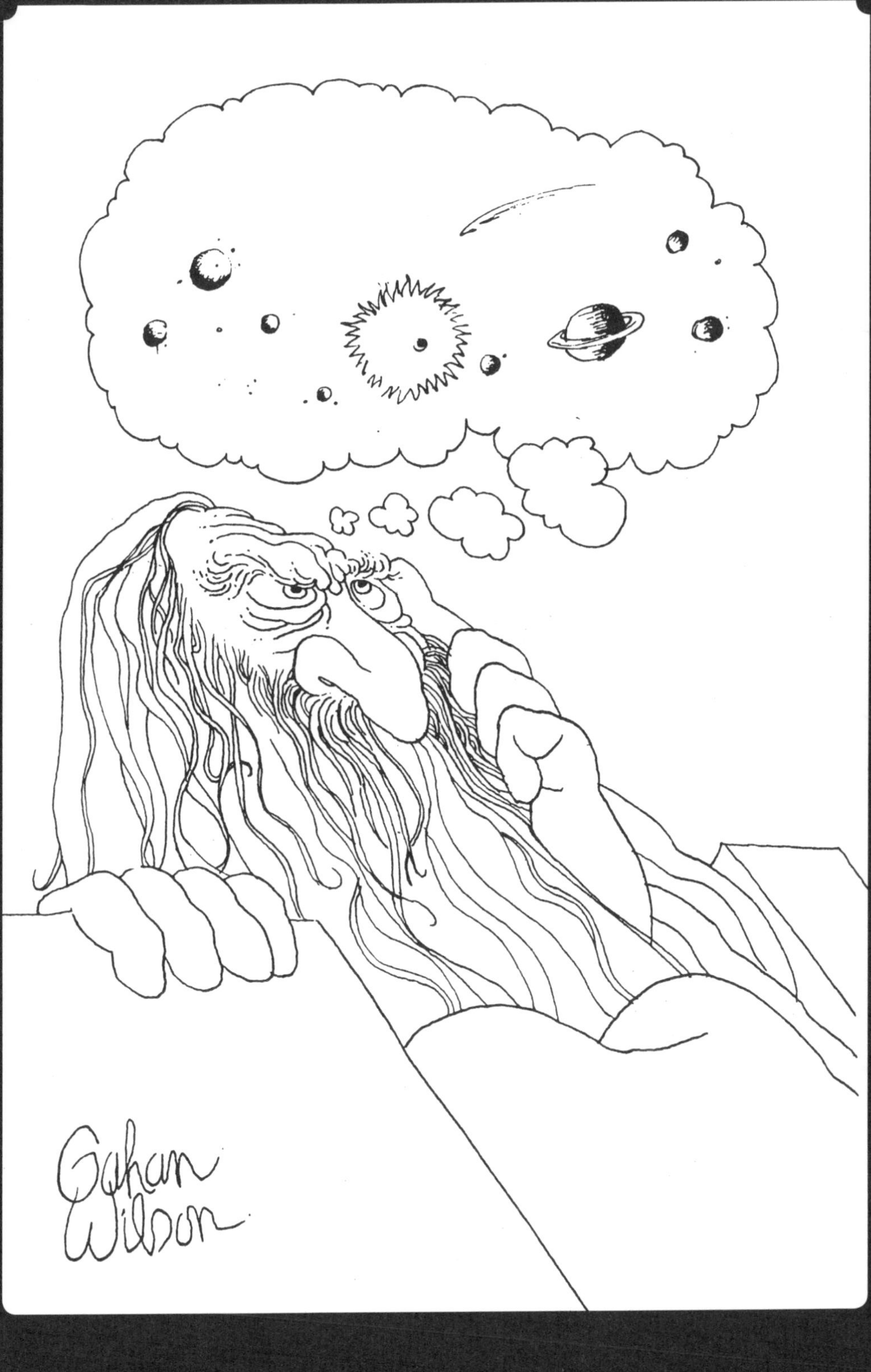
Gahan Wilson

"All right, all right! Stop it!"

"Gee, I don't know; this is kind of depressing!"

"It's that bug that's been going around town."

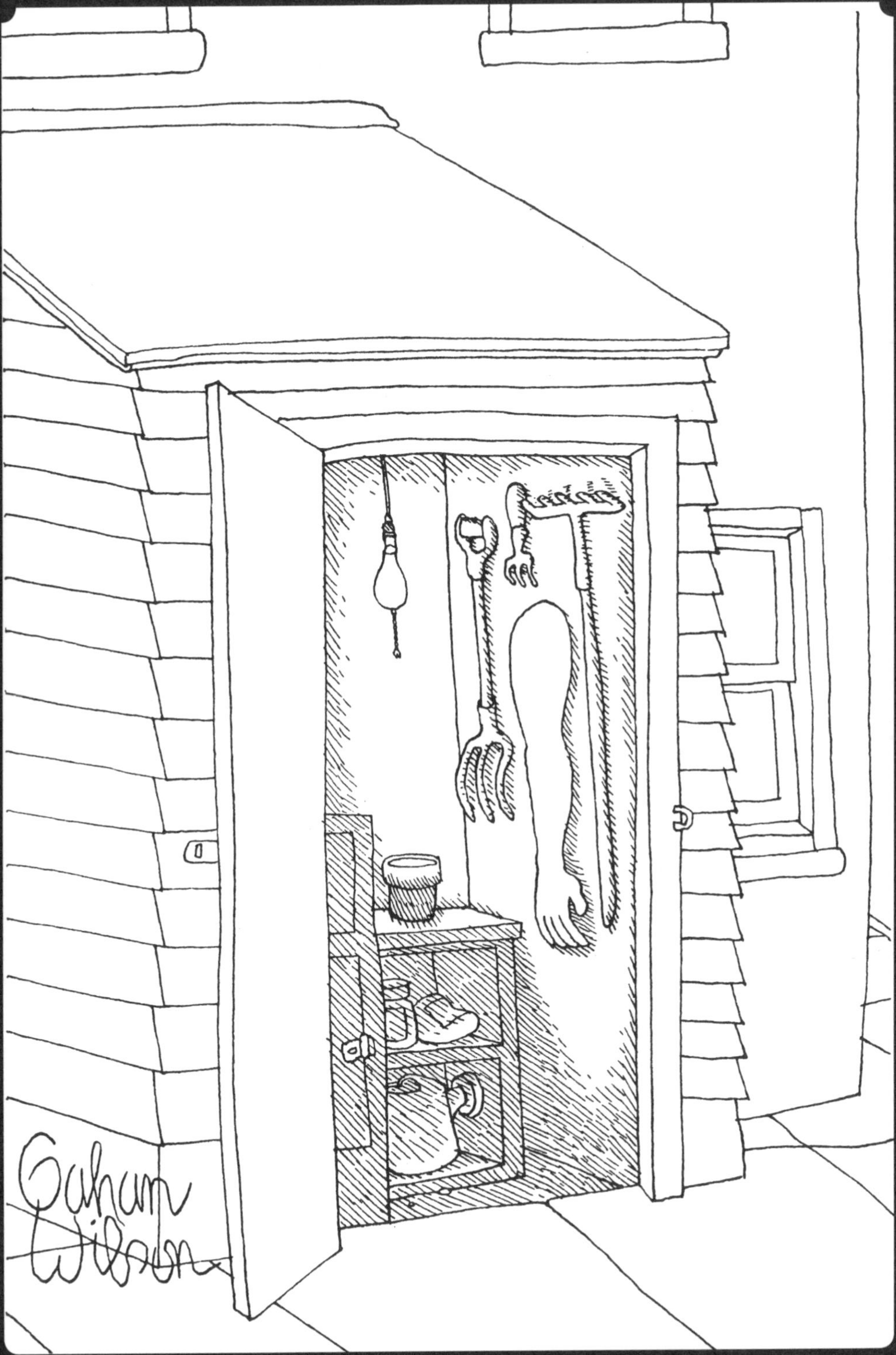
Gahan Wilson

"Tell them I'm only human, like everybody else."

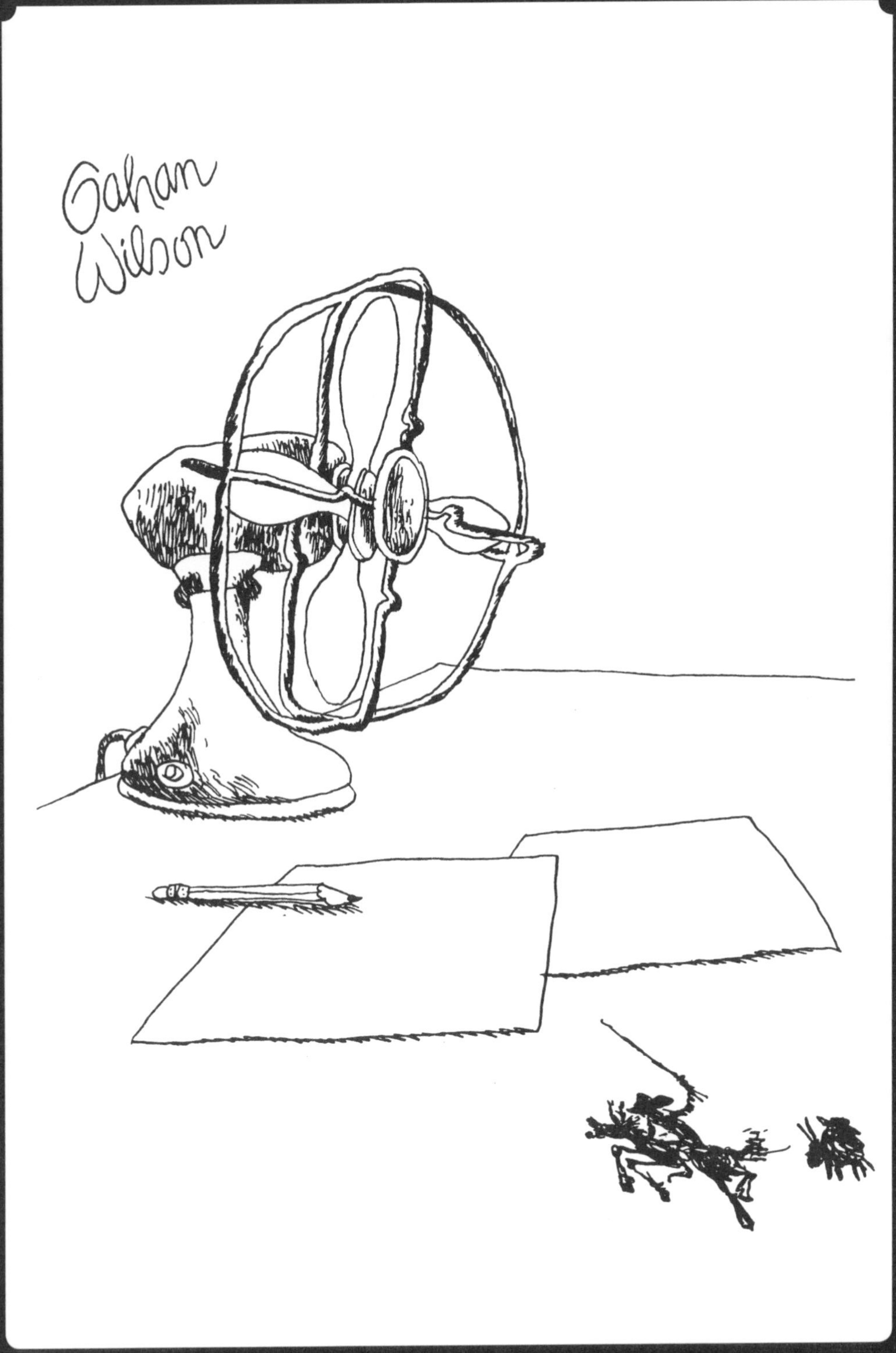
Gahan Wilson

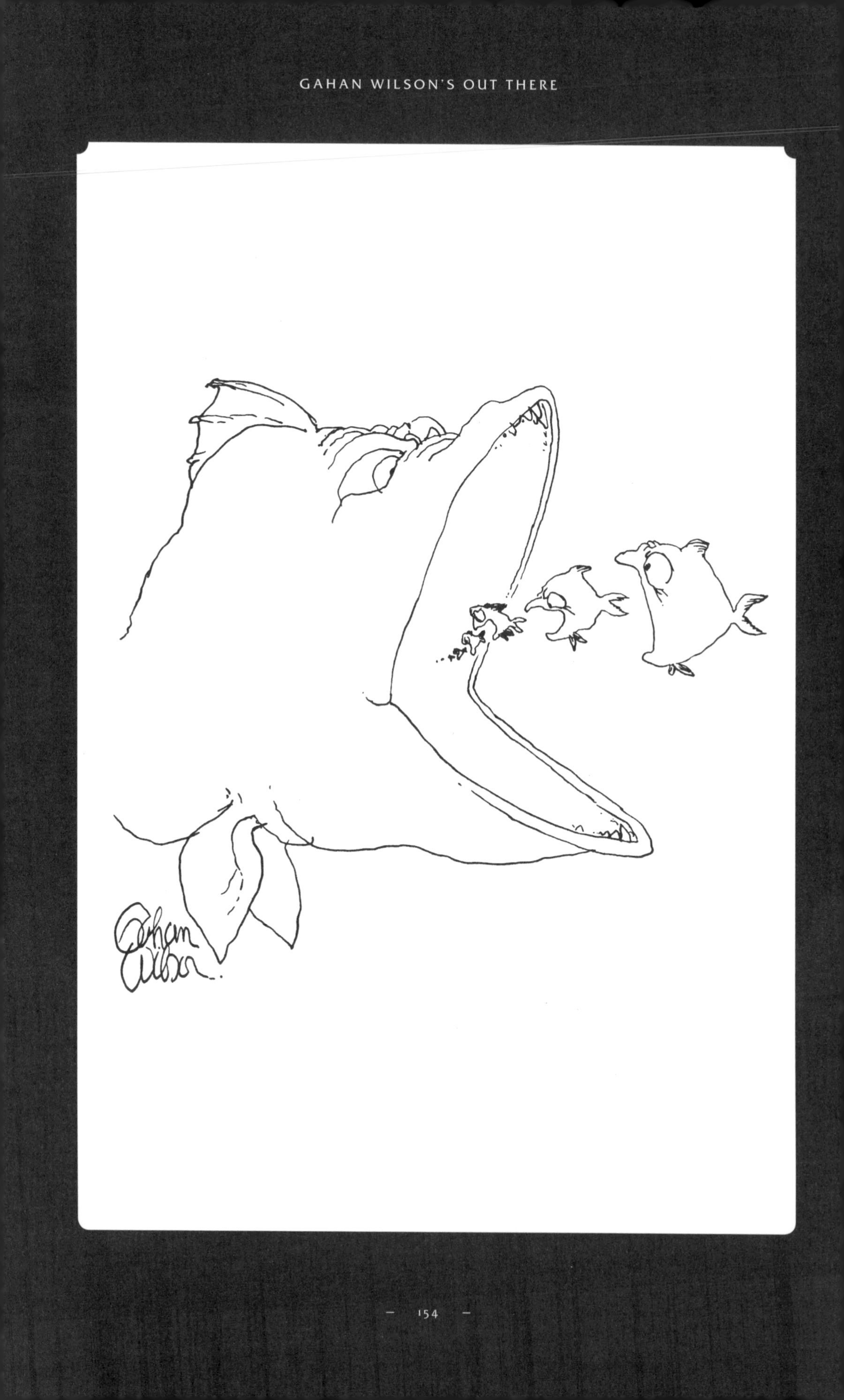
Gahan Wilson

"I'd say it's a pretty obvious case of evolution taking a wrong turn."

"What the hell's that all about?"

"I suppose you don't think this is hard work!"

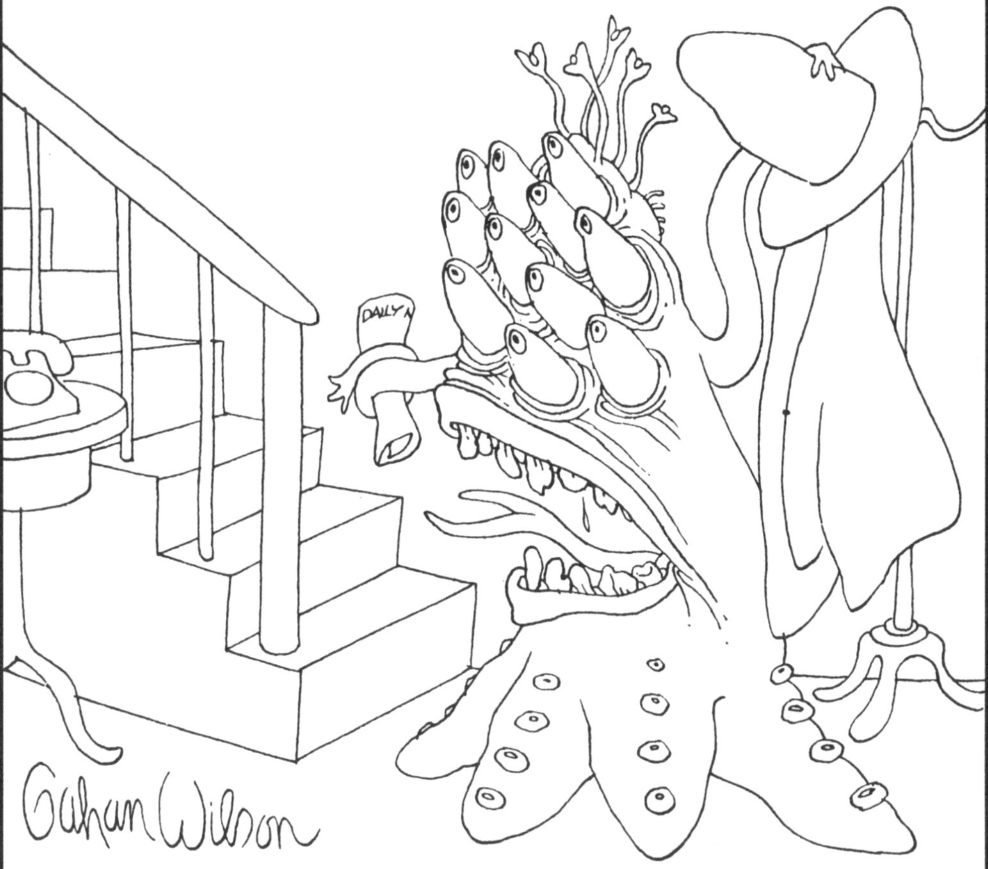
DAILY N
Gahan Wilson

"It's me!"

"*I'm afraid you have the wrong number.*"

"What is this thing that you call it a 'razor'?"

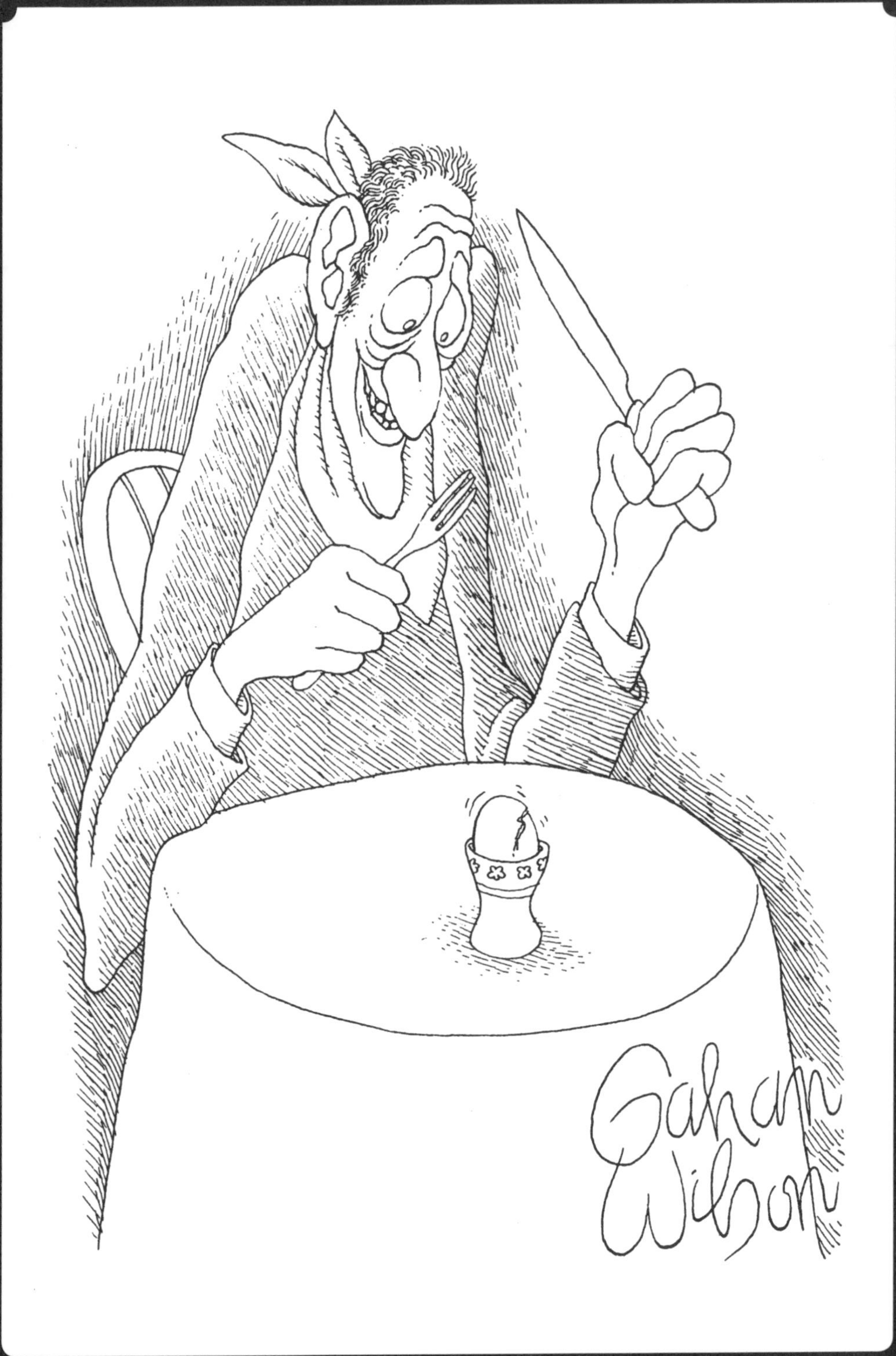
Gahan Wilson

"There's one of the real old timers!"

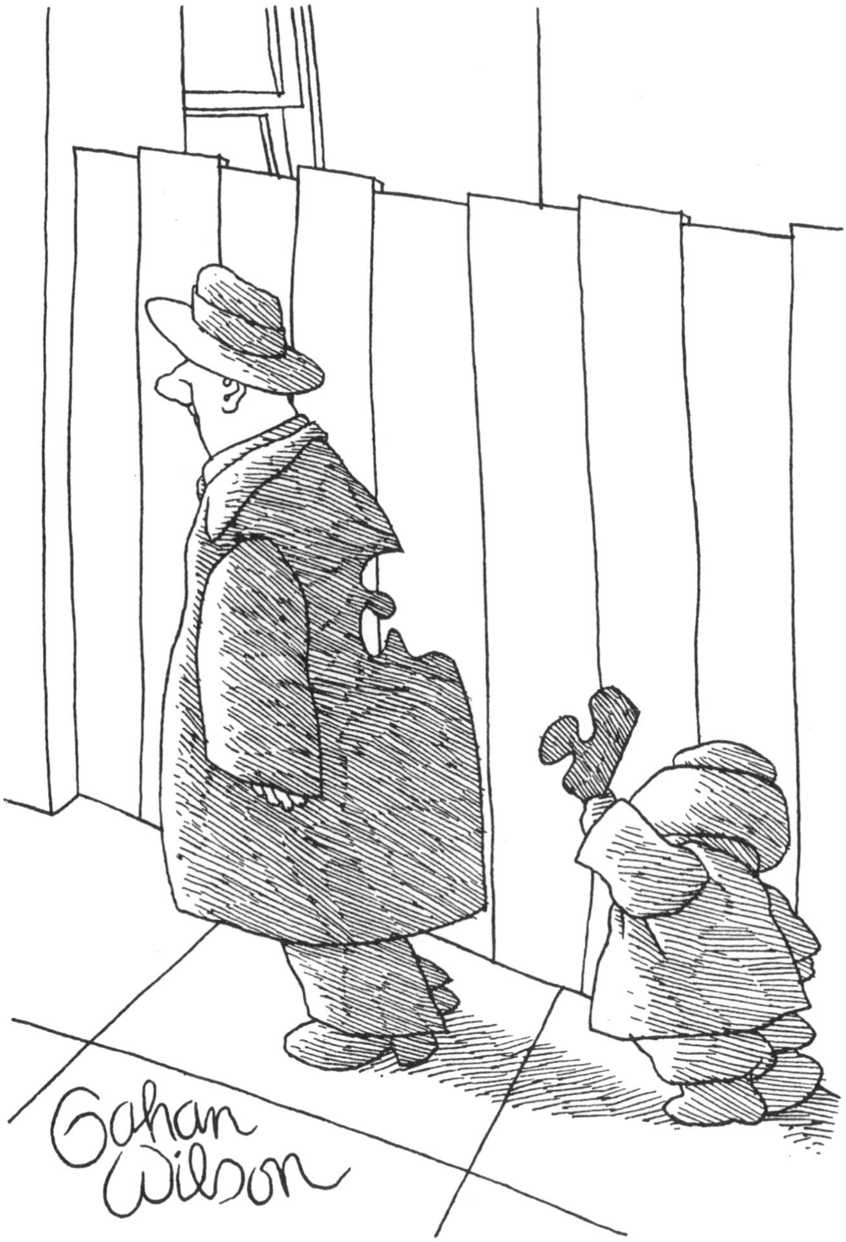
Gahan Wilson

"Hey, mister!"

"We've no idea what it is, but it makes a darling planter."

"I figure everybody else is doing it."

"Is there some way you could make the act upbeat?"

"Sometimes I wish he'd go back to Hari Krishna!"

"For some reason I keep thinking it's Wednesday!"

"Can't you get it through your thick head? In autumn you lose an hour—in spring you gain an hour!"

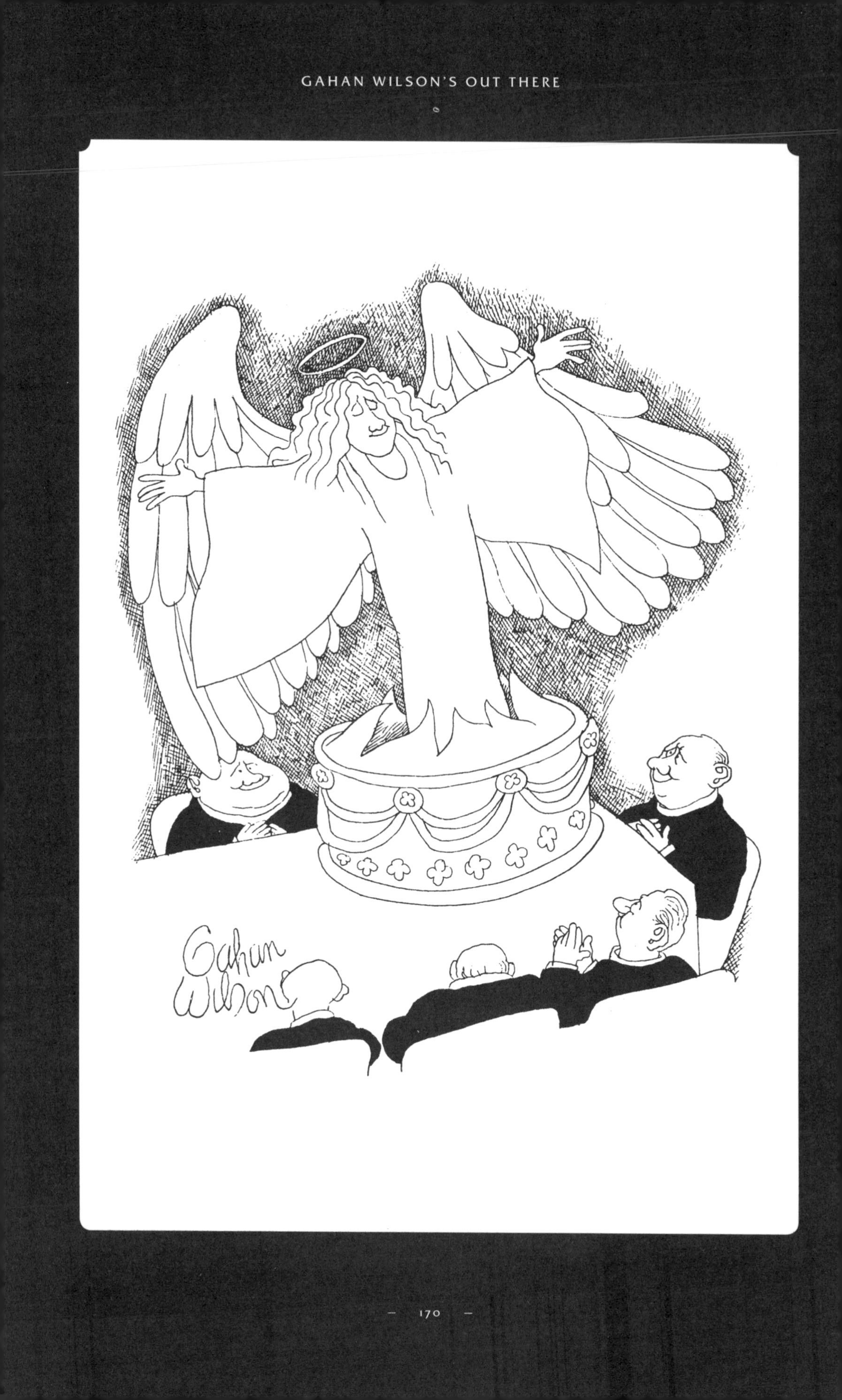
Gahan Wilson

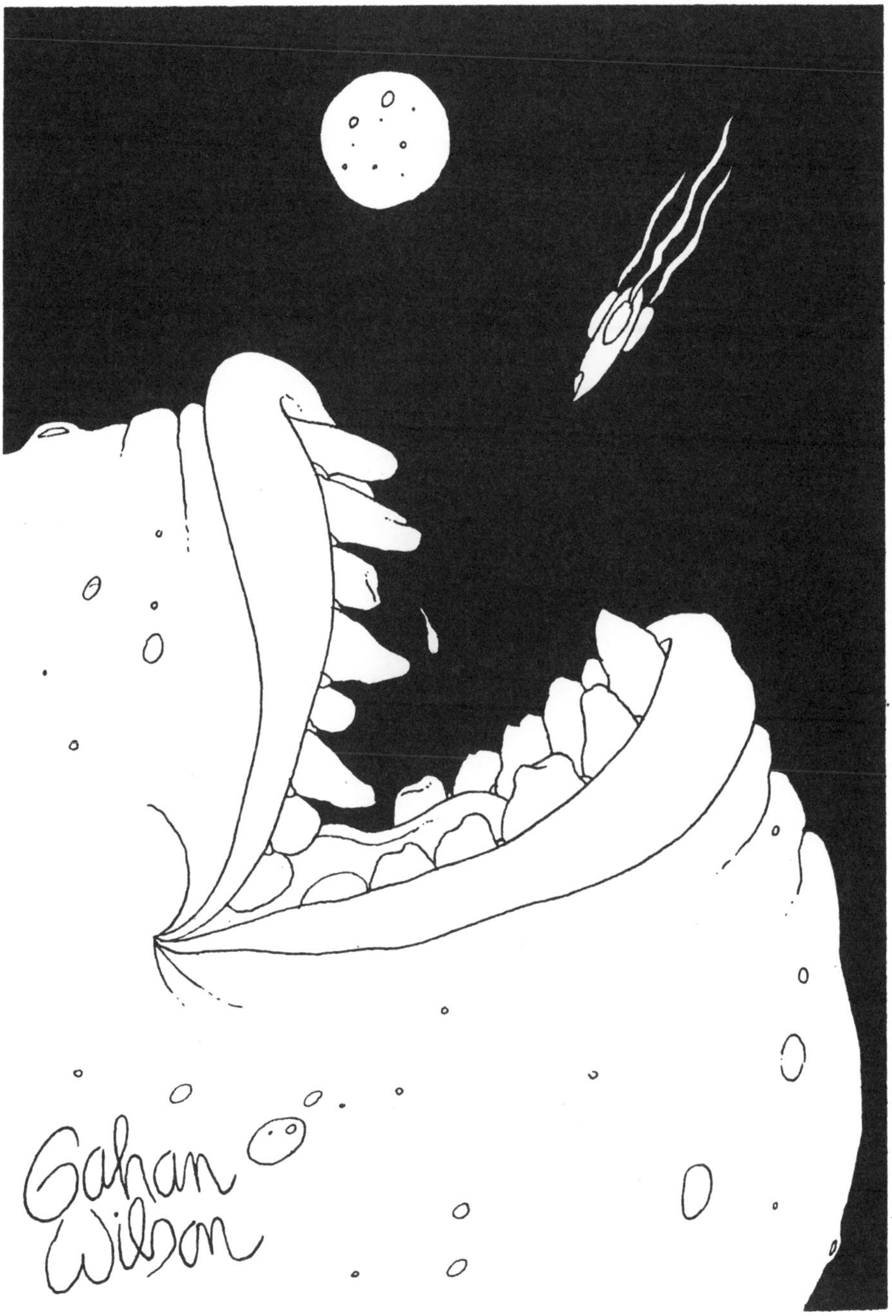
Gahan Wilson

"Oh, oh!"

"OK, kids, ask the Earthlings in!"

"*Hold still, will you? Or I'll never get the thing untangled.*"

"Of course you realize the very existence of our thirteenth
floor is the Bowker Building's best-kept secret!"

"It's this nutsy right hemisphere of mine!"

"Don't worry—it's just my kid brother."

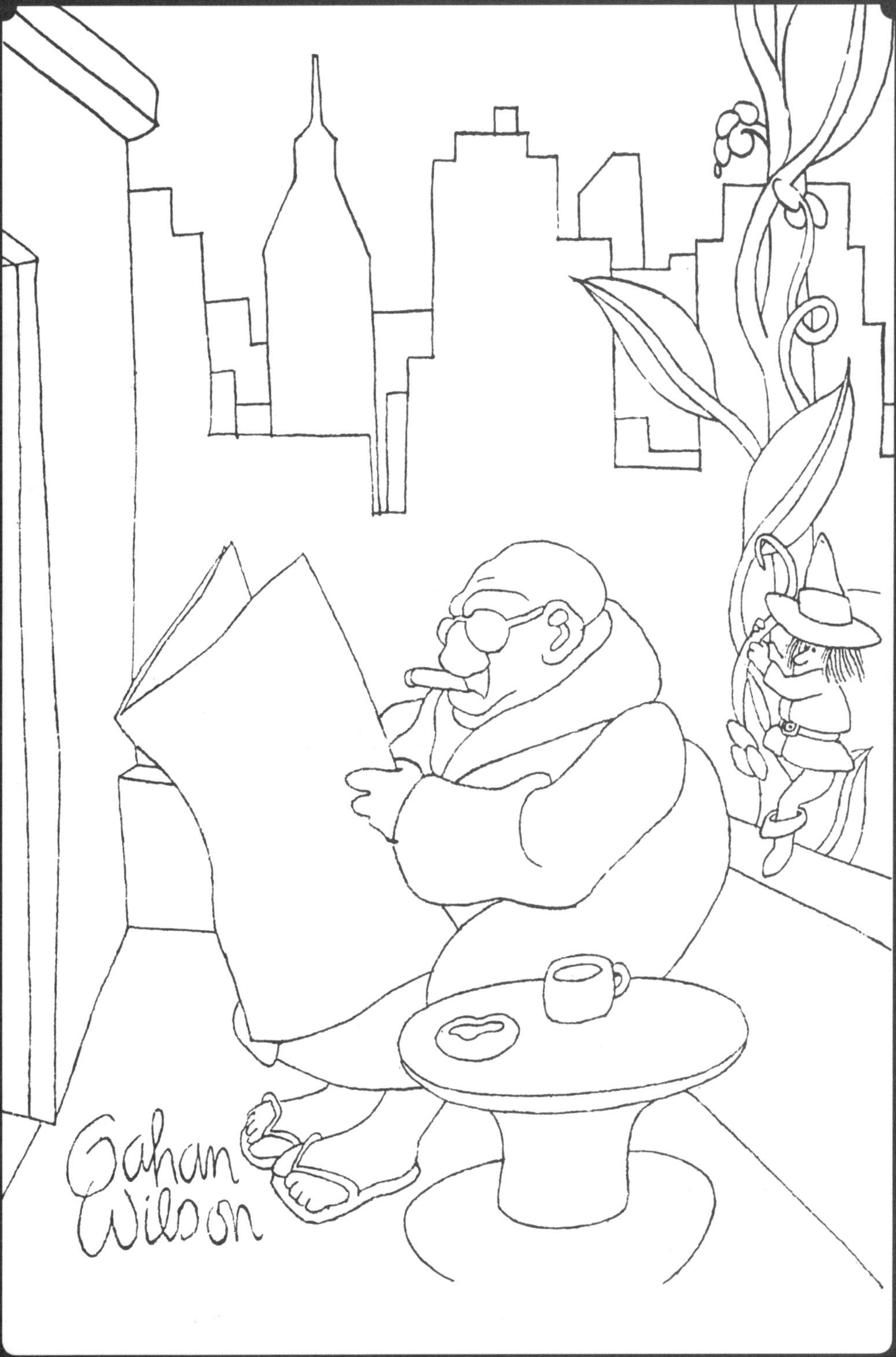
Gahan Wilson

"We were wondering if you could drop by to make up an even thirteen!"

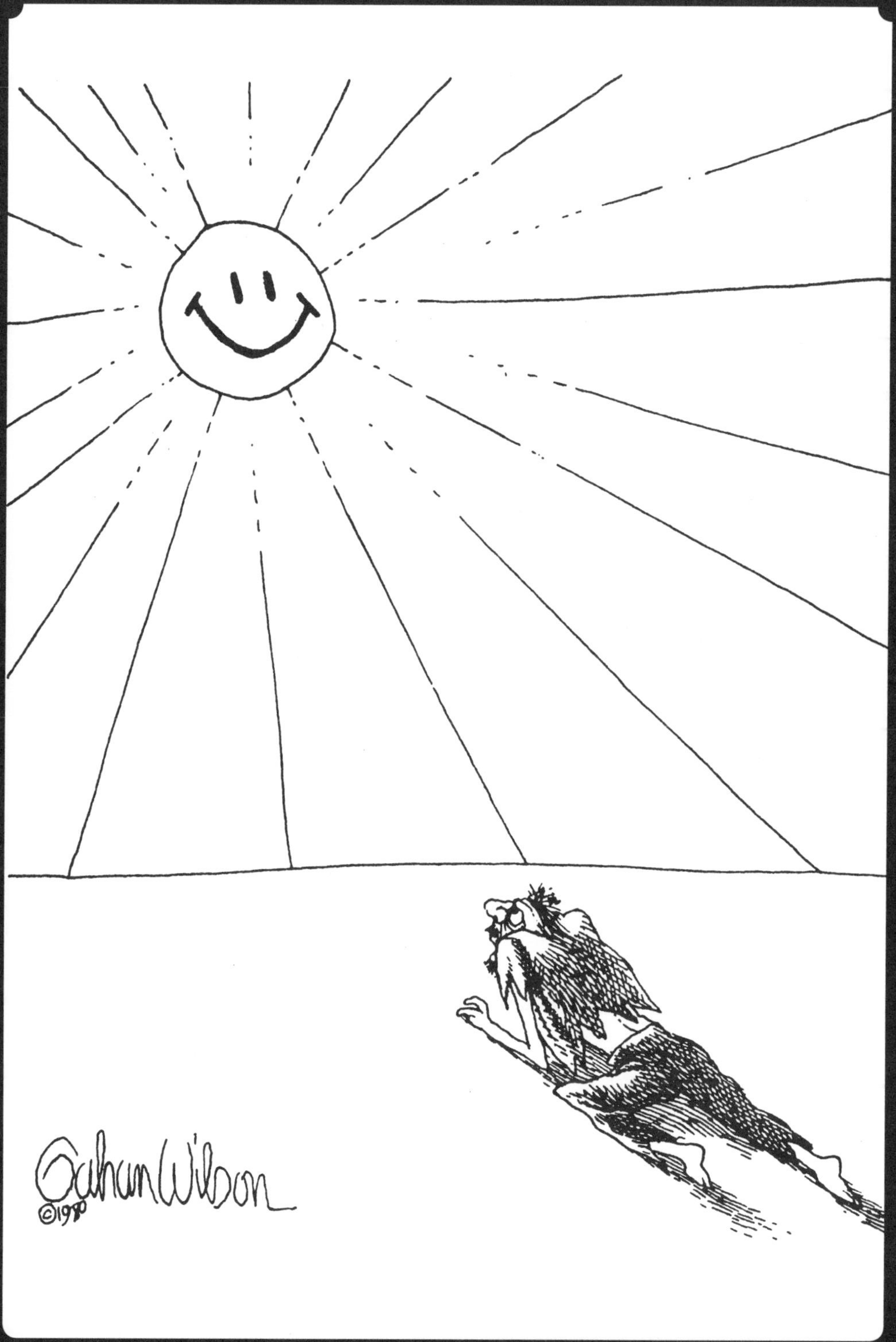
Gahan Wilson
©1980

"*That's tone control. The volume's up there.*"

"...anyhow, if I were you, I'd take every precaution, Mr. Steele."

"I don't know, Professor, this civilization is so primitive
it hardly seems worth our time!"

"Don't mind admittin' there's been one or more dark and windy nights when I wished I'd left this old boy strictly alone!"

"We're city little people, lady, if it's any
of your damn business."

"Alright, then—now what are you going to do?"

"I'm sorry, I have a very rich fantasy life!"

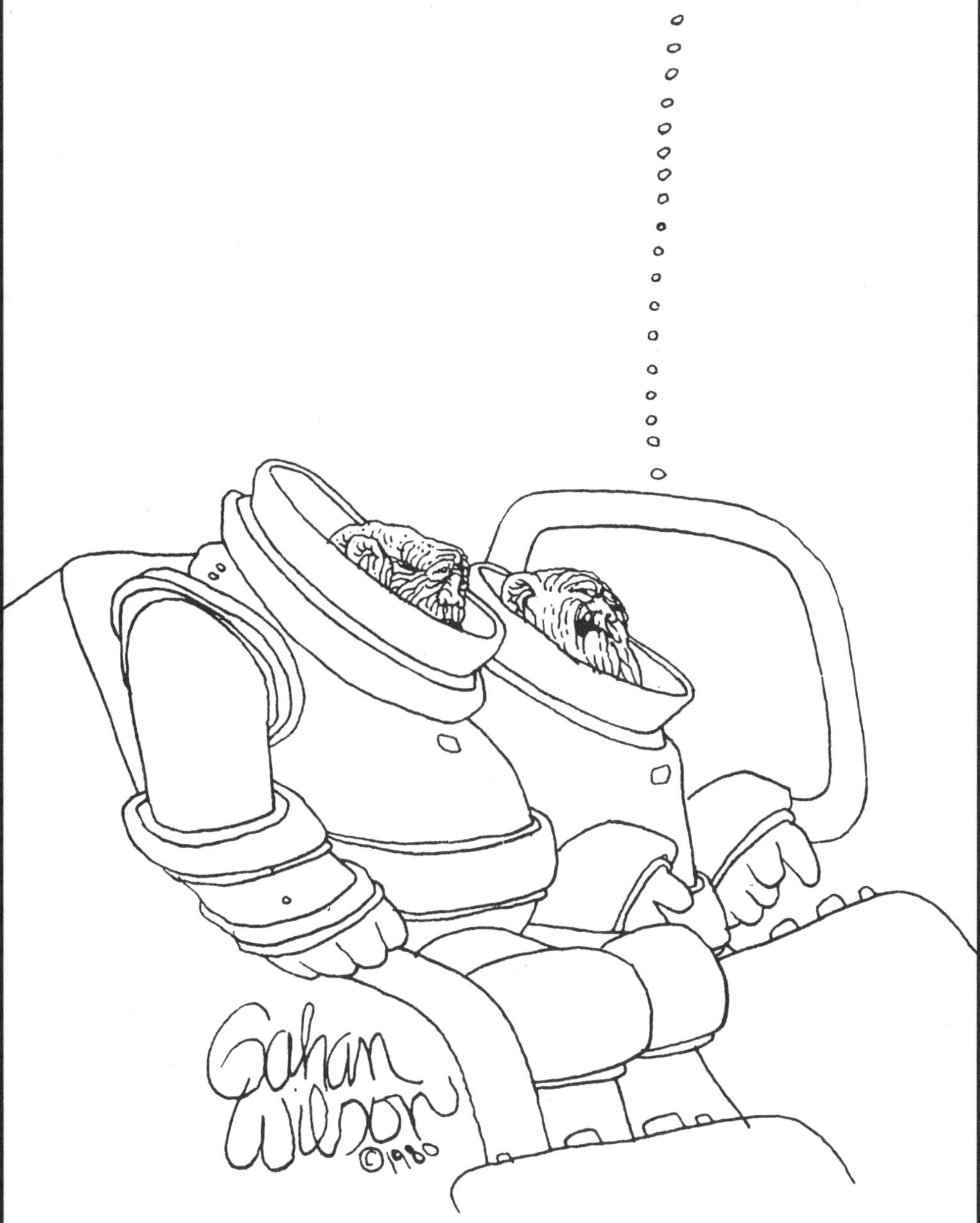
Gahan Wilson ©1980

"Well, it won't be long now!"

Gahan
Wilson
©1980

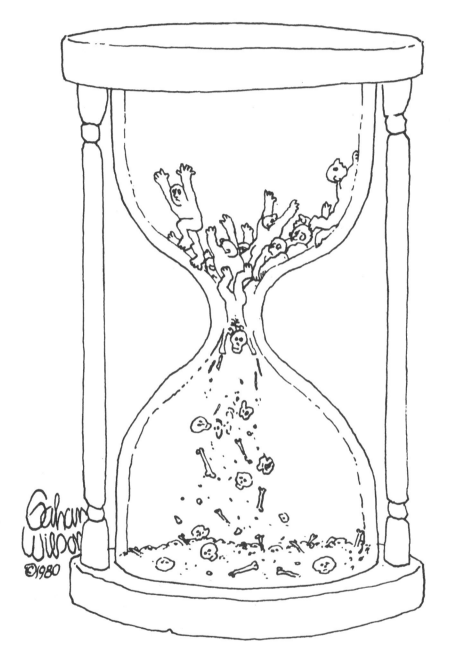

"…and this is _my_ little woman!"

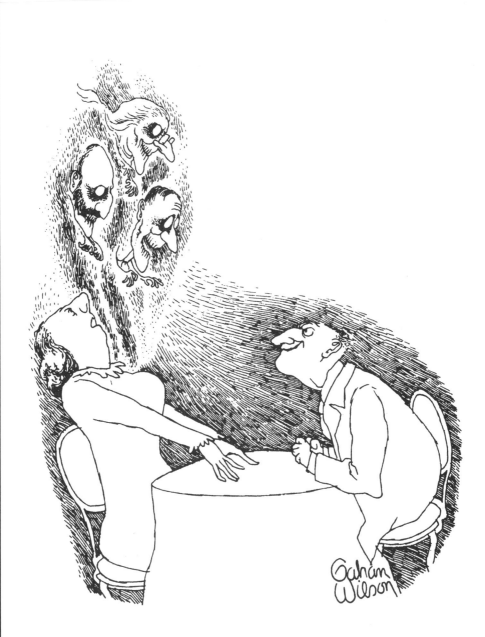

*"Congratulations, J.H.! We believe we've worked out
a technique whereby you can take it with you!"*

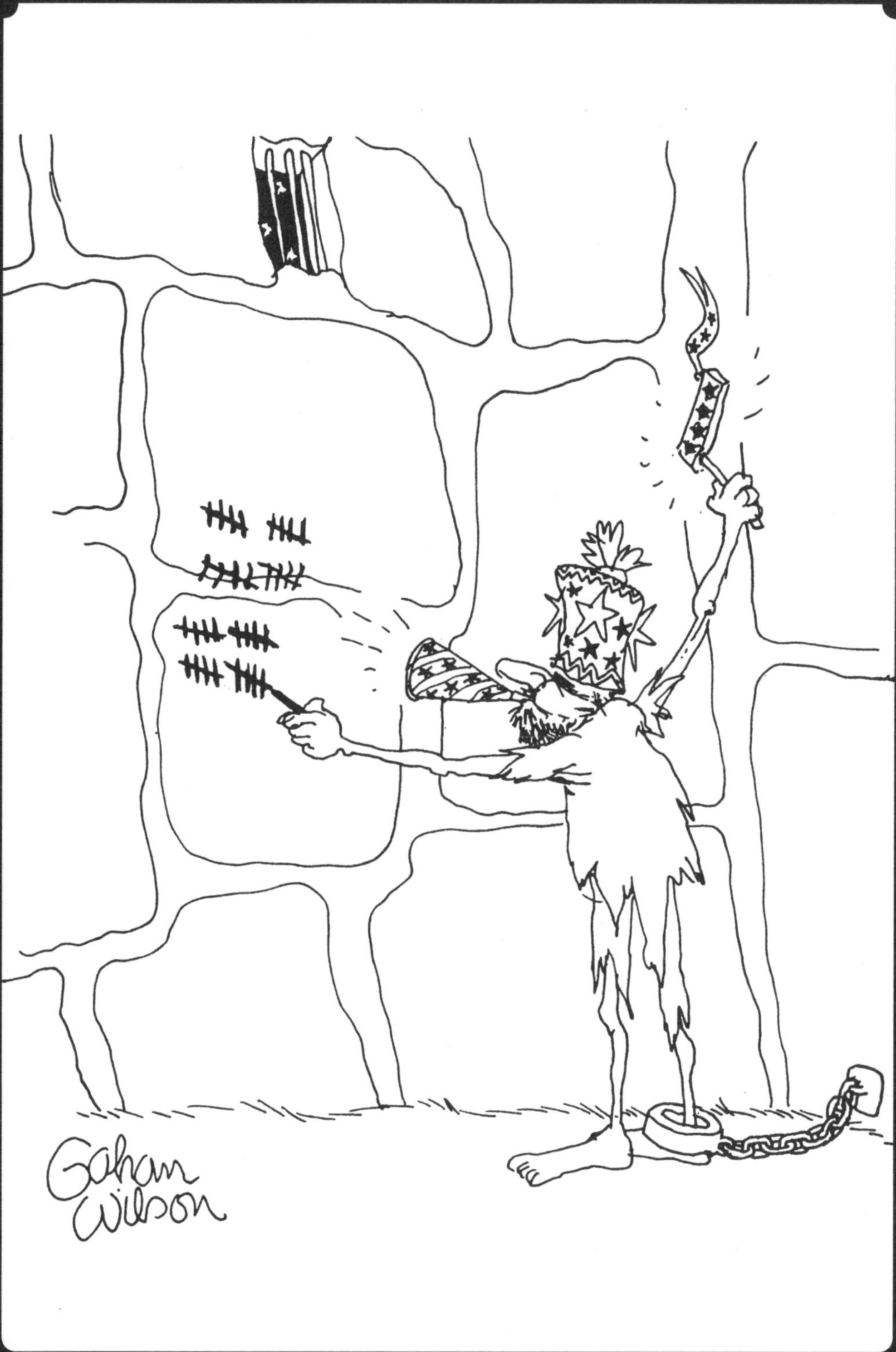
Gahan Wilson

Gahan Wilson

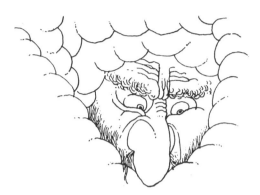

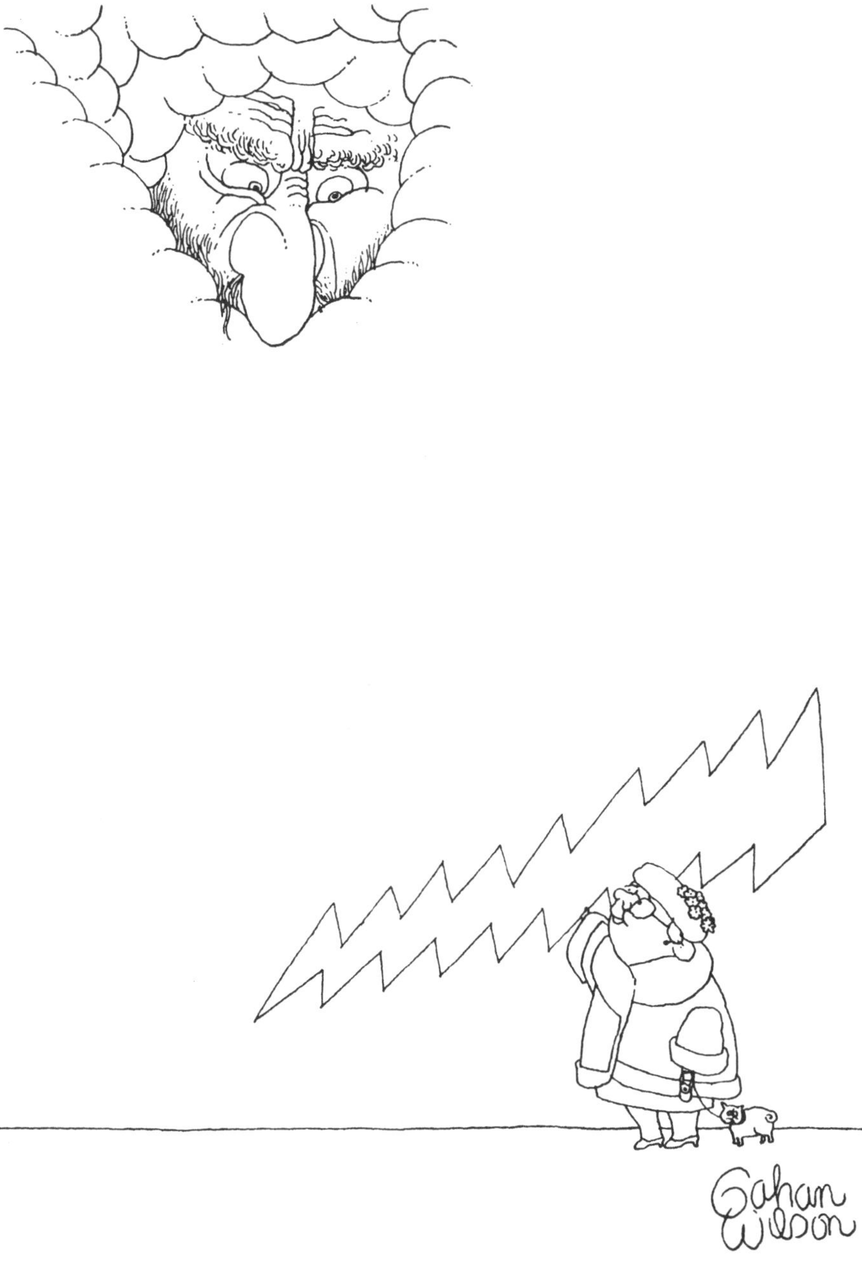

"Is this yours?"

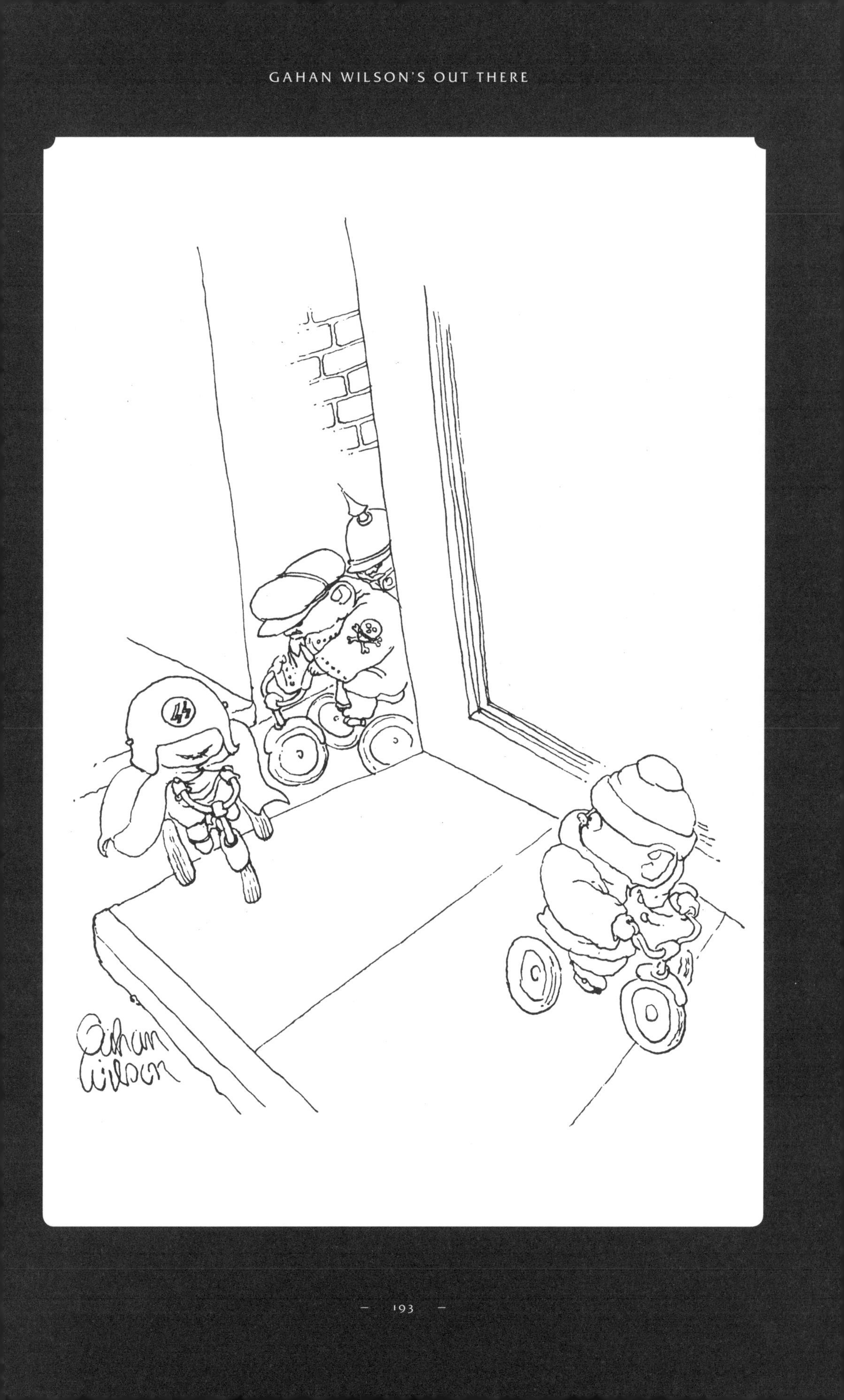
Gahan Wilson

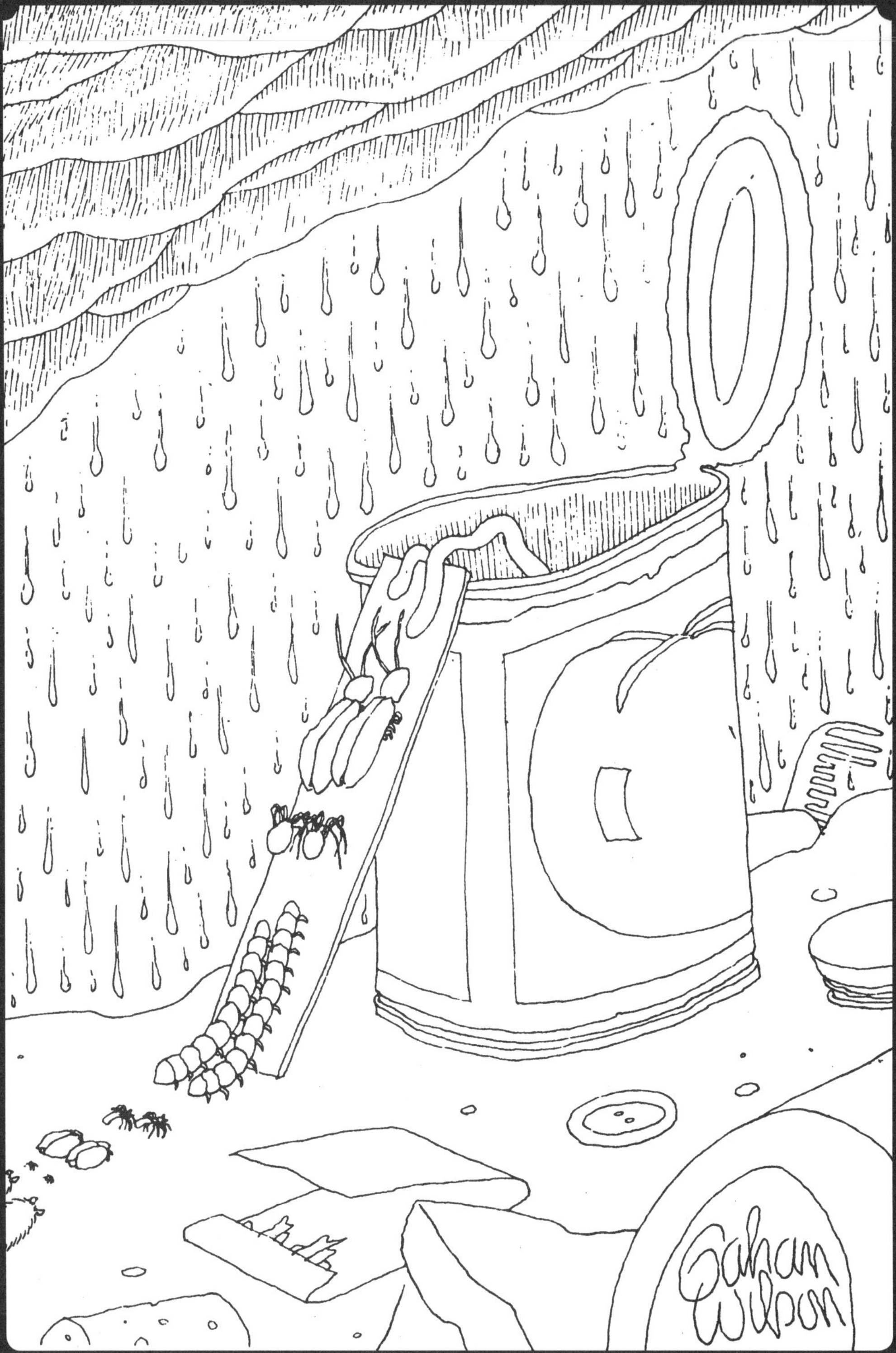
Gahan Wilson

"There you are, you naughties!"

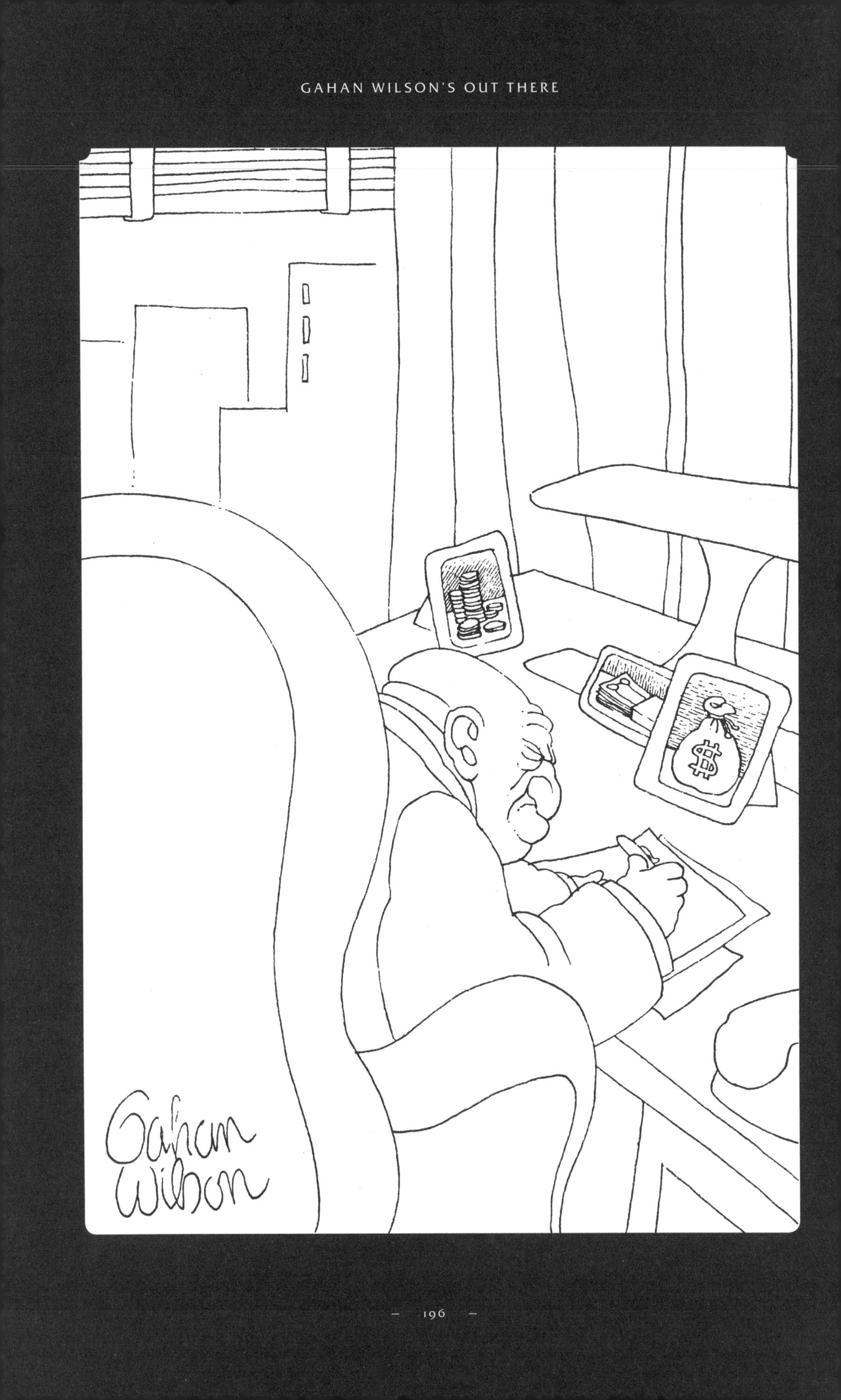
Gahan Wilson

"I was starting to wonder if you'd turn up!"

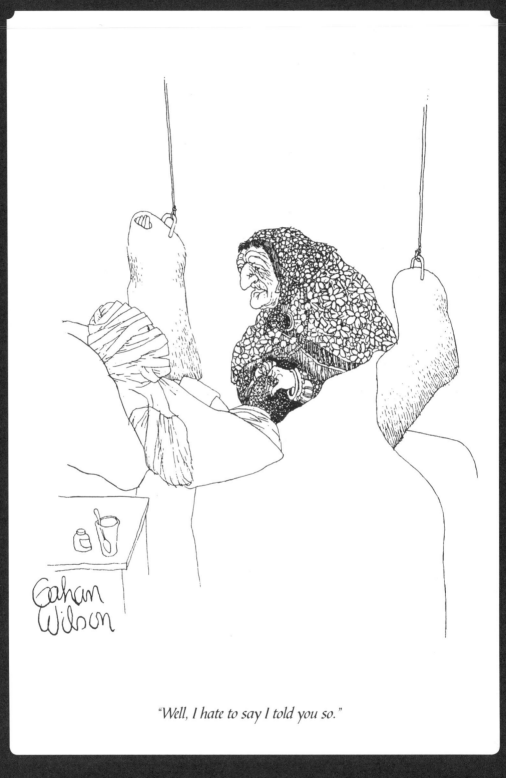

"Well, I hate to say I told you so."

SHORT STORIES

— BY —

Gahan Wilson

BEWARE OF THE DOG

nce there was an encyclopedia salesman who ignored a sign saying BEWARE OF THE DOG and went up on the porch of a pleasant cottage to ring its bell. The door of the cottage opened, and the salesman was admitted at once by a small man with a kindly face who led him straight to the parlor and served him tea and biscuits.

The salesman described the many merits of the encyclopedia, and told of the numerous advantages that would naturally come to anyone fortunate enough to own a set. The little man, who wore a long bathrobe, slippers, and gloves, said not a word, but his interest was gratifyingly obvious. In the end, he nodded firmly, gave the salesman a signed check for the full amount, and took possession of the encyclopedia set then and there.

The salesman left happily, smiling at the BEWARE OF THE DOG sign, and thinking how wise he had been to ignore it.

The little man with the kindly face watched the salesman out of sight, and then he took off his kindly face, which was actually a mask, his long bathrobe, slippers, and gloves. After that he went to the kitchen and lapped up a soothing bowl of milk for he had been a dog in disguise all along, of course, and his check would most certainly bounce.

MORAL: BEWARE THE RIGHT DOG.

"Beware of the Dog"

THE THING FROM OUTER SPACE
AND THE PRAIRIE DOGS

 rocket ship landed on the Texas panhandle one bright, sunny day, in the middle of a prairie dog colony. The top of the rocket unscrewed, with a harsh, grating noise, and out crawled a Thing from outer space. The Thing carried a death ray, a mind twister, a pain amplifier, and many other ingenious instruments of war, torture, and destruction. It drooled green drool and looked about for something to kill.

When a prairie dog peeped out from its burrow, the Thing spun on its tentacles, and shot out a blinding beam of fire from one of its weapons that reduced the prairie dog to a cloud of idly drifting ash. The Thing burbled for joy and started hunting eagerly for more of the tiny creatures.

At this point, two cleverly concealed trap doors opened in the ground, and from each of them rose a glittering, electronic cannon manned by a crew of uniformed prairie dogs. The cannons fired simultaneously on the Thing and destroyed it.

"It's a good thing we were prepared," said the captain of the prairie dogs, "But I could have sworn the humans would have launched the first attack."

MORAL: WATCH OUT WHICH FLY YOU SWAT.

"The Thing from Outer Space and the Prairie Dogs"

THE SCIENTIST AND THE MONSTER

A scientist set out to build and bring to life a new and superior sort of human being. He visualized it as being an example to the rest of us that would show the way to a better life, progress, and possibly even peace on Earth.

Unfortunately, although he had the best intentions, the scientist blundered seriously at a few crucial points, and economized a bit too much on materials. The disappointing result could be described as a monster.

The scientist, who had hidden himself in a closet the moment the monster had begun to stir, peeked out in dismay and watched the creature stagger exploratively about the laboratory. The thing was hideous, and the scientist felt a terrible guilt at having constructed it.

"What right had I," he asked himself, "to play God and bring this poor, twisted creature into suffering existence?"

Through tears of repentance, the scientist saw in sudden horror that the monster had discovered a full-length mirror hanging at one end of the laboratory and was clumping toward it.

"How terrible!" groaned the scientist. "What will happen when the pathetic being sees his ghastly image in the glass?"

The monster stood before the mirror a minute or so and then, with little coos of delight, began to mince up and down before it, turning and posturing as it did so. When the scientist leaned out of the closet a little further, so as to better observe this phenomenon, the monster saw him and ran shrieking and gagging from the room.

MORAL: MANY PEOPLE YOU FEEL SORRY FOR WOULD SERIOUSLY WONDER WHY.

"The Scientist and the Monster"

THE KNIGHT-ERRANT, THE DRAGON, AND THE MAIDEN

nce upon a time, a bold knight-errant, dressed in shining armor and riding a magnificent white charger, came across a huge dragon lurking in a dismal mountain pass. The dragon had thick, copper scales and breathed bright blue fire from its nostrils and mouth.

Now the knight knew that the principal occupation of dragons was that of guarding young maidens, so he swiveled his helmet this way and that until, sure enough, he saw one. The cruel dragon had bound her to the rocky side of the pass with heavy iron chains.

The knight took a long, thoughtful look at the maiden, observing, among other things, how poorly her white gown served to cover the sinuous curves of her body. He decided that she would do very well and, accordingly, unsheathed his sword, dismounted from his charger, and strode forth to do battle with the dragon.

Although the dragon had several tons on the knight, and at least four yards' advantage in reach, he had neglected his exercises of late, and overindulged in mead. The result was that he had gotten badly out of shape. The knight, on the other hand, was in the pink of condition, and had only recently graduated from a school where he had learnt all the very latest techniques in monster vanquishment.

The battle was, therefore, sadly one-sided from the start, and in an embarrassingly short time the knight stood with one of his feet on the dragon's neck and his sword raised and ready to deliver the final, irrevocable, chop.

But before he could begin his blade's downward swing, the maiden snuck up behind the unsuspecting knight and, with one looping blow from her heavy iron manacles, caved in both his helmet and his skull. She then turned and cast a reproachful look at her reptile guardian, which was still sprawled ignominiously on the ground.

"If you can't do better than that, Poopsie," she told it, "I'm going to get me another dragon."

MORAL: FREE WILLING PRISONERS AT YOUR OWN RISK.

"The Knight-Errant, the Dragon, and the Maiden"

THE SEA MONSTER AND
THE MAYOR OF NEW YORK CITY

ecause of an ill-advised atomic experiment, a giant sea monster was awakened from his slumber in the stygian depths. Affronted at this interruption of his peaceful slumber, the huge creature rose to the surface of the waters, determined to avenge himself on the race which had created his inconvenience.

He cruised the vast Atlantic, occasionally munching a passing ship, and pondered on the best means of expressing his extreme displeasure. When he observed that the bulk of the sea traffic tended to head in a certain direction, he went that way and thus discovered New York. He decided he would eat it up: both because the unwonted exercise he had indulged in had given him an enormous appetite and because he judged it an excellent way to chastise the pygmy beings whom had so rudely stirred him from his repose.

"If you attempt to swallow up this city," warned the Mayor of New York, speaking to the sea monster by means of a gigantic public address system mounted on a harbor tug, "you will live to regret it deeply!"

Ignoring this with a snort of contempt, the immense beast swam past the Mayor's tug and proceeded to eat Manhattan, the Bronx, Brooklyn, Queens, and Staten Island at one gulp.

Unhappily for him, along with the above-mentioned real estate, the monster also consumed, among other unpleasant items, a dozen snarling traffic jams, hundreds of homicidal maniacs, a quantity of violent riots, and an incredible amount of polluted air. Writhing and groaning from the hideous effects produced by his horrible repast, the poor behemoth struggled out to sea.

"I spoke from experience," said the Mayor bitterly, watching the sea monster's uneven retreat.

MORAL: MANY THREATS ARE KINDLY MEANT.

"The Sea Monster and the Mayor of New York City"

THE POWER OF THE MANDARIN

Aladar Rakas gave a wicked grin and raised his brandy glass.

"To the King Plotter of Evil. To the Prophet of our Doom. To the Mandarin."

I joined the toast willingly.

"May he never be totally defeated. May he and his vile minions ever threaten the civilized world."

We drank contentedly. Rakas leaned back, struck a luxurious pose, and wafted forth a cloud of Havana's very best.

"How many have been killed this time?"

Rakas tapped an ash from his cigar and gazed thoughtfully upward. I could see his lips moving as he made the count.

"Five," he said. And then, after a pause, "No. Six."

I looked at him with some surprise. "That's hardly up to the usual slaughter."

Rakas chuckled and signaled the waiter for more brandy.

"True enough," he said. "However, one particular murder of those six is enough to make up for hundreds, perhaps thousands, of ordinary ones."

His dark eyes glinted. He arched his thick, sable brows and leaned slowly forward.

"I have given the Mandarin a real treat this time, Charles," he said.

"You have, have you?"

I took a quick, unsatisfying puff at my cigarette and wondered what the old devil had been up to. I tossed out a guess.

"You haven't let him kill Mork?"

The brutish Mork. The only vaguely human emissary of the insidious Mandarin. He was, in his apish way, ambitious. Perhaps he had gone too far. It would be a shame to lose Mork.

Rakas waved the idea aside with an airy gesture.

"No, Charles. I have always liked Mork. Besides, he is far too useful

"The Power of the Mandarin"

as a harbinger of horrors to come. No, I would never dream of killing the dreadful creature."

Belatedly, a grim suspicion began to grow in me. Rakas was making quite a production out of this revelation. It would be something very much out of the ordinary.

"As a matter of fact," he continued blandly, covertly watching me from the corners of his eyes, "the only one of the Mandarin's henchmen to die in this particular adventure is a Lascar. A low underling hardly worth mentioning."

The suspicion hardened into a near certainty, but I tried a parry.

"How about the Inspector? Have you let him kill Snow?"

"Why bother? Inspector Snow. The poor blunderer. No, Charles, this murder is one of the first magnitude. This murder is the one which the Mandarin has burned to do since book one."

He looked at the expression on my face and grinned hugely.

"Of course you've guessed."

I gaped at him unbelievingly.

"You're joking, Aladar," I said.

He continued to grin.

He'd let the Mandarin kill Evan Trowbridge. I knew he'd let him kill Evan Trowbridge. I swallowed and decided to say it out loud and hear how it sounded.

"He's killed Evan Trowbridge."

It sounded like a kind of croak. Rakas gave a confirming nod and continued to grin.

I won't say that the room swam before my eyes, but I did wonder, just for a moment, if I was going to faint. I sat in my chair building up a nervous tic and thinking about Evan Trowbridge.

Who was it who stood between the malevolent Mandarin and his conquest of the world? I'll tell you who. Evan Trowbridge. Who was it who foiled, again and again, in book after book, the heartless fiend who plotted the base enslavement of us all? None other than Evan Trowbridge.

And now he was dead.

"The Power of the Mandarin"

I wiped the palms of my hands carefully with my napkin and cleared my throat. I could think of nothing else to do, short of leaping over the table and crushing in the top of Aladar Rakas's skull.

He looked at me with some concern. I suppose I looked like a man trembling on the verge of a fit. I may have been.

He sighed.

"You must understand, Charles," he said. "If only you knew how often I have ached to let him do it."

"But why?"

His eyes shown dreamily.

"Evan Trowbridge," he said. "Pillar of the Establishment. Pride of the Empire."

He had turned deadly serious.

"Do you know where the strength of a Trowbridge lies, Charles? I'll tell you. It lies in his sublime conviction that he and his kind are superior to all other men. That anyone who is not both white and English is automatically not quite a human being."

He ground out his cigar forcefully, yet precisely, as if he were sticking it into a Trowbridge eye.

"It's different here in America," he said. "Do you know what it was like to be a poor Hungarian in London? Speaking with a foreign accent? Looking alien? Liking garlic and spicy foods?"

He looked down at his huge white hands and watched them curl into fists.

"I dressed like them. I even thought of changing my name. Then I realized I would only make myself more ridiculous in their eyes."

He looked at me, and then his expression softened and he chuckled.

"Wait until you read how the Mandarin kills him, Charles. It is a masterpiece, if I do say so myself. It takes an entire chapter."

I bunched up my napkin and tossed it on the table.

"So what happens to the series, Aladar? Have you thought about that? Who the hell is going to fight the Mandarin?"

He brushed it away.

"The Power of the Mandarin"

"Somebody will, Charles. The series will continue. We will continue. I have several possibilities in mind. I have thought, maybe, a Hungarian. Maybe someone rather like myself."

We finished our coffee and parted in widely divergent moods.

I took the manuscript to my office, informed my secretary that I was strictly incommunicado, and read *The Mandarin Triumphant* from its first neatly typed page to its last.

I discovered, thank God, that it was good. Really one of his best.

I had been afraid that the hatred for Trowbridge which Rakas had just confessed would show through, and that he might turn him into some kind of villain, or, much worse, a quivering coward, but none of this had happened. The brave Britisher fought the good fight to the end. The Mandarin, after having committed what really was a masterpiece of murder, even spoke a little tribute to his redoubtable foe just before boarding a mysterious boat and vanishing into the swirling fog of a Thames estuary:

"He was a worthy opponent," said the Mandarin in the sibilant whisper he adopted when in a thoughtful mood. "In his dogged fashion, I believe he understood me and my aspirations as no man has done."

Slipping carefully from the plastic coverall which had protected him from the deadly mold, the towering man bent respectfully to the nearly formless heap which lay at his feet and, with great solemnity, he made an ancient Oriental gesture of salutation to which had once been Evan Trowbridge.

I closed the manuscript feeling much for the better.

After all, I figured, Rakas had managed to make the Mandarin series into a very successful enterprise with Trowbridge, and there was no reason to see why he couldn't go right ahead and carry on without him. It was the Mandarin who really counted, and if the heroic Englishman irritated the author all that much, I couldn't see why he shouldn't be allowed to go ahead and kill the bastard. There were a few bad moments with some of the other editors but, in the end, we all sat back with smug little smiles playing on our

"The Power of the Mandarin"

faces and waited to see how Rakas's new champion fared in the struggle against the vast criminal campaign of the diabolical Mandarin.

One very comforting development was the unexpectedly large popularity of *Triumph*. The critics who had rejected the previous books as being too much loved it. They liked the idea of the superhero getting horribly murdered. It moved the whole thing into a campy sort of area where they could relax and enjoy without being embarrassed.

We worked a series of TV and radio slots for Rakas, which was something we'd never done before, and he clicked. The public liked his sinister presence. They relished him in much the same way they did Alfred Hitchcock. There is something very reassuring about a boogeyman who's willing to joke about his scareful personality. It eases all sorts of dim little fears and makes the dark unknown seem almost friendly. This sudden celebrity pleased Rakas.

"It is very nice," he told me. "I was walking down the street the other day and a beautiful woman came up to me. 'Are you Aladar Rakas?' she asked me. And I told her I was. A perfect stranger, and that very night we went to bed. I like this being famous."

I asked him how the new book was going.

"It's coming along nicely," he said. "My hero is a Hungarian, as I warned you he might be. I have not given him a name yet. I call him Rakas, after myself, for now. Later on I will figure out some name for him. I want it to be just right, of course.

"He is not a bullhead, like that Trowbridge. He is a man who thinks. The Mandarin will have his hands full with him, you will see. I think the only real problem will be to make sure that this new hero of mine doesn't finish him off in the first three chapters."

Then he laughed, and I laughed with him.

It was just about two weeks later, about four in the morning, when the telephone rang. I knocked over the alarm clock and upset a full ashtray before I managed to bark a hello into the receiver's mouthpiece. I expected to hear some fool drunk blurting apologies, but I got Rakas, instead.

"The Power of the Mandarin"

"Charles," he said, "could I come over? I'd like to talk to you. Now. Tonight. I'm worried."

I told him he could. I slipped on a bathrobe and groped my way into the kitchen. I'd just finished brewing a pot of coffee when the doorbell rang.

He looked bad. He was pale and I think he'd lost weight. I noticed his hand shook a little when he lifted his cup.

"What's wrong, Aladar?"

"It's the book. Here." He had a manuscript in a folder and he passed it over to me. "It's not going well."

I considered giving him a little lecture about office hours and then decided to hell with it. I flipped through the pages. Everything looked fine. A man killed by a poison dart on a misty wharf. The new hero narrowly missing death by scorpion-stuffed glove. A brief meeting with the Mandarin himself in a dark SoHo alley.

For an instant Rakas saw the huge forehead, the glittering eyes, the deep hollows of the cheeks, and then the light snuffed out, leaving only a skeleton silhouette.

"You are confident, Rakas," came the harsh, icy whisper. "You consider me a puppet, a marionette."

Suddenly Rakas felt his shoulder grasped by a merciless talon which seemed hard as steel. He grunted in pain and tried to twist free.

"There are no strings on this hand, Rakas," continued the chill muttering of the Mandarin. "It kills when I want, and releases when I wish."

Then the talon wrenched away, and Rakas found himself alone.

I lit a cigarette and read on happily. It was around the end of chapter eight when I saw the beginnings of the drift.

The awful spasms of his dying, had twisted Colonial Bentley-Smith's face into a grotesque grin, and this look of dead glee seemed to mock the

---

"The Power of the Mandarin"

perplexed frown of Aladar Rakas.

"I don't understand, Inspector Snow," he snapped, "didn't you deploy your men as I asked you to?"

"I did that, sir," replied the puzzled policeman, "but they got through to him without one of us having the foggiest."

Rakas snarled and ground his teeth together. "Then we have sprung our trap upon a corpse!"

I looked up at Rakas.

"How did they get through?" I asked.

"That's just it," he said. "I don't know!"

He pulled out a cigar, started to unwrap it, and then shoved it back into his pocket.

"You've read it," he said. "In chapter seven I show how I, or rather I show how Rakas, has made absolutely sure that the Colonel's study is inaccessible. Every window, every door, all possible means of approach, are under constant observation. There is no way, no conceivable method, for the Mandarin or his minions to have snuck in with the cobra."

He sat back and spread his hands helplessly.

"And yet they do get in, *and* out, and no one the wiser."

I flipped an edge of the manuscript and looked at Rakas thoughtfully.

"Let me show you," he said, leaning forward and taking the folder from my hands. "Let me show you how it happens again." He thumbed through the pages. "Yes, here it is. Here is something just like it."

"Would you like some more coffee?"

"Yes. Sure. Here Rakas has rigged the mummy case in the museum so that there is no feasible way for anyone to open it and remove the body of the sorcerer. The slightest touch on the case's lid and an alarm goes off and cameras record the event. A fly couldn't land on the damned thing without setting off the apparatus. And yet the Mandarin does it. I don't know how, but he pulls it off."

I began, "Aladar—"

"The Power of the Mandarin"

"No. Wait," he said, cutting me off. "That's not all. Here, in chapter fourteen, here's one that really gets me. I absolutely defy you to explain to me how he manages to poison the—"

This time I cut him off.

"Aladar, it's not my job to explain how he does it. I'm merely the reader. You, Aladar, are the one to explain it."

"But, how?" he asked me, flinging his hands wide. "I would like you to explain to me how?"

"Because it's a goddam story, Aladar, and because you're the goddam author. That's how."

It took him by absolute surprise. It seemed to stun him. He sat back in his chair and blinked at me.

"You are the one who's making this up," I said, waving at the manuscript that lay, all innocence, on the kitchen table. "You made up the Colonel and the Mandarin and the whole thing. It's you who decides who does what to whom and how they do it. Nobody else but you."

He reached up and squeezed his forehead. He shut his eyes and sat perfectly still for at least a minute. Then he let his hand fall to his lap.

"You are right, aren't you?" he said. He sighed heavily and reached out to touch the manuscript gingerly with his fingertips. "It's only a story, isn't it?"

He looked up at the clock on the wall.

"My God," he said. "It's the middle of the night."

He took the manuscript in his hands and stood.

"I'm sorry, Charles. I'm a fool. I can't understand how I let myself be carried away like this."

"It's all right, Aladar," I said. "You just let yourself get too wrapped up. It happens."

We said a few more things, and then I walked him to the door. He opened it and stood there, looking dejected and foolish. I put my hand on his shoulder.

"Remember," I told him, "you're the boss."

He looked at me a little while.

"The Power of the Mandarin"

"Sure. That's right," he said. "I'm the boss."

Then the preparation for that year's Christmas rush got underway, and I found myself up to my hips in non-books to lure the prospective festive shoppers. It is a busy season, this pre-Yule observance, and Aladar Rakas got crowded out of my mind along with everything else except the confused and frantic matters at hand. At least that is my excuse for not getting in touch with him for a good month and a half.

In the end it was he who got in touch with me. I was plowing through a manuscript we'd bought on the archaeology of ancient Egypt, wondering what the copyeditor was going to say about the author's ancient use of commas, when my secretary came in to tell me that Rakas was in the outer office. I went out, covered my shock at the way he looked, and walked him back to my sanctuary. He was so thin he had become gaunt.

"It has proven more difficult than you thought," he said. "I believed you, that night, but now I am not so sure."

He had an attaché case with him. He opened it and took out an enormous manuscript. He hefted it and then laid it on my desk.

"Is that the new book?" I asked.

"It is."

I squeezed its bulk, estimating the probable wordage.

"But, Aladar," I said, "the thing's easily three times as long as any of the others."

He smiled ironically.

"You are right, Charles," he said. "And it is not yet finished. If I go on like this I will end with the *Gone With the Wind* of thrillers."

I pulled the thing to me and went through the opening pages. It was obvious he had done a lot of work on them, the changes were considerable, but the storyline remained exactly the same.

"You remember the scene where the Mandarin, or Mork, or whoever it is gets in and kills the Colonel?" he asked. "Well, it keeps on happening, Charles. No matter how I rearrange the constabulary of the good Inspector Snow, no matter if I, myself, remain on the premises, even in the room,

"The Power of the Mandarin"

itself, it keeps on happening. The Colonel always ends up being killed by that damned cobra."

"But that's mad, Aladar."

"Yes. Possibly it is because I am going mad. I sincerely hope that is the case. I was sure of it in the beginning. But now I am not so sure. The terrible possibility is that I may be sane and the thing may actually be happening."

I looked at him with, I think, understandable confusion. Rakas lit a cigar and I began to go through the manuscript quickly, skimming, turning several pages at a time when I felt I had the direction of the action.

"It goes that way all through the book," he said. "I increase the protection. I double and redouble the guards. It is all to no avail. The Mandarin wins. Again and again, he wins."

He had a weird kind of calm this time. He even seemed to be amused at his plight. He leaned forward and pointed at the manuscript with his cigar.

"At least a dozen times in there he could have killed me, Charles. Always he lets me go. Just in the nick of time, as we say in the trade." He paused. "But this last time, I am not so sure. I think he is getting tired of the game. I think he almost decided to do me in."

I turned quickly to the end of the manuscript. I found the scene easily.

Despite the almost unendurable pain, Rakas could not move any part of his body, save his eyes. In particular, he could not move his hand. He stared at it, watching it become ever more discolored under the flickering ray from the Mandarin's machine. It felt as though a thousand burning needles were twisting in his flesh.

The cadaverous form of the Mandarin arched over him, lit by the infernal rainbow of color emanating from the device. Rakas had the momentary illusion that the creature was not flesh and blood, at all, but a kind of carved architectural device, like a gargoyle buttress in some unholy cathedral.

"Your thoughts of rock images are most appropriate, Rakas," hissed the Mandarin, casually employing his ability to read men's minds. "Perhaps your unconscious is attempting to inform you that you, or at least your right

"The Power of the Mandarin"

hand, is undergoing a process unique in the history of living human flesh. It is turning into stone."

Rakas stared in horror at the graying, roughening skin of his hand. When his bulging eyes traveled back to the Mandarin, he saw that the face of the evil genius was now inches from his own. He could feel fetid breath coming from the cruel slash of a mouth.

"Shall I turn you into a garden ornament now, Rakas? Or should I spare you for a time? What do you think?"

Rakas was smiling at me.

"Shall I show you my right hand, Charles?"

It had been hidden behind his attaché case. He pulled it out and held it before me. It was bluish pale, and stiff.

"It is flesh, not stone," he said. "But it cannot move."

He touched the back of it with the lighted tip of his cigar.

"It cannot feel."

He removed the cigar and I saw that the flesh was still smooth and unbroken.

"It cannot burn."

He chuckled and slid his hand back behind the case.

"You see it is not as bad as in the story. Not yet. But it is getting close, is it not?"

I closed the manuscript without looking at it. Then I threw a part of my professional life out the window.

"Kill the son of a bitch," I said.

"What?"

"Kill the Mandarin. Get rid of him. End the series."

I took a deep breath.

"Look, Aladar, I'll admit the books make a nice bundle of money for us all, but to hell with them. They just aren't worth the damage they're doing to you. This hand business is awful but it's explainable. You can do things like that under hypnosis. But it's a goddamned frightening symptom."

"The Power of the Mandarin"

I pushed the manuscript away from me. I didn't want to touch it anymore.

"I'm telling you as your editor, Aladar, that you have absolute carte blanche to slaughter the Mandarin and wrap up the whole business. As a friend, I suggest you do it quickly."

He chuckled again. It was a fair imitation of his usual one, but it didn't have the depth.

"You don't understand, do you, Charles?"

He took the manuscript back and put it into his case. He closed the case and brooded over it for a while.

"Don't you see? I am trying to kill him. Desperately."

He looked at me and his gaze made me uncomfortable.

"With Trowbridge it was altogether different. It was a sort of chess game. Check and counter check. It was safe. Contained. But now I have removed Trowbridge, and the Mandarin is getting out. The only thing that kept that fiend in the books, I realize this now, was that blasted Englishman. Now I have killed him, and now there is nothing to stop the evil from slithering off the pages I have written."

"All right," I said. "Resurrect Evan Trowbridge. Bring him back from the dead. Conan Doyle did it with Holmes."

This time Rakas actually laughed.

"You have cited the perfect example why I cannot, Charles. Was Holmes ever really the same after Doyle killed him? No. Not except in the adventures Watson remembered from before the event. Even the most convinced Sherlockian must admit in his heart that Holmes never truly survived the tumble into the Falls."

He rapped his knuckles on the case and frowned.

"You see, Charles, that is the thing. These creatures are real. They exist. I did not create the Mandarin. I came across him. Do we ever make anything up? I doubt it. I think we only make little openings and peer through them. And openings work both ways."

He stood.

"Doyle was infinitely wiser than I. He respected what he had created.

He respected the vile Moriarty. He made bloody damned sure that Holmes took the devil with him when he died. He knew that no one else, least of all himself, would have been able to stop him. And so we are presently safe from the baneful doctor. But I have loosed the Mandarin."

Then, without another word, he turned and left.

I don't know how long I sat there cursing myself for not having done something before, such as keeping in touch with Rakas after that early morning visit, before it occurred to me that sitting and cursing was hardly likely to help. I told my secretary to plead with Rakas to come back up if he decided to phone in, and then I left the office.

I figured the best possibility was that he'd head for his apartment. It was east off the park in the sixties. I knew he seldom took a cab but always walked if he had less than fifteen blocks to go. It was a good bet that he was walking now.

He might go up Fifth, and then he might cut over; there was no way of telling. I decided that a man in his state of mind would probably take the simplest route, the one that needed the least attention, so I crossed my fingers and bet on Fifth. I hurried along and when I drew abreast of the fountain in front of the Plaza, I saw him. He was heading into the park.

My first impulse was to dash right up to him, but then I realized I'd probably just dither, so I slowed to match his pace and tried to get myself calmed down. He needed a doctor, he needed help, and it was going to take some fancy persuading. I followed him and mulled over possible gambits.

When he got to the zoo he began to walk idly from cage to cage, looking at the animals. I stopped by a balloon and banner man and bought a box of Cracker Jack. It helped me blend in, and I figured the taste of the homely stuff might bring me a little closer to earth. Rakas had stopped by a lion cage and, with slow turns of his head, was watching the beast walk back and forth.

I was standing there munching my Cracker Jacks, creating and rejecting openers, when I caught a flicker of movement out of the corner of my eye and turned to see, or almost see, someone dart back under an archway. I stared hard at the empty place. The someone had been very squat and broad.

"The Power of the Mandarin"

His suit had been a kind of snake green.

I looked back to check on Rakas. He was still standing in front of the lion's cage. I backed, crabwise, to the arch, keeping one eye on it and the other on Rakas. When I reached the arch I darted through it and looked quickly to the left and right, and I got another glimpse of the squat figure.

He'd slipped around the corner of the monkey house. He'd done it so quickly I wouldn't have seen him if I hadn't been looking for him. I remembered a filmstrip I'd seen demonstrating the insertion of subliminal images. Just one frame, maybe two, edited in so that you weren't sure if it was something you'd really seen up there on the screen or a passing thought in your own mind.

Green clothes, ape-like, and quick as a lizard.

Mork.

The Mandarin always sent Mork on before.

Then a kid's balloon burst and he gave out a squawk of fright and I found myself standing in Central Park Zoo with a box of Cracker Jack in my hand.

I went back through the arch and saw that Rakas was no longer standing in front of the lion's cage. I looked in all directions, but he was nowhere to be seen. I wondered what Evan Trowbridge would have done in a situation like this, and then I shook my head and tossed the fool Cracker Jack into a Keep Our City Clean basket. Aladar Rakas had gone mad; it was important to remember that. He had gotten lost in his own lunatic fantasy.

I left the zoo and hurried along the path leading uptown. It was logical to assume he had gone that way. In spite of myself, I found I kept looking from side to side to see if I could spot Mork. Of course there were only young lovers walking, women pushing baby carriages, and old men lost in their smoking.

Then, as I stopped to catch my breath on the hill overlooking the pond where children sail their toy boats, I saw Rakas sitting on a bench. He had the manuscript open, resting on his case, and he was writing with furious speed.

I walked up to him carefully. He was absorbed in his work, and it was only when my shadow fell across the pages that he looked up and saw me.

"The Power of the Mandarin"

"Charles! What are you doing here?"

"I was worried, Aladar."

"Oh?" He smiled. "That was very thoughtful of you. I am really quite touched."

He looked down at the manuscript.

"I am sorry to have left your office so rudely, Charles. But you know," he looked up at me suddenly, "just as I was leaving, I got an inspiration. A real inspiration. Sit down, please."

I did as he asked. I could see that he had several pages of close scribblings before him. He must have been writing at an incredible speed.

"I think I have figured out a way to get him, Charles. I really believe I know how to get the necessary leverage."

He smiled at me benignly.

"How do you propose to do it, Aladar?"

"Drag him out ahead of schedule. Manifest him before he is strong!"

I only looked at him blankly, but he was far too excited to notice.

"The Mandarin has been trying to get out, you see, attempting to push his way into life. He has been, you might say, pursuing me into existence. Well, I am going to fool him. I am going to turn and face him and pull him, willy-nilly, into reality. That should put him off his balance!"

He grinned and waved at the scene about us.

"I am going to write him into this actual location, Charles. And on my own terms!"

He rubbed his left hand over his stiff, pale right hand and cackled to himself.

"I began writing it, not on paper, but writing it nevertheless, while at the zoo, watching a lion prowl in his cage. I decided I would begin with Mork. I would not break the tradition of the stories. I had Mork pick up my trail there. I had him follow me," he pointed, "along that path."

I looked back at the path. It was, oddly enough, empty. Only dry leaves blew along it.

"Do you see that boulder?"

"The Power of the Mandarin"

I did. It stuck out of the ground like the nose of a huge, gray whale.

"At this moment Mork is hiding behind it."

He tapped the manuscript.

"I have written it here. I have put it down in black and white. He cannot get away. He is trapped. He knows I know. It's all here."

He tapped the manuscript again. "And now I am going to go over there and kill him, Charles."

He put the manuscript and the case on the bench beside him and then he stood. I opened my mouth, trying to think of something or other to say, but it all got stuck in my throat when I saw Rakas reach into his coat and calmly pull out the biggest revolver I had ever seen in my life. I hadn't known they made them that big. It was terrifying and, at the same time, ludicrous.

"I have been afraid for a long time now, Charles," he said. "Now wait here. I will be right back."

I sat and watched him walk over to the leaning rock. His black coat fluttered about him and the leaves swirled where he walked. He reached the rock, held the revolver straight before him, and walked out of sight.

I waited for the sound of the shot, but it never came. Eventually I stood and followed him. My legs felt rubbery. When I got to the rock I had to lean on it for support. I felt my way around the rock to its other side and saw him lying on the ground, partially covered with a drift of dirty city leaves. He looked up at me.

"How stupid," he said. "I couldn't bring myself to kill him."

Then he closed his eyes. I bent down, close to him. A thick, dark rivulet of blood ran from one of his ears. I brushed through the leaves until I found the revolver, and then I lifted it with both hands. I stood and walked around the rock and looked back toward the bench.

The Mandarin stood there, weirdly tall and thin, like the statue of a mourning angel in a graveyard. He held the manuscript clutched to his breast. Leaves scudded and broke at his feet. I began walking toward him.

"Not yet, you don't," I said.

I came closer.

"The Power of the Mandarin"

"The manuscript isn't finished," I said, "not even if the author's dead." I was closer.

His eyes caught the gray autumn light and glinted.

"I'm the editor," I said. "It's my job, it's my right, to see that the book is properly finished. That's the way it's done."

A leaf blew through the figure's head. I was very close. I could see the long nails on his fingers.

I dropped the gun and held out my hands.

"That's the way it's done," I said.

And then I held the manuscript.

I turned away. Some playing children had discovered Rakas and they were shouting excitedly. I put the book into the case and took it away.

Now this, what I have written, is part of the book. I have added it to Rakas's terminal scribblings and now I am going to finish the book.

I have selected this place carefully. It is miles from any other habitation. Its destruction will not endanger any bystander.

I have soaked the walls and floors with gasoline. I have piled rags around my desk and the chair facing my desk and they are also saturated with it. Everything in this room is wet except for the folder of matches, which lies beside me within easy reach. The matches are dry and ready.

Aladar Rakas discovered the Mandarin, but he couldn't quite believe in him. Even at the end he was unable to convince himself that such evil could really exist. He was too civilized a man. Too kindly and too generous.

But I am different. I have seen Rakas in the leaves and I, like Evan Trowbridge, believe in evil.

And I, like Evan Trowbridge and unlike Aladar Rakas, believe in and respect the power of the Mandarin. The devil may know what vile knowledge coils in that huge and unnaturally ancient brain, but I have only the faintest of glimmerings. I know only enough to realize that there is no question of my outwitting the monster.

I will attempt no subtleties. I will use the power I have as author to bring him here, and then I shall destroy everything, the entire hideous fabric of

"The Power of the Mandarin"

the pattern that made this situation possible. The book, the author and the creature spawned—all shall be burned cleanly away.

Now I am going to finish the book.

He is outside the door, now. He does not want to be but he must because I am writing it.

Now he has put his hand on the latch. Now he is opening the door. Now he stands there, in the twilight, looking at me with hatred in his eyes. That hatred takes a hater like myself to meet it.

He is here. Really and truly here. Not a near phantom, like the last time, but a solid, breathing being.

He is moving forward carefully, stepping high to avoid the soaked rags, but gasoline stains the hem of his grey, silken robe all the same.

Now he sits and glares at me.

He cannot move. He cannot budge, try as he may.

His eyes glow. They shimmer like fire seen through honey.

He cannot move.

Now I have lit a match and set the pack aflame.

I hope I shall never forget the extraordinary expression of astonishment on Charles Pearl's face when he realized he had committed suicide to no purpose.

He remained conscious for a remarkable period of time, considering the damage the fire was doing him, staring at me with utter disbelief as I gathered up the manuscript, including this last page torn from his typewriter.

The idiot had discovered Evan Trowbridge's strength, which was implacable hatred, but he had shared, and therefore missed altogether, his weakness, which was a lack of sufficient imagination.

Trowbridge always failed to bring me down altogether because he never quite managed to foresee the final trick of my science, the last fantastic ingenuity, the climactic trapdoor.

It would never have occurred to him, for instance, that I can live invulnerable in a pool of fire.

And so I, the hero of the series all along, have the opportunity to bring this final volume to, it pleases me to say, a happy ending.

"The Power of the Mandarin"

HARRY'S GOLDEN YEARS

A little snipped off here, a little sewn on there, a couple of tightenings, a couple of loosenings, some clearings out of the old tubes, and Harry Van Deventer was as good as new. Or almost. Good enough, at least.

Harry tied the decorative bow on the waist of his coverall and looked at himself, with pleasure, in the mirror. Harry didn't know the mirror took the gray out of his skin and made it rosy pink, he didn't know it soft-focused the wrinkles and faded the blue under his eyes, so he figured he looked pretty good. He smiled and patted his belly, which the surgeons had flattened, as an afterthought. Harry didn't know about that, either.

"Not bad," he said, softly.

The door dilated and the nurse came in. She was really a looker, really built. Harry remembered what a wild one she'd been last night and smiled. He was pleased when he remembered things. A little saliva ran out of the corner of his mouth.

"All set and ready, Mr. Van Deventer?" asked the nurse. Harry nodded. "Raring to go," he said. The nurse looked down at the floor. "I'm sorry about last night, Mr. Van Deventer," she said. "The way I threw myself at you, I mean."

She looked at him, blushed, and looked quickly down again. "I just couldn't help myself," she said.

Harry shrugged and raised his eyebrows. "That's all right," he said. "What the hell. It doesn't matter."

She looked at him with earnest relief. "I just knew you'd understand," she said.

Harry began to fidget. "So, where's the doctor?" he asked.

Outside, in the street, Harry tried to remember what had happened with the doctor, when he'd said goodbye, but he wasn't able to pull it back.

"Harry's Golden Years"

The doctor had asked him to do this and that, he remembered, take pills or something, and it had made him mad. Who did that doctor think he was? Harry was about to get mad all over again when a taxi came down and landed beside him.

"Want a ride, Mr. Van Deventer?" asked the driver.

"Yeah," said Harry, climbing in. "Only I ain't sure where I want to go, yet."

"Anyplace you want, Mr. Van Deventer," said the driver.

Harry looked at the back of the driver's neck and wondered why he always kept getting the same drivers over and over.

"Some nice place," he said. "I just been to the hospital. I want to relax."

"Just been to the hospital, huh, Mr. Van Deventer?" said the driver. "Jeez, that's tough."

"Ah, it's all right," said Harry.

The driver activated a device that judged Harry's physical condition and gauged his mood. Of course Harry had no idea what was going on. A little computer ticked over and flipped a card into the driver's lap. The driver glanced at it.

"How about Fat Lucy's, Mr. Van Deventer?" he asked.

"What's that?"

"A real swell place. You could let some steam off. You'll love it, no kidding, Mr. Van Deventer."

"Terrific," said Harry.

Then he had a second thought. An annoyed expression crossed his face.

"Hold it," he said. "How much does it cost? It ain't a clip joint, is it?"

"Oh, no sir, Mr. Van Deventer," said the driver, hurriedly. "You don't want to worry about that. I wouldn't take you to no place like that, you can bet, Mr. Van Deventer."

"All right, then," said Harry, settling back. "It's just that I heard some of you guys take people to clip joints, is all."

"You can forget about a thing like that in my cab, Mr. Van Deventer," said the driver, turning to smile nervously at Harry.

"I said all right." The driver swallowed and looked straight ahead.

"Harry's Golden Years"

Fat Lucy's was an all right place as far as Harry was concerned. Right away, right when he came in, a big blonde walked up to him.

"God, I been waiting for you all my life," she said. She couldn't keep her hands off him. "Jesus, where you been?"

"Around," said Harry.

He had a swell time. He couldn't remember the middle part too clearly, some waiter or other had said something fresh, and he hadn't liked it, but the rest of it was great. The girl got all upset when he was leaving.

"Christ, you've got to come back," she said.

"Yeah, sure," said Harry.

But he really didn't mean it. He just said it to make her happy. He couldn't help the way they all felt about him.

Back at his place, Harry had a bath and then checked his money chute. A lot of it had piled up while he was away. He didn't try to figure how much it was, he never did. He went to sleep.

While he was asleep, the accountants came in and had him sign a few papers. Years ago, when Harry had got tired of details, they'd worked it out so he could sign things in his sleep without waking up.

"The old bastard," said one accountant.

"Look," said another, "stop complaining. You're sitting pretty."

Harry woke that morning feeling restless but not sure just what he wanted to do. He turned on the television set and saw that they were doing his life story again. He sat and watched it for a while and then grew tired of it and went to the bathroom.

The bathroom was a real mess. It was all banged up. He must have got mad at something or other not working, but he couldn't remember. He'd really done a job on the shower. Anyhow, it didn't matter. They'd fix it up.

He had some trouble tying the decorative bow on his coverall, but he finally got it right. The bow had a paisley pattern and tassels on the edges.

It was a nice day, so he told the taxi driver to just fly over the city for a little. He looked down and there was the building with his name on the top. It was the biggest building in the city, and it was his. Harry never went

"Harry's Golden Years"

there any more, hadn't for years. Let them worry about it.

He glanced over at the far horizon and saw a long strip of green. He knew it was something, but he couldn't think what. Then it came back to him.

"That's the country, ain't it?"

The driver looked where he pointed. "Yeah, that's right, Mr. Van Deventer," he said.

"Let's go there," said Harry. "I had fun there, once."

"You bet, Mr. Van Deventer," said the driver, and sent a few messages ahead without Harry knowing.

By the time they arrived in the country, it was ready. The taxi landed by a farm, and Harry had no sooner climbed out when a farmer came smiling up to him.

"Howdy, stranger," said the Farmer. "Usually I don't take to strangers, but there's something I like a lot about your face."

The farmer gave Harry a fishing pole and told him how to hold it over a circular pond, which was located in the middle of the farmyard. In no time at all Harry had caught dozens of shiny fish. A crowd of country people came to watch Harry at it and to tell him what a really sensational fisherman he was.

Something or other happened just before lunch that Harry couldn't quite remember. It had to do with some guy who wasn't cheerful, like the other country people, and who had said something rotten about Harry's fishing, and that made Harry mad.

Anyhow, at lunch he was dressed in farmer's clothes because his coveralls had got stained with something or other; nobody was clear what. Whatever it was had to be washed out before it set into the cloth, they said.

The lunch was a lot of fun with everybody eating the fish Harry had caught and telling him how good they were, and then, when lunch was done, the farmer's daughter had taken Harry aside and told him how crazy about him she was, and they had gone off to the barn.

"Oh, stranger, you were wonderful," said the farmer's daughter, after they were done. "How did you get to be so wonderful?"

"I don't know," said Harry.

"Harry's Golden Years"

He was picking at the straw on which they lay, and he turned to the farmer's daughter and held up a handful of the stuff.

"Where do you get this from?" he asked.

She looked at him oddly for a half second and then gave a toothy smile.

"Why, we grow it in the fields, stranger," she said.

"Show me," said Harry.

There wasn't much she could do except walk him out and show him. She would have let the others know, but she didn't have any communicator because they don't have those all around in the country like they do in the city.

Harry seemed to enjoy the fields, and he walked on and on. The farmer's daughter grew more worried as they drew farther away. She knew everybody would figure they were still in the barn, and her instructions had been to always keep Harry within easy reach, just in case.

"What's that?" he asked, pointing ahead.

"That's a bull, stranger," said the farmer's daughter. "But you don't want to mess with it, honey. It's dangerous."

Harry frowned at her.

"What do I care?" he asked. "I'm going over there and have a look at it, OK?"

"Oh, no, stranger," she said, holding his arm. "You really want to stay away from it."

Harry jerked his arm away. "What are you doing?" he asked. "You giving me orders?"

The girl turned pale. "No, it's not that, stranger," she said. "It's just that you shouldn't fool around with that thing."

Harry's face was red now, and there were little drops of perspiration all over it. He began to breathe heavily.

"What do you mean, you bitch?" he shrieked. "Who the hell are you to tell me what to do?"

He hit her a terrible blow with his fist, which dislocated her jaw and knocked out several teeth. Then, when she'd fallen, he kicked her several

"Harry's Golden Years"

times, each time hard enough to lift her body from the ground.

Afterwards, he walked slowly away from her, toward the bull, wondering vaguely what it was he had forgotten. A country girl had said something he hadn't liked, he remembered.

The farmer's daughter managed, somehow, to drag herself far enough back to be spotted by one of the others. When they got to Harry, he was lying mangled by an oak tree, and the bull was cropping grass in a corner far away.

They flew in the medical team at once, of course, along with the head accountant who always accompanied them, just in case. The doctors patched and sewed and taped Harry together, and then the surgeon stood and snapped off his plastic gloves.

"Will he live, doctor?" asked the accountant.

The doctor sighed and shook his head.

"Yes," he said.

"Harry's Golden Years"

M – 1

Seen from across the desert, from miles away, the statue had been dwarfed and easily understood, and Henderson had smiled at its familiar outlines as he sat in the bouncing jeep. Now, climbing from the jeep at the statue's base, he found it unrecognizably distorted by its grotesque height.

Bentley, sweating in khaki, came up to him and shook his hand.

"You'll break your neck if you keep gawking up at it like that," he said, smiling.

They stood near the statue's left foot, a huge, gleaming thing of curving yellow.

"Five hundred and thirty feet from here to the top of its toe," said Bentley. "Sixteen hundred feet from the toe to the heel. Four hundred and eighty feet across at its widest point."

The two men walked to the side of the foot, and Henderson reached out to lay his hand flat against its surface. The Nevada sun had made it uncomfortably hot to touch. He moved his hand back and forth over the gleaming yellow and marveled at its smoothness.

"It's like butter!" he said.

Bentley nodded, lighting a cigarette and squinting up.

"No damned traction possible, to speak of," he said. "Makes climbing around on the thing a real bitch. And you can't dig steps into it; you can't even drive stakes to hold ropes. Folger slid off its instep, yesterday. Would have fallen to his death if he hadn't managed to grab the scaffold."

Against the side of the foot, and extending part way up the shank of the black leg, the towering scaffold looked absurdly small and unimportant next to the bulk of the statue. Henderson could see an army of men working at the top of it, slowly extending it.

"I can't decide if we're building another Eiffel Tower or playing with

"M-1"

Tinkertoys," said Bentley. "You get funny shifts in your self-image, living with this thing."

He pushed his cigarette into the sand with his foot.

"You want to wash up and all that, or do you want to get on with looking it over?"

"Let's look it over."

"Right," said Bentley. He signaled to a man who detached himself from a group standing by the entrance to one of the scaffold's elevators and came walking toward them. The man wore curved sunglasses and a leather jacket. He was lean and had an easy stride. Bentley introduced him to Henderson.

"This is Captain Harry Grant. Captain Grant's on loan to us from the Navy, and how far away from water can you get? He flies us around the statue so we can all get a better look at it and fully realize how little we understand it. He hasn't lost one of us yet."

They shook hands and the three of them began walking over to the helicopter, which stood on a little pad of concrete. Like everything else next to the statue, it looked tiny and delicate.

"Sometimes I like to get the layman's point of view, Harry," said Bentley. "What do you make of our wonder?"

Grant smiled and shook his head.

"I used to like him when I was a kid," he said, pointing up at the statue with his thumb. "But now I don't know. Now I think he scares me."

"I believe you've got just about as far with him as us scientists, Harry," said Bentley.

They climbed into the helicopter and Grant started the big blades turning. Henderson peered up at the statue through the lightening blur.

The helicopter began to climb, slowly. When it drew abreast of the top of the scaffold, several of the men turned to wave at them. Bentley smiled and waved back.

"I wish we could get that thing to climb as quickly as this gadget," he said. "I figure with all the luck in the world we might get up to its left tit by late August."

"M-1"

They had reached its midsection, now. Its red pants sparkled in the sunlight, and the two vast yellow buttons seemed to twinkle.

"The buttons are two hundred feet across," said Bentley. "You get so you can really rattle off the statistics. They have a way of burning themselves into your head."

"Have you tried digging into its upper parts?" asked Henderson. He'd never been in a helicopter before. It wasn't as hard speaking over the roar of the propellers as he had thought it would be.

"Hell, yes," said Bentley. "Once, in a fit of pique, old Wellman even let fly at it with an explosive rocket. Didn't leave a goddamn mark."

Now they were up to its black, sprawling chest. One of its arms hung down at its side, the other was raised high in a titanic salute.

"We've had expeditions on the head and shoulders times past counting. We've drilled at it, lit fires on it, poured acid over it, and usually ended up kicking at it with our feet. None of it's had the slightest effect. I honestly don't think an H-bomb would dent it."

Suddenly they were opposite its face and Henderson found the confrontation unexpectedly horrible. Somehow this nearness to the head was the thing that brought the monstrous enormity of the statue home to him. He had to look from side to side to follow the sweep of the inane grin. Sitting there in the helicopter, hovering just feet away from the swollen bulb at the end of the thing's nose, Henderson had an abrupt and hideously convincing fantasy that the statue would come to life and crush them with a pinch of its tremendous yellow fingers.

The helicopter worked its way past a gigantic black eye set into the blinding whiteness of the face, around to the side of the head where the craft swung by one of the circular ears.

"The ears are quite thin, really," said Bentley. "Only average about seven feet thick. The flat surface has a diameter of over one thousand feet. The point of attachment to the head is a piddling one hundred foot line around three feet thick. Gives you an idea of the structural peculiarities of our friend, here, doesn't it? We've mounted recording devices on the ears, just

"M-1"

to see, and we've found they don't even wiggle in a high wind. If we tried to build something like that out of what we've got on hand in our advanced technology—you'll excuse the ironic tone, I'm sure—we'd find we couldn't."

Henderson stared at the ear as the helicopter rose gently over its upper curve.

"Somebody built it," he said.

"That's right," said Bentley. "Somebody has. And they put it up here between National flight 405, which didn't see anything at all when it passed by here at 4:38 p.m., Wednesday, February the seventh, and 5:17, the same date, when the Reno air taxi flew right into the son of a bitch."

"Why didn't they see it?"

"My own theory is that they did see it," said Bentley. "They just couldn't believe it. Saw the damned thing smiling away at them with its big eyes with the little chips cut out of the sides, saw it waving at them in the moonlight— and there was plenty of moonlight, I checked—and maybe the pilot thought of a movie he'd seen once, or a Big Little Book, I don't know, and maybe he was screaming, and he just smashed into it."

They were over the top of its head, now. Henderson looked down at the shadow speck the helicopter made move across the shiny black dome of the statue's skull. Far, far down below he could see the long, thin, curling tail coming out of the rear of the bright red pants. Bentley followed the direction of his stare and smiled.

"Seven thousand feet, if you straightened it out," he said.

The helicopter began to descend. Henderson folded his hands and looked down at his knuckles. He didn't want to see any more of the statue, not just now.

Bentley lit a cigarette and shook the match out carefully.

"It's still a rumor," he said. "But it's checking out better all the time."

Henderson was watching him.

"The last word I got on it came from Schillar," said Bentley. "He believes it. He said Brandt told him he'd seen photographs."

"What do you mean?" asked Henderson. "What's true?"

Bentley licked his lips.

"They say the Russians got Minnie."

"M-1"

THE ZOMBIE BUTLER

**A** middle-aged couple by the name of Harrison, vacationing on the island of Haiti, were encouraged by their hired guide to attend a voodoo meeting. They accepted, after some hesitation, and that evening they were jeeped skillfully up the bejungled side of a mountain to a circular hut built on its peak. Their guide escorted them inside the hut and they sat, not without trepidation, on a bench by the wall.

Following a series of orgiastic dances, all done to deafening thumps of gigantic drums and the shrill keening of enthusiastically blown whistles, a simple pine coffin was carried into the room and placed on the center of the floor. As the Harrisons watched with widening mouths, a voodoo priest made odd designs on the coffin's lid in rooster blood and dashed out the brains of several small goats on its corners, all the time chanting rhythmically in a deep, hypnotic voice that reminded Mr. Harrison irresistibly of Paul Robeson.

Suddenly, with a horrid groaning of wood, the lid of the coffin swung open and an immense black, his huge eyes staring blankly ahead, sat up from within the coffin's depths, braced his huge hands on its sides, and stood. The guide, in whispers, explained to the Harrisons that they had just seen the creation of a zombie, a walking dead man who would obey its master's every order without hesitation and work night and day, inexhaustibly, at any given task.

"They make," concluded the guide, "excellent servants, of course."

"He's just what we've been looking for," said Mrs. Harrison firmly. "Especially that part about no back talk. They've gotten so uppity where we come from."

A discreet signal on the part of the guide brought the voodoo priest over to the Harrisons' bench, and, after a few moments' discussion and the

"The Zombie Butler"

signing of two American Express Travelers Checks by Mr. Harrison, the zombie was theirs.

Back in Cleveland, the Harrisons' new domestic created quite a stir. The other matrons of the town disguised their envy with varying degrees of success while the menfolk congratulated Mr. Harrison openly and speculated on the economic implications of his find.

As time passed, however, the Harrisons noticed a definite drawback to their buy. Although he walked, the zombie was, after all, dead, and the processes of corruption attendant to death, while undeniably slowed by the voodoo priest's machinations, were proceeding along the usual lines. The general effect was increasingly unpleasant, and soon the Harrisons found their social functions very sparsely attended.

"Something simply must be done," said Mrs. Harrison.

Mr. Harrison, after a little cogitation, hired the city's leading undertaker and that worthy, after several false starts, managed to ignore the constant perfume of formaldehyde; but, in the long run, his ministrations proved of no avail. If anything, reflected Mr. Harrison somberly, they added a new note of ghastliness to the zombie's steady decay.

"Ship him back where he came from," Mrs. Harrison instructed her husband, and he tried; but the health authorities, now fully aware of the zombie's status, informed him that no corpse could be shipped anywhere, nor so much as carried across the street, without a proper death certificate; and, since the Harrisons had neglected to try to obtain one back in Haiti, the zombie was theirs, forevermore.

As they grew older and more horror-stricken, the zombie served them selflessly, servile and gelatinous, and when they died it still crawled oozingly about the house, dusting the legs of the tables and chairs, and cleaning its trail from the carpets.

MORAL: A SLAVE'S CHAINS ARE HEAVY AT BOTH ENDS.

"The Zombie Butler"

THE

Dark Corner

BOOK REVIEWS

— BY —

Gahan Wilson

The more naive among the psychedelic set and the pot lot appear to believe that they have stumbled on a New Thing. They style themselves Columbuses, treading an undiscovered continent, making first contact with the angels and demons that dwell therein.

They are, of course, quite wrong. Those lands have been explored by previous voyagers, and we have the maps and logs of their journeys. Some of these bold cartographers left encouraging reports: others did not.

Among those with less happy news stood—we can say towered—the figure of Arthur Machen. His cautionary essays on what may happen to those who meddle with that which we laughingly call reality should be required reading for those who are tempted to dip their toe into the acid pool or go out with Mary Jane. Why Harry J. Anslinger has not printed up, at government expense, of course, a collection of Machen's darker tales I do not know. I am sure that the general distribution of such a book would do more to discourage would-be tasters of the stranger potions than any number of stern warnings about genes.

Arkham House, bless its gothic heart, has done another public service to those interested in the weirder speculations by bringing out the first American edition of Machen's last novel, *The Green Round*. It is not, as the dust jacket candidly admits, in a class with *The Hill of Dreams*. It has its structural flaws—too many repetitions of events, an occasional vagueness as to who is doing the narration—but it is Machen, which is quite enough.

The novel concerns a series of events that happen to, and take place in the vicinity of, Lawrence Hillyer, recluse and scholar, resident at 29 Layburn Street, London. It is full of warnings.

Where, wonders Mr. Hillyer, is the dividing line between fantasy and reality? Just what, he asks, is the difference between the waking and the dreaming state? And, finally, am I sane, or am I mad?

These are dangerous questions for anyone to ask, even for one as stable and sure as yourself, gentle reader, but for Mr. Hillyer, who has committed the supreme strategical blunder of cutting himself off from his kind, they prove disastrous.

THE DARK CORNER | BOOK REVIEWS BY GAHAN WILSON

We are weak enough as an army, says Arthur Machen; alone, in isolation, we are easy prey. Read your papers, says Machen, take politics seriously, share in the common gossip, hold on to your neighbor's hand. There are shining lights dancing along the side lanes, but stick to the highway, brother; the lonely wanderer is easily lost.

Masters of Horror is an offbeat paperback edited by Alden H. Norton and Sam Moskowitz, with copious commentary by the latter. It breaks down into two small anthologies, the first one being a resurrectionist's delight of the kind of gothic grue which made them shudder way back when, the second a spotty mishmosh of more recent ghouleries.

Unless you are an accomplished scavenger of second hand bookstores, and God help you if you are, it is unlikely you have encountered any of the ancient items. Clemence Housman's "The Were-Wolf" is straight traditional legend with that good Old Country feel; "The Transformation" by Mary Shelley, little mother of Frankenstein, is a touchingly pathetic dream-wish item concerning the redemption of someone very like her late husband; and then we have Bram Stoker's "Dracula's Guest." This last, says Mrs. Stoker, was supposed to have been the first chapter of *Dracula*, itself, but was dropped because it made the book too long. Mr. Moskowitz goes along with this, but I think the editors ditched it because they felt it would damage the novel's quiet build. You decide.

As a transition we have "The Yellow Sign" by Robert W. Chambers, which is a dandy. In his introduction to it Mr. Moskowitz seems to imply that Lovecraft went around pretending he didn't owe Chambers a good deal in the creation of his Cthulhu business. He admitted it all over the place, sir! H. P. L. was nothing if not generous in handing out credit where credit was due, and I am glad to have the chance to tromp on any rumors that he didn't. I have tromped.

The new section is a something-for-everyone affair and I confess some of it was not for me. One item, "Blind Man's Bluff" by H. Russell Wakefield, is a gem of the quiet English ARGH! school which I think you may enjoy, and there are offerings by Merritt, Keller, Kuttner and Bradbury.

‡

The ads in the *Weird Tales* of the '40s offered us creepy readers all kinds of boons: relief from the agonies of hernia by means of patented trusses, big money in radio, two-tone jackets of surpassing ugliness, muscles by Charles Atlas; even previously hidden cosmic truths (THIS WISDOM MUST DIE) could be ours for a filled-out coupon and a pittance. We were a pretty lucky bunch.

Sometimes, though, it was only promises, promises.

Arkham House began talking about the imminent release of H. P. Lovecraft's *Selected Letters*, I do believe, when they were advertising his *Outsider and Others* as a brand new book. They were still dropping hints when they brought out his *Beyond the Wall of Sleep*. By January of 1948 they even gave the price of the thing, but an obvious note of hysteria had crept into their copy. The *Letters* would appear, they said ("our printers promise"), "as soon as possible."

Well, in 1965, by golly, *Selected Letters 1911–1924* finally showed up, and now, in 1968, *Selected Letters 1925–1929* is among us. To those interested, it has been worth the wait.

The first volume was reviewed in this magazine by Fritz Leiber (May '66). Mr. Leiber stressed the point that the *Letters* were, more than anything else, the touching record of a very sick, but very brave man try-ing to claw his way through a bog of neurosis to something approaching mental health. In the same issue of the magazine there was an excellent essay by J. Vernon Shea on Lovecraft that, among other things, detailed the appalling upbringing poor H. P. L. suffered. A brute of a mother stuffed with warped ideas, a weakling father who eventually went insane—it was the sort of childhood that would have done in a lesser man's ego altogether, and Lovecraft's did not escape severe damage.

The *Letters 1925–1929* cover a period in Lovecraft's life devoted to frantic retreat and desperate reor-ganization. His marriage had not worked, his attempt to storm New York had degenerated into a fiasco, and, as if this were not enough, the Jazz Age was in full flower, T. S. Eliot, and all.

Lovecraft fled. He returned to his native Providence and tried to resume the life he'd known before his disastrous forays into the outside world. He scrabbled for roots in genealogy. He rhapsodized on his dream of Georgian days. He buttressed up his pose as an elderly gentleman who could, if pressed, think back to 1700 and beyond. In all sorts of clever and ingenious ways he attempted to become a dropout from the garish here and now.

It's encouraging to see how badly he failed. Despite their antique affectations (a typical closing: Yr. most oblig'd & obt. Servt.) the letters are, of course, obviously products of their time. There is Robert Benchley, Don Marquis, Damon Runyon, and even Walter Winchell in his humor. His cool cockiness against a background of dismayed nihilism has a recognizably John Barrymorian swagger to it. His politics smack much more of Coolidge and Hoover than they do of Tory Colonial.

He failed, too, thank heavens, in his role as a creature, probably made of silicon, who floated in outer space near Betelgeuse and viewed this Earth, and the flesh and blood which crawled upon it, with chill, impartial logic. Deny it as he may, and he does protest so much, it is painfully obvious that H. P. L. was a vulnerable and anxious heart, desperately in need of companionship, fearful of rejection, and otherwise human.

This same humanity also succeeded in crumbling away his really formidable array of prejudices, at least partly. It might even, had he lived long enough, driven him to a liberal position, though I'm sure he would have fought it tooth and claw.

If you are familiar with the members of the little group that made up his circle, and with his writings, so much the better, but it really doesn't matter if you aren't. The *Letters* stand very well by themselves as excellent entertainment. They are a charming blend of gossip, outrageous snobbery, kindly help, fascinating intellectual gymnastics, obscure erudition, and much fantastick (to use the official spelling) play. And they are about as close as you can get, these days, to meeting what must have been a remarkably lovable man.

Even if you don't believe in ghosts, even if you're not afraid of them even though you don't believe in them, *Ghosts in Irish Houses* by James Reynolds should please you, unless you're a terrible stuffed shirt on the subject. It's a darling collection of haunts ranging all the way from shy, strangled children to a whopper of a saga about the Dreaded Women of Moher who fly ragged in the storm chasing salmons by the thousands to the shore before them.

‡

F or those poorly read in the literature of the godawful, and there are far too many of you about, I recommend, without hesitation, two dandy new starter anthologies in the field: *Hauntings, Tales of the Supernatural*, edited by Henry Mazzeo, and *Strange Beasts and Unnatural Monsters*, edited by Phillip Van Doren Stern.

Hauntings, etc., has the grand advantage of being illustrated by the beloved Edward Gorey—he of the darkened hall, the wispy lady in a faint, and the mustachioed neurotic. While the interior drawings are not quite Gorey in top form, the cover is a must for anyone even slightly fond of revenants. The stories count among them such solid, and oft-reprinted, classics as Lovecraft's *In The Vault*, M. R. James' *The Haunted Doll's House*, Wakefield's *The Red Lodge*, Mrs. Oliphant's (you never heard of Mrs. Oliphant?) *The Open Door*, Collier's *Thus I Refute Beelzy*; and if you are unfamiliar with any of them, I suggest it is high time to get cracking. Perhaps too late. The only stories new to me were a haunted house tale by Manly Wade Wellman and a Faustian item by a Robert Aickman. The first struck me as being a weak choice from a good writer's work; the second is a corker. It's called *The Visiting Star*, is a marvelous account of sinister doings associated with a provincial theatrical troupe, and marks, says the anthologist, Mr. Aickman's first appearance in this country. I sincerely hope it won't be his last.

Strange Beasts, etc., has more of an excuse for containing heavily used material as it's a limited subject affair, but Phillip Van Doren Stern manages to sneak in enough new horrors to make me wish the thing had been bound in hard covers. My copy has developed serious curls at the corners and there is a spreading wrinkly area on its back. Soon it will all fall apart like Count Dracula's corpse. The last offering in the book, *The Elephant Man*, is a true account of a poor, deformed son of a bitch that will at least bring you close to tears. For the beginner, there are such basics as E. F. Benson's *Mrs. Amworth* (you never heard of *Mrs. Amworth*?), du Maurier's *The Birds*, and Stoker's *The Judge's House*. You wouldn't want not to have read those, now, would you?

Arkham House has brought out a collection of stories by Nelson Bond

(*Nightmares and Daydreams*), taken mostly from *Blue Book* magazine. I have never gone much for Mr. Bond's work; I'm not sure just why. It may have been overexposure to a wildly popular story of his, "Mr. Mergenthwirker's Lobblies," back in the '40s. Even the title of the thing is a good example of a species of whimsy that makes me, an ordinarily genial and easygoing sort, redden and swear. Then he uses a kind of wisecracking humor that irks me to a foolish extent. Then, I won't go on and on, something about his plots, their neatness, perhaps, has always irritated me beyond a reasonable point. Put my whole attitude down to a personal quirk, if you will, and buy the book. But if the idea of a Mr. Mergenthwirker running around with a bunch of lobblies puts you off, go pick up a collection of Ambrose Bierce, instead.

Weird Tales went bimonthly in 1940, shrunk to half its size in '53, vanished altogether the following year, and life just hasn't seemed the same since for the odd little band that read it, not to mention the odd little band that wrote it. It's easy to see why no one rushed in to fill the gap. *Weird Fantasy* does not attract the Hearsts and the Luces of the publishing world, because the Hearsts and the Luces are interested in making a buck, and weird fantasy is a loser. Poverty dogs it. The story behind any science fiction magazine's struggle to survive is heroic, but the saga of *Weird Tales'* constantly losing battle to turn a profit borders on the ridiculous. No sane investor would touch such a project. This is why I feel sorry for Paul and Ronald Willis. They are, respectively, the editor and publisher of *Anubis*, a new magazine devoted to weird fiction and to articles on weird fiction. It comes out four times a year (they've made it through three, gang), is probably printed with some hand-cranked device in their basement, and it gets better by the issue. Some of the stories they've published have been pretty fierce, but then some of them have been pretty damned good. They even managed to snag the likes of Roger Zelazny and E. Hoffman Price (who wrote a fascinating essay on Farnsworth Wright, editor of *Weird Tales*) for their third number, so you can see they're not just sitting around. They're planning a Clark Ashton Smith issue soon, and I, for one, am looking forward to it. If any of this turns you on, or moves you toward compassion, why not drop them a line?

‡

THE DARK CORNER | BOOK REVIEWS BY GAHAN WILSON

M ultiplying in the racks at Rexall, and spreading stealthily over the walls at the corner cigar store, are an increasing number of Black Art tracts, the likes of which, a few years ago, were to be found only in the dustiest recesses of bookstores specializing in the occult, or in the locked stacks of libraries, such as the one at Miskatonic University.

Now, the merest child can pick up a book giving him detailed instructions on how to kill his enemies, real or imagined, by means of thought waves. If the tot's interests run along milder lines, he will find grimoires on such arcane divertissements as tasseography, cartography, numerology, cartomancy, colorology, radiesthesia, oneiromancy, and metoposcopy, just to name a few, and God knows what he will do with them. His parents are by now alerted to be on the sniff for fumes of glue and marijuana, but what will they make of the pentagrams traced in sulfur on his playroom floor, or the doll that looks like Papa melting in the oven?

A happy side effect of this flood of necromantic know-how is an accompanying upsurge in the availability of the sort of fiction this department treasures, namely that of the macabre and supernatural. Of course, you and I know better, but I have a feeling that the publishers and common browsers find it difficult to distinguish between fact, so to speak, and fiction in this area, and when the one strikes the general fancy, the other tags along. Our good Doctor Asimov may be discouraged to find a reasoned work of his on atomic structure sandwiched between a treatise on tealeaf reading and one extolling the virtues of an herbal cancer cure, but the devotee of the grim fantastic can only rub his hands and chuckle at the sudden abundance of his favorite reading matter.

Avon has brought out a number of spooky books that I think of as the Harry Garrido series because Harry Garrido has done the covers for them all, and all are so much alike that from a distance—say one foot—you'd swear they were the same. It's smudgy red in the background, see? And has a strong diagonal running from the lower left to the upper right corner, and, at the top of the diagonal, there's this glowy thing. The kick-off in the series is *The Pedestal*, a novel by George Lanning which takes the classic suburbia themes of flat sex and all-around disenchantment and mixes them with a bit of M. R. Jamesian horror. It has some nice moments, but the Awful Thing and the rest of the story don't fuse to my satisfaction, and, thanks to Harry Garrido, you know what's going to happen before you open the book. Another is called *Night of the Vampire* (by Raymond Giles), and it is an unabashed romp, as the title suggests. It involves a diabolic coven, horrid monsters, and it is fun if you don't mind cardboardish characters, a creaking plot, and a hero named Duffy Johnson.

Richard Matheson's novel of the early '50s about a man with an unwanted wild talent, *A Stir of Echoes*, doesn't quite make it into the '60s for me, but I point it out for those interested. The latest of the series, an anthology edited by Charles M. Collins, *A Walk With The Beast*, has some tasty items in it, and some of them may be new to you as they were to me. I enjoyed very much the bulk of a story by Nugent Barker, *Curious Adventure of Mr. Bond*, which is a variation of the deadly inn theme, but I wish he had stopped it a little before he did. *Count Szolnok's Robots* takes an old-timey golemish approach to the mechanical man idea and has a nicely repulsive feel. And there is a very crawly item by William Wood called *One of the Dead*.

Leslie H. Whitten's *Progeny of the Adder*, takes an unusual tack by having, as its menace, a fellow who isn't really a vampire, understand, but who can, nevertheless, hypnotize his victims with a glance, drink quarts of blood, flatten dozens of attackers in seconds, and otherwise carry on like Count Dracula. There are some wild scenes, the book is nothing if not action-packed, and the repulsiveness of the ghastly lunatic is mercilessly revealed, stench and all; the problem is that Mr. Whitten's vampire is altogether too much like the genuine article for the premise of the book.

The same author takes up the same basic theme in *Moon of the Wolf*, and much more successfully. This time the fiend is not really a werewolf, but the character is far more believable, as is the world he moves in, and his exploits manage to stay pretty closely within the horribly possible. The whole book is a remarkable improvement over his first, and it will be fun to see what Leslie Whitten does next.

A Fine and Private Place by Peter S. Beagle is a whacky and gentle fantasy about a number of creatures, living and dead, who work their way through various personal problems in the precincts of the Yorkchester Cemetery, a spreading establishment near New York City about the size of Central Park. My favorite character in the book is a talking raven, which is unusual because talking animals of any description usually irk me. I prefer, for example, the Road Runner and the Coyote to Bugs Bunny and Porky Pig, although there is a serious flaw in my prejudices because the Road Runner beeps, and I know no roadrunner beeps. I think the main reason I liked the raven is because he has a sour disposition while all about him are either mystically calm or sweetly philosophic. The book, with its long, rambling discourses on Life, reminded me very much of certain plays of the '30s; it exudes a kind of wistful humanism which I found sometimes touching, sometimes irritating. *The Last Unicorn*, another book by the same author, takes place Once Upon a Time in the days when there were unicorns and traveling magicians and magical castles, and like that. The story is full of fantastical imagery and fabulous creatures, and Mr. Beagle describes it all very poetically, but, as I worked my way through the story, I found myself growing more and more impatient with the softly sad discourse of his characters, and, as their pithy aphorisms grew ever more numerous, something perfectly rotten in me yearned to see a dragon crawl out from behind a pile of rocks and give them all a good, swift clout.

Hauntings and Horrors, Ten Grisly Tales is another in the series of anthologies edited by Alden H. Norton with commentary by Sam Moskowitz. It's generously dedicated to August Derleth, in spite of the obvious fact that the same August Derleth is one of the main problems of the likes of Mssrs. Norton and Moskowitz. The Sauk City Sleuth, bless him for his enthusiastic thoroughness, has done such a good job of researching the field that it is next to impossible to unearth a tidbit of horror which is both fresh and first rate. If you come across a lovely tale of grue in some moldering book or pulp, the chances are an iodine test will reveal Mr. Derleth's prints on every page. Norton and Moskowitz, undaunted, burrow on, and I'm glad they do. The finds in this collection are, mainly, quaint, turn of the century stuff. There is, for example, the almost ungettable *The Maker of Moons* by Robert W. Chambers, and a story by Julian Hawthorne, Nathaniel's son, and one by the architect, Ralph Adams Cram. They are best savored in a padded velvet smoking jacket with a decanter of mellow port close by the humidor.

‡

Taking a sort of Baker Street Irregular tack, Sam Moskowitz has lovingly put together an anthology based on the personality and glamor of Edgar Allen Poe (*The Man Who Called Himself Poe*), and it's a grand night's entertainment. The book includes a number of short stories featuring Poe as a character, one featuring him as several characters, a little group of poems written to him or his memory, a tale begun by him and completed by another, and a mysterious piece of work which may or may not (don't look at me!) have been written by the master himself.

One very interesting inclusion is a story by a man who lays claim to have been one of Poe's friends back in the good old days at Virginia U. According to this fellow, a Douglass Sherley, Poe used to drink great quantities of a noxious-sounding brew called *peaches and honey* (italics Mr. Sherley's), gamble at cards for the sake of gold and silver coin, and walk about burdened with the appalling nickname "Gaffy." This last touch has a convincingly horrible air of reality about it that persuades me Sherley's allegations are not to be lightly dismissed. There is, near the end of the book, a poem written to Poe by his dying wife, Virginia Elizabeth, on the occasion of St. Valentine's Day. It is one of the worst poems I ever saw printed, and one of the most heartbreaking.

The Cell: Three Tales of Horror is the first collection of David Case's work to be published. The lead story, "The Cell," is the best of the lot, I think. It's either the account of a homicidal psychopath's slow disintegration, or one of an advancing case of lycanthropy. Mr. Case never says for sure, and he plays enjoyably with the ambiguity. The story is, perhaps, a little too extended, but it has a genuinely gruesome mood throughout, and the ghoulish implications of what may be in the cell, even now, are satisfyingly spooky. A second story, "The Hunter," comes very close to successfully pulling off the kind of man-against-nature sort of thing that Algernon Blackwood used to do so well; and the third, "The Dead End," also has a very good Blackwoodian flavor to it and makes excellent use of an exotic locale. *The Cell* indicates that David Case is an author who deserves to be closely watched.

The bulk of the authors represented in *Splinters: A New Anthology of Macabre Modern Fiction* certainly seem to have it in for the ladies. Offhand I cannot think of any other collection wherein the fair sex is so enthusiastically chastised and maltreated. There's hardly a full-grown woman in the book who escapes punishment, and most of them are clearly shown to be the sort who've earned their drubbing well. The book starts out with a story concerning a female which is literally a snake, goes on to a mass murderess, trips from there to a deadly rivalry between a nagging wife and a lady orchid (the author sort of passes over the fact that every lady orchid is also a gentleman orchid), and concerns itself elsewhere with a vicious dead wife who destroys her husband's second marriage, a vicious living wife who destroys her family by sealing them off from the world, a cruel teacher who bullies the wrong ugly little boy, and an unfortunate woman who is possessed by an extremely nasty demon. Even when the girls are trying to behave, and I think that last one was trying to behave, they get it from the fellows, you bet. Heads bashed in, burnt for witches, shamefully treated by gigolos, and one poor creature is even violated on her slab in the morgue. Of course there are some stories not concerned with killing or being killed by females (three), but two of these have subtle implications, if you're disposed to look for them, and after the rest of the collection, you're disposed to look for them. I have not mentioned until now that the book contains some really excellent stories, nor that I think anyone interested in the macabre would enjoy reading it, and I do so now. I highly recommend it. But they really ought to bring out a sequel where the lads get it in the neck.

‡

The gruesome tales of Howard Phillips Lovecraft revolving around the horrid doings of ancient, evil entities with unpronounceable names have, from the start, inspired a quantity of other authors to try their hands at stories concerning the same ghastly beings, and Arkham House's *Tales of the Cthulhu Mythos* (edited by August Derleth) offers generous evidence that a plentitude are cribbing yet from the perilous pages of Abdul-Ajhazred's *Necronomicon*—the fools!

Some of the best vintage *Weird Tales* elaborations on Lovecraftian themes are here presented (soft-hearted types such as myself will be pleased to find the Lovecraft-Bloch back and forth in its entirety), and there is a small anthology of brand new stories heretofore unpublished. These last count among them an item by J. Ramsey Campbell which indicates he is taking an interesting new tack with the Cult, an unsuccessful attempt on the part of James Wade to convince me that porpoises (all right, then, dolphins) are anything but lovable, and the latest of Colin Wilson's entries into the realm of Azathoth. It works out to four hundred and seven fun-packed pages. Good reading for both the nostalgic and those determined to keep au courant in Monster City. Altogether, gang—*Ph'nglui mglw'nafh Cthulhu R'lyeh wgah'nagl fhtagn*, and the last one in is a rotten Tcho-Tcho!

The Folsom Flint and Other Curious Tales (by David H. Keller) is admittedly designed for the completist. It's a memorial volume containing several of the author's better-known stories, a quantity of strictly minor material, and an affectionate and informative essay on Doctor Keller and his work by Paul Spencer. The title has the beautiful basic premise of a man trying to communicate with a Stone Age skull by means of fitting it out with dentures, blinking light bulbs for eyes, a wig, and a rubber tube attached to a small pump so that the whole caboodle may convincingly smoke cigarettes. Picture that, fantasy fans.

I am not knocking Robert E. Howard's Conan, mind, Crom forbid it, but I must admit I have always preferred his dark little Pictish hero, and so am pleased that *Bran Mak Morn* has clawed his way to the newsstands. Frazetta has done a dandy cover portraying Bran coming at you in order to disembowel you, and the book contains "Worms of the Earth," which is probably the best story Howard ever wrote, which is to say it is a humdinger.

There is living at this moment (unless, God forbid, something happened and I didn't hear about it) one of the very best ghost story writers ever to take pen in hand. He is living and breathing and capable of feeling pain, and he has not had one collection of his work published in our country. Not one. There is an excellent chance you have never even heard the name of the good fellow. It is Robert Aickman, it is, and you should write it on a placard together with a few words of protest and stand before the entrance of your favorite publisher's building with it until he breaks down and brings out an anthology of this superb author's work. I am, as I believe I have indicated in some other of these columns, a man of colossal magnanimity, and genial to a fault, but when my thoughts turn to Aickman's lack of an American publisher, I own that the sound of my grinding teeth is audible through a closed door and that dogs crawl whimpering from my presence. I mean, what do they want, for God's sake? Take Aickman's latest collection of the supernatural (*Sub Rosa*. Your friendly book dealer knows how to get hold of it, don't let him tell you he doesn't. He's lying if he tells you he doesn't. Show him who's boss; show a little guts). There is stuff in this book as good as Arthur Machen. There is stuff here that is better than Algernon Blackwood, and I speak as one who is very fond of Algernon Blackwood. There is an absolutely terrifying thing that starts out where M. R. James usually left off and then wings on out of sight. There is a political ghost story, believe it or not, ghosts on the grand scale. It is just a dandy of a collection, and if you are among those intelligent fortunates who relish goings on of this kind, I cannot recommend this book too highly. I am sorry you will have to go to some trouble to get hold of it, but I absolutely guarantee it's worth it. Perhaps, hopefully, Mr. Aickman will soon be published here. Until then: Buy British.

‡

It's said that Clark Ashton Smith may have met Ambrose Bierce in the Bohemian San Francisco of the early nineteen hundreds. Of course Smith would have been very young, and Bierce getting on to be remarkably sour, neither of them really at their best, but the confrontation would have been intriguing all the same. Few authors held less hope for our species than these two, or considered it less important in the general scheme of things.

The vast difference between them was that Bierce's understanding of man's sublime futility infuriated him and made him bitter, whereas Smith's clear vision of it braced and cheered him and spurred him on to endless, lively speculations on the awesome possibilities of impartial disaster. It isn't surprising to learn that he veered toward Buddhism in his later years, since one of the basic paradoxes of that orientation is that we should take heart, as all is hopeless. There are, in fact, many qualities about Smith visible in his photographs—a gentleness, a distance not at all aloof, a strange tranquility and a dignity—which strongly call to mind the conventional representations of the Buddha.

Smith was born and raised in a rough stretch of country east of Sacramento, an area that had been combed over and dug into enthusiastically during the Great Gold Rush and then pretty well abandoned. It made a rugged background and could well have helped inspire in him the deeply independent streak that was so much a part of him. He refused, for example, to have anything to do with public education after suffering grammar school, and educated himself by reading through the Oxford Unabridged and the Britannica, some say word by word. He lived for most of his life in the same isolated cabin he'd grown up in, put off getting married until his sixty-first year, and avoided both regular employment and having to depend upon his artistic output for a living by developing a wide variety of salable skills. He was, according to a partial listing by none other than Boris Karloff, a "journalist, wood-chopper, fruit-packer, typist, gardener, cement-mixer, miner, and windlasser."

Smith began selling fiction to the pulps in the late '20s, appearing in publications with such magnificent names as *Stirring Science-Fiction, Thrilling Wonder Stories, Amazing Detective Stories*, and—what visions of naughtiness this last one evokes!—*La Paree Stories*. His first for *Weird Tales* (September 1928) was "The Ninth Skeleton"—the skeleton was described as having "a lipless and ingratiating leer"—and it started him off on an association with the magazine that ended only with the appearance of "An Offering for the Moon" (September 1953; page 54, if you're really curious), just a few issues before *Weird* gave up its last ghost.

Smith's stories stood out rather starkly against the all-pervading, well-nigh unbelievable innocence that was the hallmark of most pulp writing. Now and then he did wander into the Golly-gee-whiz-will-you-look-at-this-planet! school, but mostly his tales were sly and subtle jibes at mankind's aspirations, chilling little fables of a startling bleakness. They were beautifully constructed, full of lovely images and absolutely sumptuous English, but they were deadly. Reading them was a tiny bit like being skillfully murdered with a Cellini stiletto, or dining well at the Borgias.

The message patiently taught the reader of Smith's bejeweled little bear traps is that man's evil and stupidity is beyond plumbing; but that for all of it, and for all of his good what's more, he is doomed to be snuffed out by forces only vaguely aware of him, if aware at all. You can see how this might have been a little rough on a reader of, say, *Wonder Stories Quarterly*, particularly when he'd just finished something assuring him that all would be well with us once we'd managed to perfect the interstellar space ship.

Smith himself printed a collection of stories, *The Double Shadow and Other Fantasies*, and my guess is that he could have used the money a copy of it would bring today. Then, in '42, Arkham House published *Out of Space and Time* for its third book, and thus began the laudable task of putting Smith's short stories between hardcovers. Now, with *Other Dimensions*, they have completed the job. This sixth and last volume is in the nature of a final wrapping-up and so contains some material that is decidedly not Smith at his best, but there is plenty of lovely work in it, and certainly no serious collector of his writings would consider passing it by. I might point out that the first book in the series has gone from $3.00 to $150.00, and that the second (*Lost Worlds*, Arkham House, $3.00 back in 1944) has touched the century mark, so you could pick this latest one up strictly as a good investment, though God help you if you're that myopic.

Now that Arkham House has completed its hard cover rescue mission on Smith, the first of the Smith paperbacks has at last been brought out (*Zothique*). I guess, as they used to say in the Walt Disney shorts on those cute wild animals, it is part of Nature's Plan. It strikes me as remarkable that no one has had the good sense to do it before now, but my sincere congratulations to Lin Carter, the editor of the Ballantine Adult Fantasy Series, and to all else at that institution who had anything to do with the project. *Zothique* is an anthology of stories that share as a common background one of Smith's most ghoulish fantasy worlds—an Earth where the sea has swallowed up all but one continent, where the sun is slowly fizzling out, and man has regressed to ignorant, ugly magic. Necromancers thrive, dark and inescapable curses abound, and extinction chews at the edges. Mr. Carter has arranged these fascinatingly morbid fantasies in a perfectly satisfactory kind of chronological order so the thing may be read as a novel, if you like. Myself I would suggest you nibble rather more cautiously at these dainties, taking them one or two at a time. A reading of *Zothique* at a sitting might do something serious to the cellular structure of your brain.

Speaking of Ballantine Books, they are also Beagle Books, or at least Ballantine Books and Beagle Books operate from the same address and begin with "Bs." Whatever, be it Beagle or be it Ballantine, they are bringing out a series of Lovecraft books, and I gather the whole thing is very official as it is called *The Arkham Edition of H. P. Lovecraft* and August Derleth is the editor. The first one is *The Tomb*, and they plan to bring out not only the writings of H. P. L., himself, but the works of other authors working in the Mythos bag: Cthulhu for the masses, in other words. A splendid project. An ad I came across for the series quotes from the *Necronomicon* in the Old Tongue, and then goes on to say that no one knows much about the Old Tongue except that it was thickly coated. This is a clear indication there are a number of cultured and sensitive individuals behind this enterprise, and I wish them well.

In mainstream publishing, as science fiction reviewers are wont to say (though I have never liked, nor really understood, the odd implication of acceptance of one's own field of interest as a kind of stagnant backwater), I came across a couple of interesting items bobbing around. The first is a collection by the famous Joan Kahn, the legendary editor of the Harper Novels of Suspense, called *Some Things Dark and Dangerous*, and it contains some excellent material: stories by such varied authors as Waugh, LeFanu, Blackwood and F. Marion Crawford;

horrific essays by such as Pearson, Prescott, and Coates. The only angle that puts me off it, and put me off by God it does, is that the thing is supposed to be aimed at children. Now why this particular group of shockers should have "Age 12 up" on its flyleaf and a foreword by Miss Kahn which makes you feel as if you were being patted on the top of your head by the town librarian, I cannot say. Miss Kahn's two previous anthologies were supposedly for grownups. Again, now that I think of it, I can't explain the classification. Perhaps it's because they were larger books and made more of a demand on one's attention span.

The other mainstream item (I'm starting to see why the word is cherished by so many) is a Literary Guild Selection which, when it came out in hardcover, got excellent notices from mainstream reviewers (I take it all back—it's a swell word), so when I saw it in paperback, I seized upon it at once. It is *Ratman's Notebooks*, it's by Stephen Gilbert, and it is, I'm afraid, completely unconvincing. It's a pity, because he has a nice basic idea, a grisly little misfit taking his revenge out on society with a pack of trained rats, but he just doesn't follow any of the rules of consistency or logical development, or staying within his premise, so the whole thing collapses early on. Nice scenes, here and there, and if they fooled with it they might make a good horror movie out of it, but the book doesn't work. Back to the Littlestream.

‡

One of the most legendary vampire books in English literature, and certainly one of the most baroquely titled,
is *Varney the Vampire, or, The Feast of Blood*, by Thomas
Preskett Prest. Varney first made his appearance in 1847, and thus
stands chronologically midway between Polidori's *The Vampyre*
(1819)—whose Byronic and Byron-based antihero, Lord Ruthven,
pretty much established the breed as we know it—and Stoker's
winner and still champion, *Dracula* (1897), who, some scholars
maintain, might never have risen from his grave without Varney's
example to lead the way.

Until recently the book was on the scarce side, there being only three known copies extant, but now, thanks to the Arno Press, you can have it in a boxed edition of three volumes, each one crammed full with tiny type, for a spine-chilling, but not exorbitant, thirty-five dollars. The magnificent blood and thunder illustrations of the 1847 edition are all there, as is the delightfully ghoulish wrapper of the 1853 penny dreadful printing, and these alone make the book a joy and a delight. T. P. Prest was the king of the authors of the "bloods" of the Victorian era: wild and wooly shockers that were gobbled up enthusiastically by an unrepentant multitude. Two other of his works have attained consider-able notoriety, one of commercial cannibalism named *Sweeny Todd,*

the Demon Barber of Fleet Street, and another of cannibalism, on the grand scale called *Sawney Bean*, but *Var-ney* remains his chef-d'oeuvre. The style is a rich, unrestrained rhetoric very like that employed by the late W. C. Fields, the plot continuous and unrelenting melodrama; yet, despite the howling mobs and the echoing dungeons, despite the duels and dire threats and hideous grimaces, the pace of the thing throughout, for all its storms and avalanches, is a slow and genteel tread. Over and over the same point will be mulled by diverse sets of characters, again and again the action will be brought to a dead halt while the author leisurely spins some side tale which may or may not have anything to do with the story at large, and the paths taken to the various horrid revelations are, one and all, slow and gently winding. A quaint and charming book of considerable historical importance.

A collection of somewhat classier writing from the same epoch is *Five Victorian Ghost Novels*, edited with an excellent introduction by E. F. Bleiler, and I flatly recommend it. Very hard to pick a favorite, but I personally enjoyed most "The Uninhabited House," by Mrs. J. H. Riddell. Mr. Bleiler has put together another fine collection for Dover, *The King in Yellow and Other Horror Stories*, a gathering of the fantastic tales of the wonderfully erratic Robert W. Chambers. If, by some awful mischance, you have not read the weird stories connected with *The King*, you now have a chance to correct your unfortunate condition, and if you think you've read all the Chambers stuff worth reading, Mr. Bleiler may have a surprise or two for you, as he did for me.

Seabury Quinn, just before his death, put together an anthology of his stories that has recently been published by Mirage Press. If I understand what he was up to, Mr. Quinn was getting together those tales he loved which have not yet received a safe berth between hard covers, as quite a few of his better works are not included. However, *Is the Devil a Gentleman?* is an excellent demonstration of the talents of the most regularly appearing author in

the history of the late *Weird Tales* magazines. Myself, I have always preferred the stories involving his psychic detective de Grandin, feeling he was really more at home in that area, but it is way past time a collection of his other works be put together, and the publishers are to be congratulated for doing it. Among the titles more likely to ring a bell in the readers' memories are "Uncanonized," "Glamour," and "Bon Voyage, Michelle."

Songs and Sonnets Atlantean purports to be a collection of Atlantean poems translated first into French by Michel de Labretagne, thence into our own tongue by a Donald Sidney-Fryer, the whole with copious notes and an introduction by Dr. I. M. Andor. Those with a suspicious turn of mind, and I certainly hope in this day and age you have a suspicious turn of mind, will soon firmly suspect that the whole thing is actually the work of one man, namely that of the Donald Fryer mentioned above. If it is, and there are firm grounds for believing it is, it is work he can well be proud of, for he has managed in his slim book, slim only in physical size, to evoke an Atlantis which is both haunting and astonishingly solid. Mr. Fryer is a profound student of Clark Ashton Smith (he edited Smith's last two collections for Arkham House and will do the same for the forthcoming *Selected*

Poems), and the influence shows, but he is very much his own poet, and he structures and plays with a surety and deftness that is remarkable. *Songs and Sonnets Atlantean* marks the first general visibility of a fine and most welcome new talent.

The Philosopher's Stone is a new Lovecraftian novel by Colin Wilson, and is by all odds his most successful experiment in the area so far. It is fascinating to see what happens when a mind like Wilson's takes off from H. P. L.'s basic premises and ground rules (and he follows the latter with scrupulous care), not only because Wilson's mind is a most interesting mechanism in itself, but also because of its contrasts with that of Lovecraft's. Both men are dealing with the basic concept that mankind is in the presence of a race of creatures possessing nearly limitless powers, that mankind will probably be destroyed by these creatures when they deign to do it, and that the universe at large really couldn't care less about the whole matter. Reservations on this last from Wilson's point of view. Lovecraft's reaction to it all was one of pity, combined with ironic amusement at mankind's plight, and more of the same for the creatures, but that mixed with awe and excited interest at the creatures' larger abilities and insights. He was obviously impressed by the enormous powers implied by the existence of the creatures, the ideas of entities with minds so vast clearly thrilled him, but he saw mankind strictly as a spectator, never as a participant, in personal hugeness. Wilson, on the other hand, sees a clear connection between the existence of such superbeings and the possibilities latent in our own minds. His monsters are scary enough, and certainly dangerous as hell, but his humans are not the pathetic, tiny pawns H. P. L. visualized; they are beings who just might, with pluck and luck, meet their erstwhile masters on something like even ground. A very interesting book.

By now you have doubtless heard of the death of August Derleth; if not, I am sorry to be the one to break it to you. The personal debt I feel towards him, for the books he made, for the work he uncovered, for the productions of the authors he helped and encouraged, is past expressing. He was a good man, a talented man, and he worked hard for what he believed in. I can't say how much I will miss knowing he's around.

‡

THE DARK CORNER | BOOK REVIEWS BY GAHAN WILSON

Although "Oliver Onions" sounds as if it might be the lead animated vegetable in a television supermarket ad or a minor comic character in one of Dickens's more involved novels, it is, in fact, the name of the man who was one of the best, if not the best, ghost story writers working in the English language.

Anyone who has done any reading at all in the field is bound to have come across his deservedly over-anthologized "The Beckoning Fair One," probably his masterpiece, and more persistent delvers have probably got a frisson off of "Rooum" and a bit weepy over "John Gladwin Says . . ." but how many have had the good fortune to be chilled by "The Rope in the Rafters," made timid over museum exhibits by "The Painted Face," and, particularly those who have had the gall to essay fiction, been mentally dislocated by "The Real People?" Not bloody many, would by this reviewer's guess, but now, thanks to Dover Publications, Inc., you can purchase *The Collected Ghost Stories of Oliver Onions* and read all of the above, plus sixteen other stories by this excellent man. Any additional pointings-out on my part are purely arbitrary, since everything in this book is well worth your time, but I might mention that "Benlian" is one of the goddamnd-est seduction stories ever written, and that the author's introduction is essential reading for all wishing to pursue the craft of conjuring ghosts with ink and paper. Mr. Onions did as much as anyone to move phantoms and other haunts from dark, Gothic dungeons to the very room in which you presently sit. There are probably only five or six others who have done as much, and this book is as good a collection of supernatural fiction as can be bought. My only complaint is that its paper covers are covered by this shiny, transparent stuff that crinkles and peels off and side tracks you into spending minutes at a time seeing if you can remove the stuff without tearing the ink off the paper underneath.

There is another super bargain available to you, and that is *Selected Poems* by Clark Ashton Smith. Probably the best way to give you an idea of the treasures within would be to list the subheadings: *The Star-Treader* and Other Poems, Additional Early Poems, Ebony and Crystal (including the fiction version of The Hashish-Eater), Sandalwood, Translations and Paraphrases, Incantations, Experiments in Haiku, Satires and Travesties, The Jasmine Girdle, and The Hill of Dionysus. Poetry was always Smith's deepest love, and this book so long in coming, is an awesome monument to his art. It contains the bulk of his work, all of the best work, and ranges from his first poems in the early nineteen hundreds to the end. Smith was heavily involved in editing and rewriting the book in the '40s; the task was taken up by others and now, at last, we have it. I wish it had dates and, more audaciously, an index of first lines but this is carping when one considers what it does have.

On a level a little less dizzying than the first two items, but still good, clean fun, we have the kickoff of a series of annual collections edited by Richard Davis and entitled The Year's Best Horror Stories, and I think the least anyone interested in the macabre fantastic can do is to give a worthy project such as this encouragement and all good wishes. The quality of the stories seemed to me to be pretty varied, but it's an interesting sampling from divers markets and authors. There are reliable old regulars such as Bloch and Matheson, comers such as Brian Lumley and Ramsey Campbell, and a really

nice bit of supernatural sociology by Robert McNear called "Death's Door," which I had read before and which well deserves being called one of the year's best.

Another event those fond of the weird may be grateful for is the arrival in our midst of an anthologist whose production and persistence are well-nigh Derlethian. His name is Peter Haining, and I know nothing of him save that he is obviously a skilled promoter and a researcher of pluck and ingenuity. Though he sometimes uses material which is possibly too familiar, he is always careful to include odd and interesting items which are almost certain to be new to you or which you may have heard of but were never able to track down. Beyond the Curtain of Dark, for example, contains a nice period piece by Mary Shelley, "The Mortal Immortal," and a nicely repulsive story by the excellent mystery writer Patricia Highsmith called "The Snail-Watcher."

Then in The Hollywood Nightmare Mr. Haining puts together all the old favorites concerning ghastly happenings in tinsel city, but he sneaks in a couple of new ones to me and has somehow or other gotten Christopher Lee to write a foreword to the thing and snagged an essay by dear old Boris Karloff on what it's like to be Boris Karloff. Going on to more ambitious efforts, we have

THE DARK CORNER | BOOK REVIEWS BY GAHAN WILSON

The Clans of Darkness that is a collection of spooky stuff concerning the Scots. It's very cleverly built as the editor starts out with aulde stories and works his way up to present day creepiness, including, en route, many excellent tales and a forward by none other than Angus Wilson. Like I say, Mr. Haining is a promoter. Also there is "Wandering Willie's Tale" from *Redgauntlet* reworked by Sir Walter Scott into an independent short story, "A Night In the Grave," and you can't do that sort of carryings on any better. There is also, most considerately, a glossary at the end to help you out with the more obscure Scot words. The best of the Haining collections I have on hand, though, is *Gothic Tales of Terror* that is nine hundred and twenty eight pages of classic stuff: some of it complete stories, some of it extracted from longer works. It cov-

ers just about every name in the area from Horace Walpole to William Beckford to Byron to De Quincey to Le Fanu to E. T. A. Hoffmann to Eugene Sue (this one the short story upon that the enormous *Wandering Jew* sprouted from) to Hawthorne to Poe, and a goodly scattering of the prolific Anonymous. Some of these are not the authors at their best, but the point of this collection is mostly to unearth items not likely to have crossed your path before. If you enjoy this kind of thing you will have a fine time with the book and, thanks to quite well done introductory essays throughout, learn all sorts of interesting and sometimes nicely gossipy things about the folk who gave us all those bleeding floors, demon lovers, and lengths of chain rattling in the night.

‡

D over Publications, in its continuing series on past masters of the macabre, has brought out a collection of stories by Wilkie Collins called *Tales of Terror and the Supernatural*. Collins wrote in the middle of the eighteen hundreds, is firstly known for his *The Moonstone*, secondly for his *The Woman in White*, and thirdly for nothing else, as far as the general public is concerned.

This book is an attempt to at least partly correct that situation by putting on view some of his shorter neglected works, and there is stuff in it that no one seriously interested in tales of terror and the supernatural should miss. True enough, there is represented that reprehensible flaw of the writings of that period, namely the ghost that is, after all, not a ghost, and my teeth once again gnashed uncontrollably at yet another encounter with "The Dead Hand," a story which starts out to tell stylishly of a gentleman attempting to share a room at an inn with a corpse which (shudder) *moves*, then goes on to explain that it wasn't really a corpse at all, folks, only this person who was very, very ill—but that shouldn't put you off an anthology containing such undeniable beauties as "The Dream Woman," "A Terribly Strange Bed," and "Mad Monkton."

Mr. Sam Moskowitz keeps popping up here, one way and another, and here he is as the editor of the revived *Weird Tales*, for heaven's sake! I certainly wish him luck and hope the project succeeds, however I have only seen one copy of the thing on any stand, that in Tuscaloosa, of all places, where I had given an inspirational lecture to an educational establishment the night before, and was killing the morning after by browsing the stands of the local drugstores. It is, by God, authentic enough as its front cover is an unpublished-up-to-now Finlay, and its back is a Rosicrucian ad all the way from San Jose. Inside we have, among other tasty items, the first R. E. Howard story sold to *W.T.* or anybody else, a William Hope Hodgson story not printed since it first showed up in 1905, an excellent essay by the editor on Hodgson's early life, and a whole bunch of lovingly compiled material from all over the place, all very much fitting and proper to be housed in *Weird Tales*. Mr. Moskowitz has started out by producing it as a quarterly,

THE DARK CORNER | book reviews by Gahan Wilson

but, obviously, he has hopes. Now if those distributors will just for once cooperate . . .

Regular readers of this magazine, and I assume we all are regular readers, will be familiar with the gentleman referred to in the title of *The Peculiar Exploits of Brigadier Ffellowes* by Sterling Lanier as he is, happily, often present in these pages. Those who are not should know that these stories are in the classic form probably best exploited by Lord Dunsany in his Jorkens tales, namely that of the gentleman-adventurer who reminisces on his hair-raising enterprises while we gather about to listen to him in the security of the exclusive club to which we all snugly belong. There is something wonderfully soothing in this format—the ghastly adventures contrasted with the coziness of the crackling fire, the wing chair, the brandy snifter in one's hand, and, above all, the sure and certain knowledge that the story you are settling back to listen to will be a humdinger. Although the spelling of Ffellowes' name seems to imply the series is approached with tongue in cheek, such is not the case. There is, now and then, some mild joshing between the Brigadier—one does not call him General—and a nasty fellow named Williams, but once the story proper is launched into, Mr. Lanier permits no kidding around. He wants to give you a bit of a turn, he does,

and he usually succeeds. Although I enjoyed the whole book and am looking forward to more of the same, my favorite exploits to date are "Fraternity Brother," "His Coat So Gay," and "The Kings of the Sea." They all have marvelously sinister overtones, and it's obvious Mr. Lanier does serious homework on his themes as his attention to authenticity in detail is excellent. Very good work, and that last favorite mentioned above has a really lovely and casual zinger at the end.

I have no idea how many stories Frank Belknap Long has written, but Arkham House has gathered up a double armful of them in *The Rim of the Unknown*, twenty-three of them, in all, crowded into almost three hundred pages of small type. The works come from the '40s and '50s, mainly, but there are five from the '30s, and a completely unrepentant shocker from 1927 that calls itself "The Man with a Thousand Legs" and lives 100 percent up to its title. Mr. Long has a way with fiendish invaders from other planets, dimensions, and what you will, and it is very much his own. A particularly pleasing aspect of his work is his relish in describing their looks, their usually baleful attitude toward ourselves, and, in careful detail, their generally dreadful digestive processes.

Another of the old pros, Carl Jacobi, has a new book out called

Disclosures in Scarlet, and it ranges in time from a 1938 epic about evil European dictator August Strausvig's really rotten plot to bring the Free World to its knees by means of singing plants from outer space, to a 1970s fantasy about a super-gadgeted electronic golf course where the thirteenth is a 1,325-yard hole with a dogleg to the right. In between is a wide variety of Jacobian divertissements, my personal favorites being "The Aquarium," a really nasty piece of work, and a sentimental bit of necrophilia named, rather demurely, all things considered, "The Unpleasantness at Carver House."

Turning from these elder statesmen of the grotesque fantastic, we come to a book written by a talent new to this or any other field, a mere lad, if the implications of the jacket copy have been correctly interpreted by me, yet when one reads Brian Lumley's *The Caller of the Black* what does one find? One finds a collection of stories which reads as if it had been culled from the oldest, most moldering back issues of *Weird Tales*, is what one finds! The earliest date on any of these is 1968, it having appeared in that year's Summer issue of the *Arkham Collector*, but Mr. Lumley has so deeply steeped himself in his source material, that being the writings of H. P. Lovecraft and his circle, that his work seems for all the world to have been written by a younger member of that spooky little group away back when in the '30s. These are unabashed pastiches, obviously written by someone enjoying himself enormously, all of them affectionate tributes to Messrs. Lovecraft, Bloch (the horrid endings where the hero rots or gets et being clearly especially dedicated to M. Bloch!), Smith, Derleth, and the rest. He uses the props, gods, italic endings, and vocabularies those gentle men held so near and dear, his tales abounding as they do with dreadful books, all too describable *things*, grisly mutilations brought on by fangs, beaks, tentacles, and the like, and, of course, cannibalism. In these pages we learn at last what finally happened to Kadath, Etienne-Laurent de Marigny, his clock, and even to Queen Nitocris, evil queen supreme, originally created for *Weird Tales* in 1928 by none other than Thomas Lanier "Tennessee" Williams. It's been a long wait.

A fellow who began things more or less as Mr. Lumley is commencing, Ramsey Campbell, has come out with a new book, *Demons by Daylight*, and a number of very interesting turns. Mr. Campbell's first volume, *The Inhabitant of the Lake*, was written mainly when he was a wee tad, and was a collection of sometimes clever, sometimes touchingly naive, but always quite enjoyable stories based firmly upon the writing of H. P. L.

Now he is older, wiser, and a good deal more frightening. I suggest we all keep a sharp eye on him. What he has done is to take Lovecraft's sinister implications out of the era of bootleg whiskey and the depression into the present one of rather more formidable mind-altering drugs and oddly unsatisfying plenty. He is also abandoning Lovecraft's extremely guarded hints as to what was going on there at the foot of the six thousand steps hard by the pit of shaggoths in favor of clear specifics as to the activities of the ladies and the gentlemen and the monsters. It makes for a chilling set of stories and promises much for what Mr. Campbell will come up with next. The possibilities inherent in Lovecraft's really sensational vision of sexual-physic-spatial-temporal (or sexual/psychic/spatial/temporal) warps has been, to date, very largely ignored by those who have been intrigued enough to write in the Mythos mood. Colin Wilson has done an excellent job of extending the intellectual aspects of H. P. L.'s mind-bending insights, but, though he has by no means ignored it, his attention to the physical and emotional end of things has been relatively peripheral. Also, quite importantly, Mr. Wilson's attention has been directed mainly to extraordinarily superior members of our species, Russellian intellectuals and the like, and folks like you and me in contact with Them has been only barely touched on in his novels. Mr. Campbell, in contrast, does concentrate on folks like you and me, people whose personalities are—no offense, mind—by and large sloppily built, confusingly motivated affairs; tottery at best, downright shoddy, now and then. When Mr. Campbell pits his fallible, commonly lonely, quite generally weak, most human characters against enormous forces bent on incomprehensible errands the results are, as you might expect, often frightening, and, as you might not expect, often touching: even heartwarming.

‡

Common sense is rightly cherished. It makes us view the advice of lawyers and financial advisers with suspicion, leads us to be cynical concerning the claims of all advertisers, causes us to waste no time in demanding a second opinion when serious illness is spoken of, and otherwise mightily helps us steer our perilous course through this confusing and often downright wicked world.

But common sense is also the prime bane to all who would write fantastic literature. Any author, wishing his ghost to walk, must first of all devise some way to fuddle or buy off this intrepid guardian, or his project is doomed. Common sense believes in hard realities, and absolutely nothing else. It steps on Leprechauns with contempt and squishes them; it slams the door on approaching vampires, breaking their noses.

One way of leading this mentor firmly down the garden path is to construct a world and a people of such obvious authenticity that the apparitions and wonders intermingled with them will also seem to be similarly sound. In *Collected Ghost Stories* by Mary E. Wilkins-Freeman, one of the best of the naturalistic school of New England writers demonstrates her complete mastery of this approach. Her Yankees are beautifully observed, as are their countryside, their houses, their clothes and daily appliances.

She was not only a sharp examiner of what went on about her, she saw it all with a lovely sense of humor, gentle, but most ironic, solidly based on human foolishness seen through clear but wonderfully understanding eyes. I have long counted a number of these tales among my favorites— Arkham House says this collection constitutes Mrs. Freeman's entire output of spooky stories—and even those not up to the level of the best ones here are very worthy of your time. "Luella Miller" is, I think, one of the funniest and most ghastly variations on the vampire theme yet done. It concerns the doings of a little pink and white, fluffy lady who is absolutely helpless and completely dependent on kindly aid, and who is mercilessly and totally deadly. "The Southwest Chamber" and "The Vacant Lot" are both spectacular productions and most cleverly combine the humor of solidly practical people finally daunted by the genuinely

THE DARK CORNER | BOOK REVIEWS BY GAHAN WILSON

spooky events they're unfortunate enough to have to confront. There is also an extraordinary tale, "The Hall Bedroom," about a man going, sense by sense, to another kind of place than our own. And much more very good stuff, indeed, and an intelligent and useful introduction by Mr. Edward Wagenknecht.

Another way to make common sense nervous and faltery is to confront it with a hearty and confident faith that the strange events and creatures being spoken of so folksily are just plain, down-to-earth facts. There isn't any writer better at this back country, no nonsense approach than Manly Wade Wellman, and he now has a handsome book out from Carcosa called *Worse Things Waiting*. It's 352 pages of small type containing a couple of poems, twenty-six short stories, and two novelettes. The bulk of it, until now, was completely out of the reach of all save particularly ingenious collectors. And, if that's not enough, folks, it's lavishly illustrated by none other than Lee Brown Coye.

Wellman loves vampires, and there are a good dozen or more in *Worse Things*, some of them given the classic treatment as in "School For the Unspeakable," which starts a really nasty bunch of bloodsucking brats off on their highly satisfactory eternal damnation, "When It Was Moonlight," wherein E. A. Poe

devises a new way to destroy one of the living dead, and another featuring none other than Count Dracula as its hero; but Wellman really shines when he puts his vampires into an atmosphere predominately bucolic, where the characters, fiends and all, are solid country people who speak solemnly in quaint dialects, and who all, in one way or another, firmly respect the old time religion. One of the best of these is the novelette "Fearful Rock," which pits the evil Persil Mandifer and his disgusting son Larue against Sergeant Jaeger, member of the Union Army, simple man of God, and staunch reader and user of John George Hohmun's *Pow-Wows; Or, Long Lost Friend*. It's a lovely fight, and Jaeger survives it to return in the second novelette, "Coven," so that he might give the whatchacallit which flaps snickering through the night along the Missouri-Arkansas border its deserved comeuppance. Among the short stories that I enjoyed best would be "The Undead Soldier," which makes good use of the fairy-tale device of the ominous repetition of a spooky phrase to bring the menace ever nearer to our throats. "Come Into My Parlor" has a swell vegetable monster, and then there's such as "Larroes Catch Meddlers," "The Pineys," "Dhoh," and "The Hairy Thunderer." These last two, by the way, are among a group of stories using American Indian legends and themes. Wellman was writing about Indians as if they were real people long before the idea caught on generally. The illustrations by Coye show that he is in top form, which is to say they are absolutely ghastly, horrific, and to be kept out of the hands of all but the stout hearted and the brave. A grand job of putting together a book.

Another way to confound poor old common sense is to place it in an atmosphere so uncongenial it does not know how to get its bearings, or what to do next, and if there is a place on this globe more uncongenial to practicality and the supremacy of reason than Wales, I do not know of it. The tireless Mr. Peter Haining in *The Magic Valley Travelers* has put together a charming collection of stories and whatnot by Welsh folk themselves, or those that know enough about the place to evoke it effectively. Here's stuff by Machen, Dylan Thomas, Richard Hughes, Mary Shelley, Caradoc Evans, Charles Williams, and other luminaries, plus a piece by Traditional and another by Anonymous. The land of Merlin and Arthur and God only know what, and common sense hasn't got a prayer.

‡

[Further excerpt from lost issue.] Hodgson's Carnacki, Mycroft & Moran have published *Number Seven, Queer Street* in order to introduce Margery Lawrence's Miles Pennoyer. Pennoyer is in the grand, unabashed tradition of the British psychic detective. He belongs to the best clubs, dwells in a comfortable bachelor apartment overlooking the Thames, permits himself only the occasional fine Havana lest tobacco damp his occult abilities, and engages in constant and remorseless battle with the powers of evil. His Watson, Jerome Latimer, himself a gentleman of impeccable credentials, does not rush the telling of his friend's adventures, but has the sense to present them in the thoughtful and leisurely fashion they demand. Not that there are not some very spooky moments in these tales, mind, but we know always that the keen mind and stout, kindly heart of Miles Pennoyer will triumph over even the most determined ghost or villain. Highly recommended to those who have the good sense to enjoy this sort of thing.

‡

I t is a pleasure to be able to lead off this Dark Corner with an announcement which is bound to create so much pleasure, namely that—and of course it is at last—we have among us *Lovecraft at Last* by Willis Conover. The first I heard of the project was an ad occupying the entire back page of the Fall '73 issue of the brave but doomed second coming of *Weird Tales* (I hope I am not the one to inform you this revival did not survive).

The ad was full of complicated information printed in small type and took minutes to read, but the gist of it was that *At Last* made available important Lovecraftian material never printed before; that a free facsimile of H. P. L.'s last manuscript was offered (his final working of *Supernatural Horror in Literature*) if you would but clip, fill out, and mail the coupon provided, and that all monies would be refunded if the buyer expressed dissatisfaction within fifteen days of receipt of the book. The years between have seen a flurry of handsomely printed apologies for delay, the promised *Supernatural Horror* (looking for all the world like four actual pages of yellow sheet typed with Lovecraft's ancient machine, badly needing cleaning, and spidery additions in his hand), and now, at last, *At Last*. It has been worth the wait.

The book is not, nor does it pretend to be, a work of scholarship. It does not presume to psychoanalyze Lovecraft's private motivations, nor reveal to a startled world what actually ailed his father (I know, by the way—the old fellow was slowly turning into a frog!), nor does it attempt anything like a full biography. What it does do, and beautifully, is convey what it is like—I use the present tense on purpose as Conover has built a kind of time machine—to be a fifteen-year-old kid who, by a touching combination of brass and naivete, has activated a regular correspondence between himself and the awesome H. P. L. Conover was involved with the production of one of those amateur publications devoted to fantasy, bless their hearts, and he figured it would be a swell idea if he could get some of the more towering professionals in the field to contribute, say, for example, Howard Phillips Lovecraft. He sent a nervy letter of inquiry off to Providence and got back a generous and sympathetic reply. Staggered, fifteen-year-old kids do have some contact with reality, he wrote again and again was answered, and so the material for this delightful volume grew, postcard by postcard and letter by letter. Now thanks to Conover's loving, painstaking labor—the delay in publication is amply explained by a glance through his book—we can share his experience.

The layout and development are, I think, unique. You read this or that letter in print, or read a reference to such and such a Christmas card, and there, right next to the quote or description, is the card or letter itself! I have no idea how Conover managed to get, say, the ink colors so flawlessly reproduced, I expect patient dedication had a good deal to do with it, but the effect is so completely convincing that collectors in this area are advised to tread cautiously lest they find themselves spending small fortunes for clippings from this book. As the correspondence proceeds the characters lose shyness by degrees and confidences mount and you are presented with a moving and extraordinarily encouraging look at a maturer and healthier Lovecraft than has been heretofore presented. He has fought and won through so much that plagued him during his earlier years, and his comments on that suffering younger self make fascinating reading. But I think I'd best leave off describing what happens further and leave it to you to read it page by page

and impact by impact. We have seen books of varying quality representing varying research into Lovecraft's life and work. As his legend and influence inevitably grow, we'll see many more. The newer ones will supersede and render obsolete the older, profound interpretations tending to get more complicated as they go along, but *Lovecraft at Last* will, I believe, remain with us for it is no third hand interpretation, above all no explanation—it is Lovecraft himself, and his young, awed admirer, and they're both alive.

Another book that has been looming for some time and has finally joined us is *Xelucha and Others* by M. P. Shiel. Shiel is, of course, one of the very best. He is most famous for his novel *The Purple Cloud*, but a number of his short stories have been heavily anthologized and are well known. "The House of Sounds," "Huguenin's Wife," and "The Pale Ape" fit into this category, and these are represented in this collection, but there are a number of others much less familiar and well worth your time if you have not yet come across them. The title story is an excellent example of Shiel's knack for decadence and is highly informative regarding the dietary customs of graveyard worms. Shiel is always disturbing, but I found one of these, "The Primate of the Rose," bad enough to give me quite a nasty little dream. Now, hopefully, they'll get on with the long promised collection of *Prince Zaleski*.

Brian Lumley has a new book out with Arkham House (*Beneath the Moors*) that, I am relieved to say, is quite good—really by far the best thing he's done. I'll admit to being a little worried about him after getting through *The Burrowers Beneath*, which was tiring to read and must have been exhausting to write. The thing never came to life, and though there was continuous and strenuous tugging at the hawsers, poor Lumley never seemed to be able to get the damned thing pulled together. The exercise must have done him good, however, because after a slightly faltering start, he lopes easily from page to page and carries the reader effortlessly to a really dandy climax featuring a statement by a fellow named Williamson which is as grand a sample of a solid, down-to-earth mind colliding with the Ghastly Impossible and struggling to grasp what in hell happened since Bram Stoker utilized the same strategy in *Dracula*. Mr. Lumley is coming along well. Also there is a highly successful underground horrorland that is solid, consistent, and well designed to give you a bit of a turn, even several in a row.

The back of the jacket of Basil Copper's *The Great White Space* contains high praise for the author by a number of formidable folk; the copy encourages expectation of high Lovecraftian fun. The cover art is intriguing, and so I settled down with a happy sigh to have a good, ghastly read, but did not. Copper has the thesis down, all right, but doesn't seem to know what to do with it. His scientists travel through strange places in wonderful machines, they come across huge and ancient artifacts, hear flapping wings, disinter weird creatures which instantly rot, and do all the other fine, traditional things we all enjoy so much, but none of it ever adds up to a meaningful whole which makes the entire thing an exercise in frustration. Perhaps the promise of excellent moments here and there is what makes it such a disappointing book.

I think my public record is very clear concerning August Derleth, that I hold him in the highest respect and my gratitude to him for his work with Arkham House truly knows no bounds, so the reader will understand that when I got a copy of *The Watchers Out of Time* and an angry letter concerning the book from Donald Wandrei almost in the same mail, I found myself faced with a painful decision. Mr. Wandrei's thesis is that it is time, past time, to give up pretending the stories in this book which are attributed to the authorship of Lovecraft *and* Derleth are anything of the sort, and that the